M000017967

# Unleashing
# the Power of
# Parental Love

# Unleashing the Power of Parental Love

*4 Steps to Raising Joyful and Self-Confident Kids*

Gary M. Unruh, MSW LCSW

Lighthouse Love Productions, LLC
Colorado Springs, CO

© 2010 Gary Unruh. Printed and bound in the United States of America. All rights reserved. No part of this book may be reproduced or transmitted in any form or by any means, electronic or mechanical, including photocopying, recording, or by an information storage and retrieval system—except by a reviewer who may quote brief passages in a review to be printed in a magazine, newspaper, or on the Web—without permission in writing from the publisher. For information, please contact Lighthouse Love Productions, LLC, 1277 Kelly Johnson Blvd., Suite 220, Colorado Springs, CO 80920.

Although the author and publisher have made every effort to ensure the accuracy and completeness of information contained in this book, we assume no responsibility for errors, inaccuracies, omissions, or any inconsistency herein. Any slighting of people, places, or organizations is unintentional.

First printing 2010
ISBN 978-0-9824204-4-7
LCCN 2009925597

**ATTENTION CORPORATIONS, UNIVERSITIES, COLLEGES, AND PROFESSIONAL ORGANIZATIONS:** Quantity discounts are available on bulk purchases of this book for educational, gift purposes, or as premiums for increasing magazine subscriptions or renewals. Special books or book excerpts can also be created to fit specific needs. For information, please contact Lighthouse Love Productions, LLC, 1277 Kelly Johnson Blvd., Suite 220, Colorado Springs, CO 80920; www.unleashingparentallove.com.

*To all the moms, dads, and children
who have allowed me to be a part of
their lives and demonstrated to me
the miracle of love unleashed*

# CONTENTS

# ACKNOWLEDGMENTS

WRITING A BOOK IS as much about the supporting cast as the author: family, friends, contributions from mental health professionals, and, above all, an excellent editor.

Mary McNeil meets the qualifications of an excellent editor. Mary quickly learned the recipe for how to give me just the right mixture of straightforward feedback and encouragement. Thank you, Mary, for making a dream come true. The book would not have happened without your expert guidance and caring.

To my family, friends, and especially Charlene Pardo, who helped me start my book—your support and feedback on this book have been invaluable.

My wife Betty and our four children have been an inspiration to me throughout my life. From Betty I witnessed daily the amazing power of unleashed love with our children. What a treasure you are, Betty. Laura, Eric, Christine, and Jason—what an example and joy you are to me. I learned about the good being at the center of children from each one of you. No matter what curves life throws you, your continual responses are about the good in life. The foundation of this book was inspired by all of you.

Thank you, Mom, Dad, Ken, Phil, Stan, and Aunt Betty for your love throughout my life. You've all contributed mightily to what I have learned about the power of love. Mom and Dad, thank you for all your loving support and multiple opportunities you made available to me. What a challenge that little red-headed, freckle-faced boy must have been—a kid who ran before he walked. (Little did they know they were raising an ADHD child!) Big brother Ken, I would never have found my passion for being a counselor if not for your unending belief in me. Phil, thank you for always seeing the good in me. And, Stan, what a constant support you have been throughout the writing of this book—always seeing the glass three-fourths full when sometimes I wasn't sure where the glass was. What a joy it is to experience your unleashed love. Aunt Betty, your continual happy smiles and comments to me—even when I was only four years old—are a profound memory that has been a continual source of joy. You are special.

Many mental health professionals have made outstanding contributions toward understanding human nature and effectively restoring mental health. I feel deeply indebted to a number of these individuals both professionally and personally. Using and adapting their contributions has been immeasurably helpful in my efforts to help children and their parents restore and maintain their mental health and loving relationships. Here's a list of these professionals and a brief summary of their key contributions:

- Sigmund Freud: childhood development and the role of defenses, particularly unconscious projection
- Erik Erikson: stages of childhood development
- A. Thomas and S. Chess: the nine temperament traits that are a part of every human being
- Paul Ekman: in-depth understanding of emotions
- Carl Rogers: the concepts that humans are fundamentally good and that reflecting emotions is essential
- Abraham Maslow: the hierarchy of needs, especially the fourth and fifth levels—esteem needs and self-actualization
- Haim Ginott: the central role of emotions and how children thrive when adults focus on emotions first before behavior
- Dan Goleman: the central role of emotions in healthy human functioning

- Thomas Gordon, *Parent Effectiveness Training*: the importance of a collaborative, cooperative (democratic) parent-child relationship

- Aaron Beck: cognitive therapy (the interplay between beliefs, thoughts, emotions, and behavior) and interventions to restore mental health based on this interplay

Through their rich contributions, these professionals have made it possible for thousands of children and their families to experience the gift of life more fully. With deep gratitude, thank you.

The staff from About Books has been exceptional. Allan Burns, the senior editor, reviewed my first ten pages and gave me the necessary encouragement to launch the book. Deb Ellis and Debi Flora and their staff have been a continual joy to work with. Thank you for making this part of the process enjoyable and rewarding.

These people have made writing this book such a rich experience. Once more, I thank each and every one of you for your meaningful contributions.

# INTRODUCTION

EVERY PARENT WANTS TO raise a self-confident, joyful child. Achieving this goal is one of the most challenging and rewarding tasks you will ever face. As a father of four children, a grandfather of seven, and a professional counselor of children for thirty-nine years, I know what it's like. But all too often the challenges end up causing you and your child to feel discouraged and defeated.

Do you need to accept those feelings as just part of parenting? Absolutely not! This book will teach you parent-friendly skills and steps for approaching your parenting challenges with hope and the anticipation of a successful outcome for both you and your child.

After counseling more than twenty-five hundred children and their moms and dads, I clearly saw three basic, underlying aspects of the relationship between children and parents. These three aspects form the basis of the skills you will learn as you read this book:

1. A basic need of every child is to feel "I'm good" and "I'm lovable" and to avoid feeling "I'm bad."

2. Emotions are a direct expression of your child's core being, his or her identity. Validating these emotions is essential to establishing "I'm good."

3. Fully expressed parental love establishes the belief of "I'm good" at the center of your child. The result: flourishing self-confidence and abounding joy. I call this fully expressed love "unleashed parental love."

Unleashing your parental love is at the heart of this book. You love your child and want to focus on the good within him or her. You know what fully loving your child is like during good times: The joy is tremendous for both of you. The key aspect of love is focusing on the good within your child, which is easy—when your child is obedient and contented. But how do you focus on the good when your child is disobedient and difficult to manage?

You'll find the answers to that question in the pages of this book. But in case you're feeling skeptical, let me assure you, you *can* continually focus on the good in your child even during the difficult times. That's what the skills of unleashed love enable you to do: focus continually on the good in both the fun times and the difficult times. We are not born with these skills, however; they must be acquired. I've seen many, many families gain these skills, and I have every confidence that you can as well.

Along with the steps outlined in the following pages, here are some of the key activities you will learn to do with and for your child:

- Establish healthy guilt within your child
- Match your temperament traits to those of your child
- Match your important life beliefs to your child's unique personality
- Establish your child's passion
- Change your child's behavior in the best way possible—with close to 98 percent success with the majority of expectations you establish for your child
- Advocate for your child with teachers and extended family

The journey we will take together throughout this book will result in your child acquiring an engrained belief of "I'm good" and "I'm lovable." Your child's self-esteem and joy will flourish. You will feel immeasurably fulfilled, knowing you have accomplished the most important task and privilege of your life: being a good parent.

### CHAPTER 1

# Love Works

"HI, MICHAEL. I'M GARY. How's it going today?"

Michael shook my hand cautiously, his head turned slightly away from me, eyes focused on the floor.

"Have a seat. Do you know why you're here?"

Michael tried to find a comfortable position on the sofa. "Yeah, I'm sick to death of being teased all the time about my weight, and my parents are always trying to help me, but what they say doesn't help." His voice started to shake, and tears welled up in his eyes. "I can't help it that I'm fat." He grabbed a tissue and wiped his nose. Then, looking me in the eye and raising his voice, he said, "And I'm really tired of my parents trying to tell me every little thing I can eat and yelling at me to stop eating—even when I'm still hungry. I wish they'd just leave me alone."

I talk with families like Michael's every day. They're not made up of bad kids or bad parents, but they've gotten stuck along the way, and they're not sure why. The parents are doing the best they know how, but they're frustrated with their inability to help their children succeed and be happy. Is there any worse frustration than to see your child unhappy and not be able to do anything about it?

Without exception, the parents who come to my office say they love their children. I'm sure you would say the same. But why, when parents try so hard to show their love, do difficult situations not get resolved? Kids end up feeling, at best, that their parents don't understand them and, at worst, that their parents don't love them.

The following pages will answer that question, so in the words of Rodgers and Hammerstein, "Let's start at the very beginning, a very good place to start," by focusing on what loving your child really means.

## What Is Parental Love?

First, some good news about parental love: All parents have the instinctive capacity to love their children. Sounds like a no-brainer, doesn't it? Perhaps in some ways it is. The problem occurs when parents rely only on their instinctive love without taking it further. Contenting ourselves with instinctive love would be somewhat like following our instinct to eat without concerning ourselves with what we're actually consuming. We'd feel full, but our health might suffer. So it is with parental love. By relying on our instincts, we might believe we've filled our children with love, but the emotional health of our kids and our family might be at risk. Kids tell us this when they say, "You don't understand me" or "You don't love me" or "You don't care." Fortunately for your children, by reading this book you've chosen to move beyond the instinctive and to explore the best possible way to love or nurture your child.

> Contenting ourselves with instinctive love would be somewhat like following our instinct to eat without concerning ourselves with what we're actually consuming.

Nature and nurture are the two fundamental aspects of your child's development. *Nature* refers to a child's inborn personality or temperament traits. (We'll look at this subject more closely in chapter 4.) *Nurture* describes the impact and influence of a child's entire environment on his or her development. I like to refer to parental nurturing as "parental love," which we'll define as follows:

> Parents behave and speak in ways that consistently transfer the message—through devotion, tenderness, and affectionate attachment—that their child is good or lovable.

So, what do I mean by "lovable"? The word tends to bring up images of cuddly teddy bears or puppies, but in relation to your children it goes far beyond warm fuzzies.

Feeling lovable means your child has acquired qualities from your parenting that result in the following firm belief: "I am a good, joyful, worthy person, able to attract caring, love, and acknowledgment of who I am from others."

In this book, loving your child means imparting the belief that he or she is fundamentally good. "I'm good" is your child's conscious experience of believing he or she is lovable.

Why do I place so much importance on a child feeling "I'm good"? A child's response to being corrected is either "I'm good" or "I'm bad"; there is no in-between.

"I'm good" far outweighs "I'm bad" as the best foundation for changing your child's behavior.

Children consistently tell me they either "feel good" or "feel bad" about their parents' responses to them. When Dad angrily asks, "Why can't you be more responsible?" the child doesn't have the ability to think (at least until adolescence), *Dad's had a bad day* or *Dad's just looking out for my best interests*. Every time a child tells me about a negative comment from a parent, the child ends with a self-blaming comment, such as "I make Dad mad all the time" or "I'm bad." This "I'm bad" response certainly motivates a child to change, and change will happen most of the time. After all, who wants to feel "I'm bad," especially when that idea comes from the most important people in a child's world, parents? Unfortunately, self-confidence and feeling

> A child's response to being corrected is either "I'm good" or "I'm bad"; there is no in-between.

valued are not being established with "I'm bad" as the motivator for change.

Here, put in very simple terms, is how you know parental love is working in the best way possible:

> You consistently hear, see, and feel your child feeling "I'm good" in response to your parenting. Parental love = your child feeling "I'm good."

This book will teach you how to get this "I'm good" response consistently from your child. Perhaps you're thinking, *I've really messed this up. My child already thinks she's bad. Have I ruined her? Is it too late for my family?* Every parent says this to me at the beginning of our sessions together. Good news! No, you have not ruined your child, and it is not too late to turn things around. Applying the unlimited power of parental love always has a profound impact on your child, no matter at what age you start. Take it to the bank. Your investment will provide significant returns. I've seen improvement in every family in my practice.

Parental love: Parents behave and speak in ways that consistently transfer the message—through devotion, tenderness, and affectionate attachment—that their child is good or lovable.

## Emotions: The Focus of Parental Love

The primary focus of parental love is your child's emotions and feelings. Daniel Goleman's excellent book on emotional intelligence confirms the central role emotions play in human lives.[1] Let's spend a moment to gain an understanding of emotions and feelings.

Surprisingly, no commonly accepted definition of *emotion* exists. In my clinical experience, Paul Ekman's list of core emotions is the most accurate representation of human emotions: anger, fear, sadness, happiness, surprise, and disgust.² I've modified this list by excluding surprise because it does not seem to be as basic as the other emotions, and I've also changed happiness to joy. The *Oxford Dictionary* defines "happiness" as a feeling based on luck or good fortune. "Joy" is defined as a vivid emotion of pleasure. Happiness comes more from external, material things; joy comes from internal, basic qualities, such as solid relationships, self-confidence, and strong values. Feeling joy has a more profound impact on your child's well-being than happiness does. Joy is also part of our definition of "lovable." Seeing your child frequently expressing joy indicates he or she is feeling lovable. Parental love is working!

Emotions are subjective and nonlogical (as opposed to thinking, which is objective and logical). The words *emotions* and *feelings* are typically used interchangeably, but in this book I define feelings as an individual's *unique experience* of one or more of the five basic emotions. These basic emotions are much like the primary colors—red, yellow, and blue—and feelings are the multiple variations of these primary colors and can range anywhere from basic orange, violet, and green to burnt umber, fuchsia, and aquamarine! For example, we all express anger in different ways. Some of us may shout and throw things; others may shout and pound on the nearest table; some express their anger in low, menacing tones; others may shout first and lower their voices after their initial outbursts.

Most of a feeling comes from one or more of the five core emotions, but thoughts mix into the feelings, as well. When someone asks, "How do you feel about that beautiful sunset?" you don't just say, "Joy." How weird would that sound? You feel the intensity of joy as the foundation of the feeling, but you express it with thoughts: "I can't believe how awesome the colors are. I feel so invigorated watching the clouds and light shift and change."

Now, what do feelings, thoughts, and sunsets have to do with your child feeling lovable? Many times children, as well as adults, do not respond with their feelings when asked what they feel; they only respond with their thoughts. When this happens, you can't validate the child's feelings. For example, here's an exchange between a mother and son:

"Billy, what do you feel when I take your computer time away from you for calling your sister a name?"

"You're so unfair; you're never that hard on my sister."

This response contains only thoughts. You need your child to verbalize feelings along with thoughts so you can validate the emotions. In this situation you can get at the emotion by adding a feeling word to the thought—for example, "It sounds like you're upset about how unfair I am."

> Your child's emotions are the most basic representation of who your child is. For this reason, parental love must first focus in the best way possible on the child's emotions.

I trust you're getting the idea that your child's emotions are really important; emotions are the primary source for developing your child's sense of goodness and identity, "who I am." A child trusts and relies on her emotions twenty-four hours of every day. The most basic and important feeling for children is either "I'm good" or "I'm bad." Children evaluate how people treat them and how they feel about themselves in these terms. Bottom line: Your child's emotions are the most basic representation of who your child is. For this reason, parental love must first focus in the best way possible on the child's emotions.

## Be the Adult

A fundamental requirement of parental love is for parents to be the adults when dealing with their own emotions and their child's emotions. By "being adult," I mean parents must acquire the ability to deal effectively with their own emotions as well as their child's emotions. Note the order of expressing parental love: Deal first with your emotions, then with your child's. You will not be able to handle your child's emotions if you aren't in control of your own. That doesn't mean you should ignore or "stuff" your emotions. Rather, you should become aware of them and proceed to deal with your child after you have adequately understood and effectively managed your own emotions. It's a three-part process: (1) become aware of your emotions, (2) understand them, and (3) effectively manage them.

Notice I said parents need to *acquire the ability* to deal effectively with both their own emotions and those of their child. Let's have a show of hands of how many of us were taught before we became parents how to deal effectively with emotions. I don't need a magic mirror to know that fewer than 5 percent of you raised your hands; that's the approximate percentage of clients I've seen who feel they were prepared to deal with emotions before they started parenting. Clearly, you are not alone if you feel unprepared to deal with emotions effectively. One of the primary purposes of this book is to help you acquire this ability.

Based on my experience, I know you'll succeed if you follow the principles in these pages. Let's look at an example of a mom who learned how to deal with her own emotions.

Jim continually trips his sister, and Mom has tried everything to stop him: warnings, threats, life sentence to his room—but nothing works. Mom is a typical parent. When Jim trips his sister, Mom becomes immediately frustrated and in a microsecond responds the way she always does: with a long lecture, yelling, menacing looks, and some type of consequence.

Here's how Mom responded after learning about the three parts of dealing effectively with emotions. After calming down from the 110th tripping episode, she took some time to reflect (becoming aware, part 1) on the intensity of her frustration. She reviewed the long lecture, her harsh voice, and the prison term she doled out to Jim. Yes, the frustration was too strong. (Mom is well on her way to understanding her emotion, part 2.) The biggest understanding? Mom felt like a complete failure as a parent. Then she realized her frustration was as much about feeling like a failure as it was about

Jim's tripping behavior. Mom worked through this feeling by accepting that she doesn't yet have the skills to deal with this tripping problem but that she should use the parental-love approach more thoroughly. (Mom is well on her way to dealing effectively with her emotions, part 3.)

Mom has learned through parental-love counseling that a parent needs to focus on the child's emotions first. Based on her awareness and understanding of her own emotions, Mom has become able to lay out the following first step: If she can't focus on Jim's emotions right away because her frustration is too high, she should leave the situation until she can focus on Jim's emotions. After several attempts, Mom gets it right: She either leaves right away because of too much frustration, or, when she effectively manages her frustration, she focuses on Jim's emotions. That's a high five, Mom. Way to go!

Are you wondering whether you can be your own therapist like Jim's mom—know when your frustration is too strong, understand why your emotion is so intense, and then deal effectively with your emotions so you can focus on your child's emotions?

You've actually done it before. You know you can control your emotions when your child accidentally drops a bowl of spaghetti. You know she didn't mean to make a mess, and when she cries, you have no difficulty gathering her into your arms, comforting her, and then working together to clean up the floor. If you've done this much, you're well on your way to making your child feel lovable. But what happens when your child consistently lies to you after you have explained multiple times why lying is destructive? Setting aside your feelings at that point is much more difficult. Difficult? Yes. Impossible? No.

You can do it! This book will give you plenty of practical information about how to understand yourself in situations like this and specific guidelines about how to help your child deal effectively with his or her emotions.

Let's summarize. Setting aside your emotions temporarily is the first step in dealing effectively with your child's feelings, thoughts, and behavior. It's the first of four parental-love requirements:

Set your thoughts and feelings aside temporarily, at the beginning of a problem-solving situation.

Even though your child may not realize it, through this requirement you are demonstrating a most powerful type of love: selfless love. This powerful type of love is the cornerstone of parental love. You're putting the well-being of someone else ahead of your own: a fundamental requirement for loving someone else. What a lesson for your child to learn from you! (Of course, this selflessness needs to be balanced with knowing when you need to stand up for what is important to you.)

> **Parental-Love Requirement 1:**
>
> Set your thoughts and feelings aside temporarily, at the beginning of a problem-solving situation.

Why is setting aside your emotions so difficult? When you feel strongly about something, you automatically believe the other person should feel and think the way you do—that's especially the case when you're trying to improve your child's thinking and behavior. It's typical human behavior but ineffective parenting behavior.

Conversely, when you set aside your emotions and thoughts, you make room for your parental love to operate at its fullest capacity—to feel, validate, and acknowledge your child's feelings and thoughts according to his or her world, not your world. This is the second parental-love requirement:

Start with your child's feelings first and the behavior second. In his book *Between Parent and Child*, Dr. Haim Ginott identified the crucial importance of focusing on the child's feelings.[3] Be at the center of your child, where thoughts and feelings reside. Start where your child is, not where you are.

> **Parental-Love Requirement 2:**
>
> Start with your child's feelings first and behavior second.

# Your Child's World

Sounds confusing, doesn't it? Validating according to your child's world. To explain, let's go right to Jim's world, his experience.

Jim's case is based on hundreds of children I've seen who purposely hurt their siblings. Jim feels his parents love his sister more than they love him. On the surface he's angry, but deep down he feels unlovable. He doesn't know it; he's not aware of being unlovable; all he feels is the emotion coming from it, anger. He handles his deep hurt by hurting his sister, who is loved more than he is. Jim expresses his hurt by hurting the person (his sister) who hurt him. Destructive? Of course. But it makes sense to Jim (though certainly not to adults). Until Jim feels his parents can experience or understand his world completely, no change will happen.

In contrast to Jim's world, here's a snapshot of Mom's world: *Jim is being destructive, and he needs to stop it right now. This is destroying his sister. I will not allow my daughter to be abused. What's wrong with Jim, anyway? What if Jim is this way to girls when he's older? What am I going to do?*

Is Mom correct in this thinking? Absolutely! Then what's unacceptable about her thinking? She must start with Jim's emotions and feelings, not his behavior. By the way, I'm not saying Mom should ignore her son's tripping behavior while she shows Jim understanding of his world. Consequences need to occur to minimize these episodes until the real cause, Jim's emotions, can be dealt with effectively.

The problem will be resolved most rapidly by Jim feeling his mother understands his world: *You love my sister more than you love me.* Only then can the behavior be dealt with. Incidentally, saying, "I understand, *but...*" will not work. Jim will need to be convinced. Mom will need to spend five or more minutes asking questions and validating feelings. Here's a brief example:

"Jim, what are you feeling about your sister?"

"I hate her, Mom."

"You're really upset, aren't you?"

"Yeah. You never get mad at her when she does something wrong!"

"Tell me more. I didn't realize you were so angry. That's really got to be—"

"You know the other day, when she…?"

> Being understood when a difference occurs is one of the *deepest* needs of your child.

You get the idea? Later on I'll give you detailed instructions on how to go through this validation process. One of the parental-love dialogue guidelines is you talk 25 percent of the time and your child talks 75 percent of the time when first validating feelings. When you encourage your child to talk more than you do at the beginning of a problem, your child receives a very important message: "Your thoughts and feelings are really important to me." Validation and understanding are accomplished. If you take nothing else from this book, I hope you will grasp this one concept: Being understood when a difference occurs is one of the *deepest* needs of your child.

Furthermore, you have the means to meet this need! When you do, your child's sense of identity and self-confidence will flourish.

Being in the child's world is being at the center of where your child is thinking and feeling. When you operate at that center, here's what your child experiences and processes at some level: "Mom is understanding the way I'm feeling and experiencing the situation. She's not immediately judging me as bad or wrong." This is parental love at its highest level! The result is your child feeling "I'm understood, good, acceptable, and valuable."

# The Birth of Self-Confidence

The most critical time for your child to feel understood, good, acceptable, and valuable is when differences occur. This is the fertile ground from which self-confidence grows with abundance. As we all know, the more self-confident we feel, the more we experience joy and fulfillment as an adult.

Since self-confidence is such a critical outcome of parental love, let's identify its four features:

1. *Knowing and comfortably expressing one's deepest feelings and thoughts.* For example, "When I got angry, I felt hurt when I heard you tell me that I did a lousy job washing the car. I'm sorry that I handled my hurt by yelling at you. But it really felt like a putdown" versus "I'm fed up with you telling me how messed up I am. I'm out of here—and don't expect me back home tonight."

2. *Minimal defensiveness.* For example, "You're right; I really didn't do that well on my essay. The ending needs to be more than just one sentence, and the beginning needs to be a little more creative" versus "My essays are never good enough for you. Everyone does them like this, and I'm handing it in just the way it is. If my teacher gives me a D like you say she will, it's her problem. Nobody likes her, and everyone gets at least a D on these essays."

3. *Accurate understanding of oneself and others; own your part first.* For example, "You said my brother always ends up getting hurt when we wrestle. I can see what you're saying. I guess it is actually true. I'm going to stop the part I play in this stuff. Let me tell you what part my brother is playing in it…" versus "It's all my brother's fault and you don't do anything about it. I won't do anything until he stops his…."

> The most critical time for your child to feel understood, good, acceptable, and valuable is when differences occur.

4. *Assertiveness.* For example, "I don't want to be disrespectful, Mom, but here's the way I felt and what I saw happen when I was late for my curfew" versus "I'm not talking, no matter what you try to take away. You can't make me talk. I don't care anyway."

Here's the formula for your child to develop self-confidence: Parental love = your child feeling "I'm good" ("I'm lovable") = your child's self-confidence.

Now let's take a look at some real-life parenting examples through the lives of two children: Michael—whom we met at the beginning of the chapter—and Karen. Michael's parents utilized their parental love to the fullest after effective counseling, and Michael developed significant self-confidence. Karen's parents struggled with utilizing their parental love capacity, and Karen likewise struggled to feel lovable and confident.

## Michael's Story: Parental Love Working Well

A word of caution before you read Michael's story: Please don't feel discouraged if you feel you can never reach the level of functioning Michael's family achieved. The good news is that all the families who complete counseling do acquire parental-love skills and do feel satisfied with the noticeable positive impact on their parenting and their child's self-confidence. Your goal should be noticeable, continued improvement, not some idealized "perfect" outcome. The results of parental love will be different for every family because every family is different! I encourage you to stay with me as I support you on your journey to acquire parental-love skills. I know you can do this! And remember, it's never too late to start implementing your parental love fully.

As you recall, fourteen-year-old Michael told me at his first session that he was upset by kids teasing him about his weight and the way his parents interfered. Over several months of weekly counseling, I worked with Michael and his parents (in separate sessions) to help them understand and learn to demonstrate parental love. Toward the end of counseling, Michael and I focused on how well he was coping with his overweight condition. Our conversation went something like this:

"So, Michael, how are you dealing now with being overweight?"

"You know, I've accepted it for now. I'm different than a lot of other kids, but, hey, everyone's different [demonstrates knowing and comfortably expressing one's feelings and thoughts]. Nobody's the same physically. This is what both my mom and dad have told me, and it makes sense. They say what matters is what kind of person I am. I feel I'm really okay just the way I am. Of course, there's always room for improvement [demonstrates knowing and comfortably expressing one's feelings and thoughts]. I do want to do more about being as healthy as I can, so I'm exercising by walking with my dad three times a week."

"That's wonderful, Michael! It sounds like you've figured out quite a bit about yourself. Now, what about the teasing? How are you handling it?"

"Well, I still don't like it. But since I've accepted that this is the way I am now, it hardly bothers me at all [demonstrates minimal defensiveness, knowing and comfortably expressing one's feelings and thoughts]. Besides, I know why they're teasing me. They don't feel very good about themselves, so they point out how different I am to somehow try to feel better about themselves" [demonstrates accurate understanding of others].

"So, what do you do when kids tease you?"

"Most of the time I just move on. Sometimes I joke about it, like, 'Why don't you guys go pick on someone your own size?' or 'I hope you feel better about yourself for noticing' [assertiveness]. My parents say, 'Sometimes you need to speak up, but make sure you're not attacking others, and never make more than one or two comments'" [assertiveness]. Cocking his head slightly, and looking at me out of the corner of his eye, he asked, "Did you tell them that, or are they that smart?"

I just smiled and asked him what his parents were doing about his weight other than walking with him.

"Oh, not much. We stopped having certain foods at home. It's funny; everyone else decided to do this for me. Isn't that something? They sure do love me. I'm so lucky to have a family like them [demonstrates accurate understanding of oneself and others]. My sister still gets her private stash of candy sometimes, but that's okay. And at the dinner table, my dad sometimes says when I take too many servings, 'Is that your stomach or your mind making that decision?' It makes me stop and think, so I usually don't take it [demonstrates comfort with knowing and expressing one's feelings and thoughts]. But that's about all they do. They spend most of their time telling me what's good about me instead of all the stuff I'm doing wrong."

Here's what happened when I met with Michael and his dad at the end of the session. Dad came in and sat down on my large couch right next to his son. Michael immediately put his arm around his dad and shifted even closer to him. He then told his dad what we had talked about. Dad looked at me with a smile and said, "Isn't he something else? We sure are lucky to have a son like him." They smiled at each other, and at the end of the session they walked out with their arms around each other's shoulders, chuckling and discussing what they would do next.

Clearly, this family was well on its way to success. What a vivid picture of how powerful love can be!

# Karen's Story: Parental Love Difficult to Provide

Now let's take a look at a teenage girl who was not as fortunate as Michael in regard to both her temperament traits and her parents' nurturing. Whereas Michael's personality included temperament traits of calm, openness, optimism, adaptability, persistence, and a great sense of humor, Karen—also fourteen years old—was quiet, moody, unpredictable, slow to adapt, withdrawn, and only minimally aware of her feelings. Recently, she had made friends in the "Goth" crowd and started wearing black clothes, heavy eye makeup, and an eyebrow ring. She refused to do her homework, so her grades had dropped to Ds and Fs from the previous year's Bs. Karen was generally quiet and sullen. She never did what her mother asked, and, if pushed, argued and yelled. Karen's mom, Joan, wasn't trying to do things with her because when asked if she wanted to go shopping or to a movie, Karen always said no.

In the first session, Joan asked Karen why Karen would never talk to her. Slouched as far into the corner of the couch as she could, as far away from her mother as possible, Karen deepened her creased frown but remained silent. After several requests from her mother with no answer, I gently made several inquiries to Karen—also with no response [demonstrates nonassertiveness, defensiveness]. I asked Joan to leave, and on her way out, she said to Karen with tears running down her face, "I'm not doing a very good job parenting. I need a lot of help from Gary."

Karen was silent for several moments. Then, "I hate my mom."

"Tell me more," I said.

"Oh, never mind; you would never understand!" [demonstrates defensiveness].

"I can tell you feel strongly that adults never understand you, but I'd like for you to at least give me a chance."

Karen looked up briefly at me from the corner of her eye, then said, "She's always gone, and she never spends time with me. My dad always asks about my grades and complains about my clothes.

There's nothing wrong with my clothes. And I hate school, but I like my Goth friends; at least they accept me and don't always nag me. Before the divorce, I was daddy's girl, and now all he does is bug me. I don't know what happened" [demonstrates limited but some understanding of oneself and others].

I asked whether her parents had any reasons for nagging her, trying to see whether she understood what part she was playing in the problems.

"I'm not doing anything wrong. School is boring. I'm sick of them always bugging me. I wish they would just leave me alone and let me do what I want" [defensive, inaccurate understanding of oneself and others].

"I thought you wanted your mom to spend more time with you."

"No, I guess I really don't. She has her boyfriend. I really don't care anymore."

"Many times we give up and say we don't care when really we do, because it hurts too much to care."

She looked up, discouraged. "This isn't going to help. Can I go now?" [defensive, inaccurate understanding of oneself and others].

The combination of Karen's difficult temperament traits and a stressful divorce contributed to her low self-confidence, and she certainly didn't feel lovable. On the positive side, Karen was able to maintain her Goth friends, which gave her a sense of acceptance and made her feel good. By the way, did you notice that with just a little support, Karen opened up more? Why? She felt validated and that someone was interested in hearing about her world—two essential parts of parental love.

Karen did receive important parental-love messages from her mother. Joan valued Karen by starting counseling and acknowledging to her daughter that she needed to parent Karen better. These messages conveyed to Karen that she was worth loving and set Karen on the path toward feeling lovable.

By the way, don't expect your child to show you that he or she has received these messages when the differences have reached this level of hurt. In fact, expect no positive reaction and some rejection from your child at the beginning stages of problem solving. Later, when the hurt is not so intense, kids such as Karen tell me in one way or another that they were and are aware of their parents' loving efforts.

Both Karen and Joan were carrying a heavy load; they felt very little hope. Without knowing it, Karen demonstrated hope by her partial openness to me when I validated her feelings and made an effort to be in her world. Without outside assistance, the risk would have been high for Karen's family to experience worsening family dysfunction. (Later on we'll revisit this family and learn more about how Joan and Karen made great strides toward Karen becoming more self-confident.)

Now that you've witnessed what the results need to be, how do you go about exercising your parental love? You need to fine-tune a powerful part of love: selfless love. When you do, you'll build great self-confidence in your child, the subject of our next chapter.

### CHAPTER 2

# Building Your Child's Self-Confidence

"CAN YOU HELP US build our child's self-confidence?" This is the most frequently asked question in my counseling practice. Parents typically go on to explain why they want this help: "She gets teased more than other children"; "He gives up on anything that takes any effort"; "She never wants to try new things"; or "When homework is too hard, he just will not try." Self-confidence questions are always a serious, major concern of all parents. What is the answer?

Self-confidence in your child can be significantly increased when you fine-tune your parental-love capacity. As I mentioned in the last chapter, here's how that will look:

| Parental love | = | your child feeling "I'm good" ("I'm lovable") | = | your child's self-confidence |
|---|---|---|---|---|

Now let's break down the elements of this equation:

*Parental love*: Parents behave and speak in ways that consistently transfer the message—through devotion, tenderness, and affectionate attachment—that their child is good or lovable.

*"I'm good"*: Feeling good, or lovable, means your child has acquired qualities from your parenting that result in your child's firm belief: "I am a good, joyful, worthy person, able to attract caring,

love, and acknowledgment of who I am from others."

Building your child's self-confidence is a matter of putting together these elements by practicing four parental-love requirements. Chapter 1 lays out the first two, but I've listed them here as well, as a reminder:

> Feeling good, or lovable, means your child has acquired qualities from your parenting that result in your child's firm belief: "I am a good, joyful, worthy person, able to attract caring, love, and acknowledgment of who I am from others."

1. Set your thoughts and feelings aside temporarily, at the beginning of a problem-solving situation.

2. Start with your child's feelings first and the behavior second. Be at the center of your child, where thoughts and feelings reside. Start where your child is, not where you are.

3. Establish behavioral expectations that will enable your child to be successful 98 percent of the time. (Forget about your behavior requirements for success.)

4. Dialogue effectively:
   ✔ Avoid judging.
   ✔ Avoid negative comments.
   ✔ Be calm.
   ✔ Talk no more than 25 percent of the time; allow your child to talk 75 percent of the time (the 75/25 rule).
   ✔ Make only one or two points at a time.
   ✔ Keep the transaction brief.
   ✔ Acknowledge your mistakes.

# Success—Most of the Time

Who likes to fail? No hands raised. That's why the 98 percent success instruction is so important. Let's say you're trying to get your ten-year-old to clean up his room. Here's the typical parental response. (If I had a dollar for every time I've heard this room-cleaning story, I'd be living in a home in Hawaii on top of a cliff overlooking the ocean.)

"You've had one hour to clean this up. What are you doing? You need to be more responsible and have more respect for yourself." (Actually, the mini-lecture goes on for at least three minutes.)

"I don't know. Why can't I just close the door so you don't have to see the mess? Why should you care?"

"It's sloppy, and it looks bad. (Oops, there's the "B" word. We've all said it too many times!) You need to take some pride in your things and in our home."

Now let's see how the 98 percent success instruction works. Start by setting an expectation you think will have the best chance to be completely successful, but 98 percent will do. In this case, you realize you've set the bar too high, so you adjust your expectation, stating it clearly and without judgment to your child.

> **Parental-Love Requirement 3:**
>
> Establish behavioral expectations that will enable your child to be successful 98 percent of the time.

"I see you haven't cleaned up your room yet. It looks like I've asked you to do more than you can do for now. Let me help you. I'll do this half while you do the other half."

The room gets done (you're happy); your child feels lovable (he or she is happy); and together you've taken another step toward building self-confidence.

Success reinforces "I'm good." If you're looking for motivators to change your child's behavior, you've found the best one. (Doesn't

cost anything either. What a deal.) Success is a primary motivator for changing
behavior. Consider it in your own life. It's
very tough to change your eating habits to
lose weight, but once you've dropped five
pounds, aren't you more motivated to go

> Success is a primary motivator for changing behavior.

for ten? Don't you feel more inspired to prepare a meal on Tuesday
when the family raves about Monday's dinner?

The 98 percent plan becomes essential when you notice a problem
repeating itself. You want to fix the problem as soon as possible; the
98 percent plan will do the trick. Let's look again at the room-cleaning illustration. You might be thinking, *A ten-year-old should be able
to clean his room by himself*, and I'd probably agree with you. A ten-
year-old with low self-confidence, however, might struggle with the
task. So, as his mom, you've already created a "success scenario" with
the "I'll do half; you do half" expectation. Maybe you'll have to do
that a few more times before you move to "I'll put your clean clothes
in the dresser, and you put your dirty clothes in the basket, pick up
the trash, and make your bed." As your
child's self-confidence improves, he can
do more and more on his own. Maybe
a few weeks from now, you'll just be his
cheerleader when he finishes each task
related to cleaning his room. Ultimately,
of course, your goal is for him to do the
entire project on his own. (You'll still
want to offer lots of praise when he's
done, though. You might even take the
opportunity to show him how far he's
come: "Remember when I had to do half

> Low self-confidence requires lower expectations and almost immediate and visible success; high self-confidence allows for more challenging expectations without need of such immediate success.

of this job for you? Wow! You've come a long way! Great job!") Low
self-confidence requires lower expectations and almost immediate
and visible success; high self-confidence allows for more challenging
expectations without need of such immediate success.

# Dialogue Effectively

The fourth parental-love requirement, dialogue effectively, gives you the most specific directions for how to put your parental-love equation of actions and words together for the best result—your child's self-confidence. In the above room-cleaning example, the mother helping her child do half the room includes most of the essential actions and words for effective dialogue. She doesn't judge; she speaks calmly; she makes only a couple points and does so briefly; and she acknowledges her mistakes.

### What It Looks Like at Home

Now that we know the equation for achieving your child's self-confidence, let's take these parental-love requirements out of the counseling office and into your home. Remember, start where your child is by dealing with your child's emotions and feelings first; acknowledge and validate them (requirement 2), putting yours aside (requirement 1). Deal with behavior issues second, with a goal of 98 percent success (requirement 3). When you've entered your child's world, follow the effective dialogue principles (requirement 4): Avoid judging; be calm; do not talk more than 25 percent of the time (75/25 rule); make only one or two points at a time; keep the transaction brief; and acknowledge when you make a mistake.

In the following pages we'll see a typical exchange between a parent and child that does not reflect the parental-love requirements, and then we'll look at a healthier exchange.

Parental-Love
Requirement 4:

Dialogue effectively.

### "It's All About Me"

Andrew came home from his first day of middle school. The door banged open. He slammed down his book bag and yelled, "I hate that math teacher; she's so mean!"

Just as he was catching his breath, his mother poked her head around the corner, pointed at him, and said, "Andrew John"—he knows he's in trouble when she uses his middle name—"pick up that bag right now, go to your room, and stay there until you can say something nice about Miss Evans."

"But, Mom, she—"

"Don't 'but Mom' me. You heard me. And I don't want to hear that *hate* word one more time."

Case closed. Court adjourned. So there!

Andrew stomped upstairs to his room, turned on the TV as loud as he dared, and flopped onto his bed, trying to calm down. *When I get mad and use unacceptable words, I always get sent to my room. Nobody understands me. She doesn't care. When I come home, I shouldn't bring up things that make her mad. What's wrong with me that I get so mad?* Andrew was establishing "I'm bad" in his emotional databank.

Back in the kitchen, Mom paused over the kitchen sink, looked out the window, and thought for a minute. *What am I going to do about Andrew getting so angry at Miss Evans, and how am I going to get him to stop saying he hates people when he doesn't get along with them? It seems the problem is getting worse, and I don't know what to do but send him to his room! I'm such a failure.*

Now let's look at an equally frustrating after-school scenario that implements the parental-love requirements.

### "It's All About My Child"

Beth threw down her backpack, slammed the door shut, and yelled at the top of her lungs, "Mom, where are you?" As she rushed past her mom in the kitchen, she burst into tears. "I hate my English teacher. She's never fair. I wish she'd be abducted by aliens and just disappear off the face of the planet!"

Mom grabbed a box of tissues and followed Beth to the couch, where she was sobbing on the armrest. Mom handed Beth a tissue and sat calmly next to her. "Sounds like you're very upset from a hard day. Tell me more."

Red-eyed, Beth faced her mom. "I'm sick of that old hag. She never gives me a chance. I didn't hear her say the paper had to be typed. Mom, I finished the report, but I did it in pencil." Sobbing again, Beth continued. "She said my grade would be reduced 10 percent. Can you believe that?"

"I can tell by your comments that you're really angry and hurt." Mom adjusted her voice to an extra-caring tone and moved closer to Beth, gently touching her daughter's hand. "This is really painful, isn't it, sweetie?"

Beth scowled, pulling away from her mom. "Of course it is! Wouldn't you be saying the same thing?"

"I would be angry. Of course, I would." They embraced. *Beth's getting a little calmer.*

*Glad Mom always listens to me.... Wish my teacher wasn't always disagreeing with me.*

Does this scenario make you uncomfortable? Does it sound wrong? Most parents hearing this for the first time feel bothered. Did you just write off Beth's mom as too perfect to be real? After all, what parent *always* listens and *never* disagrees? Actually when parents follow parental-love procedures most of the time, children frequently relate this type of "perfect" statement. Remember, I'm reporting from the child's world; it's black-and-white, and children are always inspired when their feelings are validated.

You want your child to feel this type of support from you at the beginning of a dialogue. You can achieve this by focusing on the emotions before you address the behavior. Remember: Listening validates your child, establishes "I'm good" deep inside her, and results in increased self-confidence. Beth's behavior will be dealt with only after the emotions have been handled adequately.

Maybe you're feeling discouraged after reading how Mom handled Beth. You're thinking, *This sounds impossible. I can't see myself saying those words. It's like a foreign language. Forget it. I don't think I can do this.* Wait! Hold on! That's what all my clients say at first. And they (and you) are right; talking to your child in this manner is like trying to speak Russian when the only Russian words you know are *nyet*, borscht, and Moscow! But making a change or learning a new skill always feels awkward at first. Trust me. Soon you'll be speaking Russian, er, the dialogue of parental love, with ease. Every client

> Listening validates your child, establishes "I'm good" deep inside her, and results in increased self-confidence.

who has finished the parental-love counseling has gone on to implement parental-love requirements the majority of the time. The dialogue Beth's mom pulled off was her best. Sometimes, though less and less, she goes back to her old ways. But she keeps growing in her skills, and I'm confident you will as well. Incidentally, it might make you feel better to know that fewer than 1 percent of the clients I've worked with come in with even a basic understanding of how the parental-love requirements work. But if they can learn how to build self-confidence in their children, I have no doubt that you can too!

# FAQs

By now you probably have a few questions—and maybe even a few objections—rolling around in your mind. Let's pause to address those I hear most often.

*I can see the benefit of validating Beth's anger, but I hope you're not saying you agree with slamming the door, using the word* hate, *and blaming everything on the teacher—are you?*

Absolutely not! All the things Beth did to show her anger are unacceptable. Underneath Beth's anger is hurt. Mom supports Beth as acceptable and valuable; she hasn't yet addressed the behavior. (Chapter 8 will give you the details about anger and hurt.) As I mentioned, validation of feelings first, behavior change second.

*I'm still not quite getting why I should focus on the feelings first. Isn't it more important to stop inappropriate expressions of anger?*

This procedure is confusing because inappropriate behavior does need to be stopped. Unfortunately, starting with a child's inappropriate behavior is the typical way adults handle problems with their children. Feelings, however, are the most important cause of unacceptable behavior. The most long-lasting, productive behavior changes are a result of your focusing first on the energy source of behavior and the most basic representation of your child's feelings and thoughts. Through this step your child acquires the most basic knowledge, acceptance, and understanding of him- or herself.

Now let's unpack these parental-love requirements to make them practical and successful for you.

## Start Where Your Child Is: Two Steps

In figure 2.1 a gap occurs between the parent's expectations and the child's behavior. This gap represents not starting where your child is, as in our previous examples of Karen and Andrew. Both parent and child are frustrated and unsuccessful with this gap. The diagram then shows the parent joining the child, starting where the child is.

## Doomed for Failure

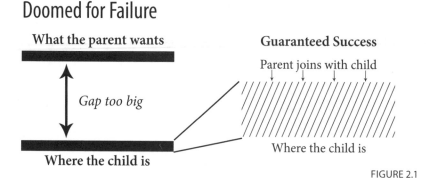

FIGURE 2.1

## Stretch but Doable

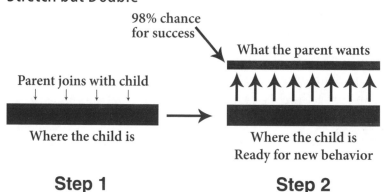

FIGURE 2.2

In figure 2.2, you see the two-step process of starting where your child is:

Step 1: Be in the center of where your child is: emotions and behavior.

Step 2: Present your child with behavior that's a bit of a stretch but still doable—the activity of a child gradually moving up from unacceptable to improved behavior.

Doable improved behavior means there is a 98 percent chance of the behavior working. I call this the "stretch-but-doable" rule.

> Doable improved behavior means there is a 98 percent chance of the behavior working. I call this the "stretch-but-doable" rule.

Let's go back to Beth and her mom for an example of how to implement these steps correctly.

Beth has trouble writing essays. She only writes a few sentences per paragraph, not enough for the teacher. And she usually includes too many ideas in each sentence, at least four or five. Let's listen in on how Mom approaches the problem. Beth has just written two paragraphs like she always does: too few sentences, too many ideas per sentence.

"Beth, I've told you not to put more than one or two ideas in one sentence."

Beth stiffens and turns her head. "Fine. You do it if you think I'm so dumb."

The conversation results in total frustration, anger, and no success. Obviously, the gap between Mom and Beth is too wide (fig. 2.1). Now let's look at the adjustment Mom makes to be in the center of where Beth is.

"Writing a paragraph is really—"

"I hate writing. I don't like it when you try to help. You think I'm stupid. I could do this if I wanted to."

Mom moves closer and tries to make her voice gentle. "I know you can. Writing paragraphs is very upsetting to you. We're going to—"

"Of course it is. Wouldn't you get frustrated if you had a teacher as demanding as mine?" (Less anger.)

"I would feel like you do. It's really hard, isn't it?"

Beth looks down sadly. "Yeah, I just hate writing."

"Let me help in a different way so this isn't so—"

"Like how?"

## Four Features of Self-Confidence

1. Knowing and comfortably expressing one's feelings and thoughts
2. Minimal defensiveness
3. Accurate understanding of oneself and of others
4. Assertiveness

"Let's you and me come up with some ideas for the first paragraph and then put two of the ideas in each sentence. Maybe then we can try to make a three-sentence paragraph."

Beth frowns. "Okay, but then you have to leave after the first paragraph is done, and I'll do the next one myself."

"I'll leave for the second paragraph."

Mom has successfully completed the first step of starting at the center of where Beth is. Now the frustration is low and Beth is ready to modify her behavior—trying to write several sentences with only two ideas in each sentence. She's now ready for the stretch-but-doable second step, actually implementing the plan Mom suggested.

"Okay, let's start by identifying a thought or two for several sentences," Mom says.

Beth and Mom come up with six ideas; Mom writes the first sentence, and Beth writes two more sentences. The first paragraph is done! Beth is surprised Mom did the first sentence; she's never done this before. (Good job, Mom!)

Now Beth is ready to move up to another level: doing the next paragraph by herself, starting with identifying four to six ideas to put in two or more sentences.

With the first paragraph done, Beth looks at her mom and says, with urgency in her voice, "Mom, you said you would leave. Leave! Please, now!"

"I did promise that, and you did such a good job on the first paragraph."

"I know, I know. I can do it."

"I'll leave right now, if you will accept my seeing what you did without shouting at me when I come back."

"Okay, okay!"

Mom leaves, and soon Beth yells from her room, "Come take a look, Mom."

Mom reviews Beth's work and sees that the paragraph is an improvement over previous ones. She notices one misspelling and two grammatical errors but chooses to comment only on the success of one or two ideas per sentence. "Great, Beth! You put the right number of ideas in each sentence." (To comment on all the mistakes would have been a stretch that wasn't doable—not a chance for achieving 98 percent success.)

"See, Mom, I told you I could do it by myself." Self-confidence beams from Beth's face.

Mom smiles and touches Beth's arm. "Yes, you certainly did."

By following both steps in starting where her child was, Mom achieved her parental-love goal: Beth felt "I'm valuable," "I'm lovable," "I'm good," and not "I'm bad." Wow, what a great piece of work Mom did!

This might seem like hard work at first, but the joy you'll see on your child's face and the success you'll feel as a parent will make the labor worth it all!

## FAQs 2

*In the first paragraph-writing go around, Beth and her mom were both so frustrated. This is where I'm stuck; my child and I both end up frustrated. How can we get past it?*

It is true that in the initial step of Mom's being in the center of Beth, Beth was very frustrated and her mom had to feel frustrated too. Expect this level of frustration at first. The initial stages of conflict are very frustrating with little to no surface appearance of success from your child. After you have successfully mastered the above two steps, be assured you are making a difference, even if you don't see indications of success from your child at the beginning of a conflict. With this knowledge and continued practice, you will become less and less frustrated. Keep trying.

*I'm really bothered by how the mother almost did the first paragraph for Beth. In my opinion, this is enabling. Beth really needs to do this on her own. How is she ever going to get to the point of independence? Isn't her mom teaching Beth to stay helpless?*

At the initial stages of therapy, I hear this question quite often.

Obviously, this issue is of great concern. The last thing we want to do is make our children dependent and irresponsible. On the surface, Mom's involvement looks like enabling, or doing what Beth should be doing herself.

The key point here is to find the level of assistance that establishes your child's success 98 percent of the time initially and then gradually help her to be more independent and responsible—but only as she continues to experience mastery and success most of the time.

Staying too long at the initial level of success with continued significant help would definitely be a form of "enabling." Enabling, as you have used the term, refers to doing for someone (often an addict) what he could and should be doing for himself. If Beth's mom wrote every opening paragraph of every essay all semester long, we could safely say she had slipped into this type of enabling—not a good thing. Webster's dictionary defines "enable" this way: "to provide with the means or opportunity; to make possible, practical, or easy." And that's what Beth's mom is doing in our scenario. She is not teaching her child to be irresponsible. Rather, she is, in a sense, offering Beth a helping hand— teaching by example and then encouraging her daughter to do for herself what she can.

*Okay, I guess I can see the reason for this approach. I'll have to try it myself to see whether it works, but what parent has the time to do all this stuff? I don't think it's realistic, especially since I'm a single parent.*

> The key is to find the level of assistance that establishes your child's success 98 percent of the time initially and then gradually help him or her to be more independent and responsible—but only as he or she continues to experience mastery and success most of the time.

At first glance, this task seems to take a lot more time than what you may be doing now. Over the years, parents have informed me that at the beginning, this approach does take a few more minutes than they're used to. Implementing a new approach to any type of

problem solving will be more time in-
tensive at first. Once you've tackled
a few situations using this method,
though, the length of time required to
complete the two steps compared to the
old approach is about the same. The big
benefit of this approach is the outcome:
emotional growth, success, and satisfac-
tion for both parent and child. (For more help in monitoring the
parental-love requirements, see appendix A.)

The big benefit of this approach is the outcome: emotional growth, success, and satisfaction for both parent and child.

To encourage you to invest the extra few minutes this approach
requires, let me comment on a couple of benefits of implementing
effective parental love that I haven't mentioned yet.

First, your child learns from your example how to apply the parental-love requirements in his or her relationships with peers and
adults. These skills are a significant asset for your child in establishing quality relationships, whether it be with friends, a future spouse,
or future coworkers. With successful implementation of parental
love, your child will feel lovable ("I'm good") and in turn will attract
emotionally healthy people. Also, having seen the good in him- or
herself, your child will see and reinforce the good in others.

Second, your child will become an expert on his or her emotional world, the part of the human condition that plays the most significant role in determining behavior. Through your parental love,
your child will acquire the skills to know his or her feelings clearly,
particularly the ability to label and work through feelings. All four
features of self-confidence will have the best chance possible to be
fully developed. With these essential skills in place, life's many positive and challenging conditions will be managed in the best way possible. As an added bonus, all of these parental-love benefits work in
adult relationships. I'd encourage you to use them whenever possible.
For example, you might just find that difficult coworkers become less
challenging when you meet them where they are, focusing on their
emotions first before you address whatever issues they're presenting.

Before we go to the next chapter, let's summarize what we've learned in these first two chapters:

- Your child's emotions are the most basic representation of who your child is.

- Practicing parental love means your child is experiencing you being at the center of his or her world. Parental love requires the parent to be selfless: first, temporarily putting aside your thoughts and feelings when problem solving and then validating your child's feelings and thoughts. This is selfless love.

- Implementing parental-love requirements means your child is consistently receiving the message that he or she is good or lovable. The characteristics of this relationship are devotion, tenderness, and affectionate attachment.

- Your child feeling lovable is the result of implementing the parental-love requirements. Feeling lovable means your child believes: I am a good, worthy person, able to attract caring and love from others and acknowledgment of who I am.

- Self-confidence is the result of parental love. There are four features of self-confidence:
  1. Knowing and comfortably expressing one's feelings and thoughts
  2. Minimal defensiveness
  3. Accurate understanding of oneself and of others
  4. Assertiveness

Now let's turn to a discussion about your parenting beliefs, the subject of our next chapter. How can you make sure your most important beliefs are transmitted to your child in the best way possible?

### CHAPTER 3

# When Good Beliefs
# Go Bad

"GARY, I DON'T KNOW what I'm going to do. Aaron lies all the time. No matter how often I explain why lying is wrong, he continues to lie—even when he knows I know he's lying! I'm really afraid. Lying is a big deal to me. My dad made it clear to us kids that lying was the worst thing a person could do to another person. If we lied, we got spanked; so we didn't lie. No questions asked. It was that simple. I've spanked Aaron, taken away privileges, and even grounded him, but it doesn't stop the lying. What if he grows up to be a liar?"

Aaron's dad is stuck. And most of us can relate. As parents, we've all been there, and we'll be there again. Unfortunately, it's part of the parenting territory. Whether our children lie, don't do or don't hand in their homework, use marijuana, argue, defy authority, don't follow through with chores, or misbehave in other ways, we all get stuck in trying to change our child's actions. Nothing we try works. We may go to a workshop, read a book, or talk with a friend about different ways to handle the problem. We think we have the answer, but no matter which approach we try, the problem persists. Aaron's dad had tried everything he knew to break his son's habit of lying. He landed in my office, dejected and discouraged, as a last resort.

# "Stuck in the Middle with You"

Important news flash: Dad and Aaron (and you and your child) can get unstuck! There is a solution to this dilemma.

Dad needs to begin by exercising more of his parental love. He must start where Aaron is: emotions first, behavior second. That's going to be a bit difficult for him to do, however, and here's why: In the previous chapters we said a parent needs first to deal effectively with his or her own emotions before addressing the child's. What do you think about Dad's emotions as he expressed them to me: "I'm really afraid" and "Lying is a big deal to me"? They're pretty intense, too strong to set aside even for the sake of maximizing his parental love.

Strong emotions cloud our problem-solving ability; they dominate reason and logic and will take over in a situation that triggers them. Remember the old adage about the person who can't see the forest for the trees? In this case, Dad's emotions are definitely the trees! Since Dad really needs to focus on the "forest" of Aaron's emotions, what should he do?

> Strong emotions cloud our problem-solving ability; they dominate reason and logic and will take over in a situation that triggers them.

He needs to do two simple, yet difficult, things. First, Dad must understand why his emotions are so strong, and, second, he must find a way to manage his emotions effectively.

In this family's situation, Dad's strong emotions are coming from his deep-seated belief system about what makes a person "good" or "bad." Sound familiar? As children, we experienced ourselves—"I'm good" or "I'm bad"—just as rigidly as our kids do now. And our present-day parental beliefs were formed based on the way "I'm good" and "I'm bad" were communicated to us by our parents. (I'll explain this in more detail in a moment.) Here's my definition of parental beliefs:

Parental beliefs are a set of logically based, passionate, emotional convictions—specific morals, principles of good behavior, and values—that are essential for a child to be a "good" person. Parents want their children to share and practice these beliefs.

Each one of us is passionate and certain about our parental beliefs. (In this chapter, those "priority" beliefs are the ones we're most interested in.) As adults, we experience no stronger emotions than those associated with being "good" or "bad," particularly in relation to our children. Of the five core emotions mentioned in chapter 1, four are associated with being "bad": fear, anger, disgust, and sadness. Powerful emotions, aren't they? No wonder the feeling of "I'm bad" is so difficult and powerful! Aaron's dad feels each one of these emotions when his child lies. His memories of his own childhood lying play vividly in his mind in high-definition color and surround sound. By the way, as you may recall, only one of the core emotions is associated with being "good": joy.

Let's sidetrack for just a moment and talk about the power of joy. Even though only one core emotion is associated with "I'm good," joy is more powerful than all of the other four emotions when it is the predominant emotion felt **Joy is the result of parental love.** by a child or adult. Do you find that difficult to believe? I've seen it over and over in my practice. Once people adequately address the other four emotions through understanding and problem solving, joy always becomes the most prominent emotion in their lives. As you read through this book, you will see how joy is the result of parental love.

Going back to Aaron's dad, now we can understand why he's stuck. Dad's belief system about lying is the same as yours: Lying is bad. You may not feel the intense emotions Aaron's dad does, however, because your parents may have instilled your belief about lying using the principles of parental love. But in his case, his father's strong emotional and physical reaction planted a deeply rooted belief: "If I lie, I'm bad." This belief sets off all four negative core emotions every time Aaron lies, with fear being the most basic: fear of not being lovable, of being "bad," and of not being valued by a parent.

Throughout this book I have said feeling lovable is the most basic need of a child. (And you'll probably read it a few more times before we're through.) If parental responses focus too much on how bad the child is (from the child's experience), the child will always feel fear. Some fear is important as a motivator for change. Too much fear minimizes self-confidence and maximizes "I'm bad." Here's a useful rule of thumb: Focusing on your child's behavior first with a lot of frustration causes too much fear; focusing first on and validating your child's emotions (being in the center of his or her world) minimizes fear. (We'll look more closely at fear in chapter 8.)

> Some fear is important as a motivator for change. Too much fear minimizes self-confidence and maximizes "I'm bad."

When Aaron lies, Dad's most basic emotion is fear. His self-talk goes something like this: "I know how scared I felt [fearful] when my dad caught me in a lie; he was really mad at me [feeling unlovable]. I can never allow my son to feel bad about himself like I did. It's awful. I must immediately stop my son's bad lying behavior." Most of this self-talk—and the emotions causing the self-talk—is unconscious. No wonder our emotions are so strong when we get stuck trying to change our child's negative, "bad" behavior—particularly when we did the same "bad" behavior ourselves. By the way, the impact of your parent's frustrated reactions toward a sibling's "bad" behavior can have a negative impact on you as well. You sensed the frustration your parent felt toward your sibling, and you became extra careful not to do what your sibling did to make your parent so angry.

To get unstuck in regard to your child's behavior, you'll first need to become aware of your belief system. (Dr. Aaron Beck's cognitive therapy program outlines the role beliefs play in behavior.[1]) Don't worry; I'm not asking you to consider changing those beliefs that work for you, only the ones that don't work. I just want you to change how you experience what you believe. Now, before you roll your eyes, wave your hand, and dismiss this as a bunch of psycho-mumbo-jumbo, read a little further and let me explain.

> To get unstuck in regard to your child's behavior, you'll first need to become aware of your belief system.

## Beliefs from the Ground Up

Let's start by looking at how your belief system was created.

The image of welding provides a great illustration of how your beliefs became part of you. As a child raised on a farm, I had many opportunities to see this process firsthand. The welder places the two pieces of metal he wants to connect as close together as possible. Then, with his helmet on (think Darth Vader), the welder lights a torch-type nozzle. A flame ignites, and the work begins. With his torch in one hand and his welding rod in the other, the welder places the rod on both pieces of metal, holds the torch to it, and watches carefully as the rod melts and spreads to cover both pieces, welding the two together. He lifts the rod, shuts off the torch, and *voilà!* the two broken pieces are as good as new.

Likewise, when you were a child, your developing beliefs were like one of the metal pieces, and your parents' beliefs were the other. They used parental love or fear and anger as the torch and rod through thousands of intense emotional exchanges with you. In either case, your beliefs were welded into place at a deep level within you. The method they used—love or fear—determined whether you feel good or bad when you respond to your child's violating your belief.

Acquiring a belief is an intense, heated process. No wonder we are so passionate and certain about our beliefs.

# Better Clarity

Let's apply our welding illustration to Aaron's behavior. In Aaron's situation, the welder is Dad, with all of his heated emotional lying belief and Aaron's lying behavior. Dad wants to weld his telling-the-truth belief into Aaron's belief system. So far Dad's been unsuccessful. Here's why (Can you guess?): He's not starting where Aaron is. We'll get to the specific steps needed for Dad to make the best weld possible in just a little bit, but first let's look at two more aspects about beliefs: (1) Most of our beliefs are unconscious, and (2) we project our unconscious beliefs onto others.

*Beliefs Are Mostly Unconscious*

Here's what cognitive neuroscientists have to say about the unconscious: We are aware of only about 5 percent of what causes our decisions, actions, emotions, and behavior.[2] A car suddenly pulls out in front of you. You don't think about what to do; you react defensively from your unconscious memory. So it is with our beliefs, especially when the "welding" process was intensely uncomfortable. When Aaron lied, Dad was not aware of how his intense belief was created; but unconsciously, all the emotions and events related to it from his childhood were turned on inside him; they were the source of his intense emotional responses. Dad was aware only of his intense feelings of failing as a dad. Incidentally, when our beliefs have been welded into place by pleasurable emotional experiences, we will be conscious of them in high-definition awesome joy. Enthusiastic scuba divers believe diving is the best recreational activity and dive whenever possible. When scuba divers talk or think about scuba diving, they are instantly aware of all their past emotions and experiences related to scuba diving. Similarly, if you have learned

> We are aware of only about 5 percent of what causes our decisions, actions, emotions, and behavior.

that good people don't cheat, for example, and your parents taught you this belief with parental love, you will likely embrace this belief with a positive attitude. You'll be completely aware of how they did it (with memories of "I'm good" feelings), and you'll express the belief to your children in the same way your parents did.

We need to digress for just a moment to look at three important points about this unconscious business: repression, suppression, and denial. (Are you feeling like you're in a Psych 101 class? There's no test; you get an A just for reading the next several paragraphs.) Parental love is significantly improved through becoming aware of how the unconscious part of your beliefs work.

Repression, suppression, and denial all achieve the same result: hiding uncomfortable memories. *Repression* happens automatically. It's the mind's way of protecting us from the results of hurtful experiences. Repression keeps the detail of Dad's memories about lying unconscious. *Suppression* of uncomfortable events is done purposefully. A clerk was rude to you at the store this morning. You could choose to think about it all day or you could choose not to think about it; choosing not to think about it is suppression. *Denial* explains both repression and suppression: Either unconsciously or consciously, emotions and events are shut out of our awareness as if they never happened.

What can you do when the unconscious emotions attached to your beliefs interfere with starting effectively where your child is? (A lot of talking and your raised voice is your clue there's something unconscious going on.) Here's what one mom did when her son Cole lied to her. (This had happened several times before, and Mom was getting good at stopping her long, intense responses.)

Mom pushed hard on the short lecture button and turned the volume way down; she knew she needed to say something brief and then take a ten-minute timeout before continuing. "Cole, what do you think I feel about your lying?"

"But, I didn't—you never trust me."

"I'm going to think about this for ten minutes, and then we're going to deal with it."

Mom exited to her room and quickly checked her notes about how to proceed. She had already become aware that lying was a red flag from spankings she got as a girl. Now she was able to decide what to do with a little more logic working.

Back with Cole, she continued. "How do I feel when you lie?"

"I know—you hate me."

"No, I'm sad that somehow you don't feel safe telling me the truth. I want to find out why you don't and then find a way for you to feel safe to tell me."

Here's what you can do to become aware of your unconscious memories. Try writing down your memories about the intense emotions involved in forming a belief. Talking with a friend or spouse who will not judge you is another way to get at the details of your emotions. The sole task of the friend or spouse is to listen and support your emotions. Judging increases "I'm bad" and results in suppression or denial, which is what you're trying to move away from.

How can talking or writing help? Both these practices will significantly increase awareness of the unconscious. Even if you feel skeptical, you've got nothing to lose by trying them. (What's the worst that could happen?) And don't give up after a minute or two. Try these approaches several times: two ten-minute periods of writing and/or several conversations with another person. It takes this type of continued effort to open up the unconscious. (If you haven't made progress after several attempts, consider enlisting the help of a licensed counselor or therapist.) Look for fear as the basic emotion. Aaron's dad had a lot of fear.

Are you wondering how simply becoming aware of the detail of a belief will allow you to mange the emotion adequately? Repressed emotions are always stronger than conscious emotions. When we are aware of our deeper emotions, we can make sense of them and understand them, and most of the negative energy will be reduced. After a person is in a car accident, most of the memories and emotions are repressed. If left repressed, trauma will set in, and an excessive fear of driving may result. On the other hand, if the person talks in detail about the event and the emotions, the fear will be reduced significantly within several weeks.

> When we are aware of our deeper emotions, we can make sense of them and understand them, and most of the negative energy will be reduced.

## We Project Our Unconscious Beliefs

We need to cover one more aspect of beliefs in our psych mini-lecture: unconscious projection—something we all do without knowing it. Sigmund Freud and his daughter Anna are credited with identifying this most powerful defensive mechanism.[3]

Sometimes unconscious projection is harmless. We've all said things such as "Don't you think this rainy weather is depressing?" or "Don't you think Jane's tipping only 15 percent in that expensive restaurant is about the most cheapskate thing a person could do?" When we say something like this, we're assuming others see the situation just like we do. In effect, we are projecting onto others what we feel as though everyone feels the way we do. Maybe they do, maybe they don't. Not a problem when we're talking about weather. It's another story when we assume the other person has the same beliefs we do on emotional issues. Most of us do this without thinking; that's the unconscious part, thus the term "unconscious projection." It's human nature, but left unattended, this habit is one of the major causes of parent/child conflict.

Let's dig a little deeper into how unconscious projection works, so we can recognize it and stop it. Let's start with the projection part.

Just like a movie theater projector projects images onto the screen, when we project, we place our attitudes, feelings, and beliefs outside ourselves onto another person. As I said before, all of us do this every day. It's the way humans engage with each other. It's automatic; we don't think about; it just happens; it's unconscious.

Here's the problem with unconscious projection: What if the other person doesn't see a situation the same way you do? What if your friend holds a different belief than you do about an important issue? If both individuals are not aware that they are projecting their belief onto the other person, each will try to convince the other about the absolute correctness of his or her belief. Have we all been there and done that? Of course—daily.

Unfortunately, conflict is always the result of unconscious projection. The destructive part of unconscious projection onto a loved one is that it results in personal attacks, which results in the other person feeling "I'm bad."

Aaron's dad was doing this to Aaron; he was unconsciously projecting his emotions and experiences onto Aaron about his belief—some of it acceptable (the destructiveness of lying) and some of it unacceptable (spanking, angry lecturing). The remedy for Dad? Stop the action, become aware of his belief, delete the destructive parts, include the constructive parts, and get to the center of where Aaron is. Then he can craft a step-by-step building process for helping Aaron see how telling the truth will work for him.

That concludes our mini-lecture on the two important aspects about beliefs. Let's apply this information to Aaron's lying problem.

We've already established that because Dad cannot set aside his intense emotions, he's unable to get to where Aaron is. Again, here's what happens: When Aaron lies, an unconscious high-def video gets turned on in Dad's memory library about when he lied to his dad. It includes the lying experiences, what his dad's face looked like, the words used, the spanking, and most of all, the vivid emotions of feeling bad about disappointing his father and fear of his dad's disapproval. All wrapped up it resulted in Aaron's dad believing "I'm bad," "I'm unlovable." The video runs undetected by Aaron's dad, but it fuels his strong emotions and accompanying lectures to Aaron. And the cycle keeps going round and round with no satisfactory resolution.

In review, to break this cycle, Dad must stop interacting with Aaron. Then he needs to become aware of the emotional details of his belief, the emotional memories of how his belief was welded into place. As I outlined earlier, this awareness can occur through writing about these details, talking to a nonjudgmental friend or spouse, or seeking counseling. The awareness and understanding will adequately reduce the emotions and allow Dad to set them aside and start where Aaron is.

## Next Steps

Aaron's dad returned to my office several weeks later. He'd followed the steps outlined here, and he'd dug a bit deeper into his childhood videos on lying.

"Gary, I'm really feeling unsettled about all of this. I've tried your idea of talking with a friend about my memories of being spanked when I lied. Man, I didn't realize those memories, or videos as you said—for me they're feature length, not clips—were so emotional. It took about half a box of tissues to get through it. Now I can see where all of my emotion toward Aaron is coming from. I know you said to stop what I was doing. I've done that. I know now I'm supposed to deal with the lying without all the negative emotions. Walk me through the next steps. I'm miserable."

"Carl, take a deep breath. I've got good news: Feeling uncomfortable and anxious is normal for the first part of any human change. In fact, discomfort is necessary to motivate us to change. The bad news about feeling uncomfortable is that many parents choose to deny the discomfort—it just hurts too much—and keep on making the same mistakes. They are in denial, but you are not. Can you keep talking to your friend and maybe add journaling?"

"Yes, he's been really good about listening. About the writing"— he looked at his shoes, and I could hardly hear him—"I'm really not that good at it, but I guess that doesn't matter. No one will ever see it. Okay, I'll try. How much more video viewing do I need to do?"

"Probably until the tears and fear stop and anger starts at your dad. Some people feel pity for their parent, but a lot of people feel anger; both are normal. Anger in this situation is good. Make sure you thoroughly review the videos in detail. Don't hesitate to use the pause and slow motion, and don't forget adequate audio. Pay attention to specific events and the feelings associated with the situation—both your dad's and your feelings, as well as Dad's facial expressions, tone of voice, anger, and so forth. Remember to talk or write about these feelings. Just thinking about these events will not give you the best results. Do you think you need to review the videos more?"

"I must be making progress. During one of my video viewings with my friend, I let out a line of swear words I haven't used for quite a while. Do you think I'm ready for doing something effective with Aaron? Will I need a lot more counseling?"

"Sure, I think you're ready to engage effectively with Aaron. You're really doing a good job of owning your part of the problem first and then dealing with Aaron's part of the problem. Impressive—particularly for a male! Most males find looking at themselves difficult; they frequently do not own their part in a parent-child conflict.

"You asked if you would need a lot more counseling. Before making this decision, follow the guidelines we've talked about, and see if the results are satisfying. You've dealt with your emotions adequately enough that your thinking can be a lot clearer. Here's what's next: editing. I think you're now ready to go the editing room and see how your childhood video should have been, using the parental-love approach. What do you think?"

Carl shook his head, grimacing. "Sounds a little weird to me and like it's a waste of time, not to mention embarrassing. Why would I need to edit the video showing my dad doing it right? I'm an adult; I understand what he did wrong, and I know how he could have done better."

"Okay, maybe it sounds a little weird, and it does feel a bit embarrassing. You're an adult and 'shouldn't' need to see and feel a better way to have been parented. After all, adults don't need to be valued like kids do, right? Well, if I had a loud 'wrong answer' buzzer, I'd push it. Adults *do* need to feel valued. It's important when we are reviewing difficult childhood memories to imagine these events occurring with parental love. This imagining exercise will help you work through some of the difficult memories and help you become more comfortable about feeling lovable. Your embarrassment comes because it's uncomfortable to feel this kind of love when you haven't had it much as a child. Our need to be loved stays with us until death. It's healthy and normal. And it's never too late to ask for it. But at first, it's uncomfortable because we've become used to not having it. Strange, isn't it, how the mind works?"

Carl swiped at his eyes. "Here come the tears again. I guess that's a pretty clear confirmation of what's brewing inside me. Okay, I'm convinced. I'll go back to my editing room, do the rewrites, and 'show' the movie to whoever will listen. It will still be hard, though."

"Carl, keep up the effort. Acknowledging these repressed feelings will always hurt at first, just like cleaning a fresh wound. When we take the time to get every speck of dirt out, though, the wound heals cleanly and much faster than if we allow contaminants to remain. So it is with the initial hurt of painful memories: Continued acceptance will heal the emotional wounds, and they'll hurt less and less as you continue with the acceptance and awareness. A scar will be there, but the hurt will be significantly reduced—maybe some issues will completely go away. Are you ready for the editing job?"

"Yeah, as ready as I'll ever be, I guess."

"Great. Your finished product will be a video that shows you receiving what you needed from your dad. First, as you view and feel the detail of your memories with your dad, you will find little to no valuing and respect from him. Delete those sections. Remember, all of us wanted—and continue to want—to feel valued when we encountered a difference with someone else, especially a loved one.

"Next, edit the video to include the valuing and respect. Play this edited video over and over until you are really familiar with its sounds and images. This is the starting point for how to eventually treat Aaron. What do you think?"

"It's sounding doable. Like you say, 'a stretch,' but I'll try it. It's still so embarrassing, though."

"Try to put up with the embarrassment. Embarrassment is the mind's way to keep the memories repressed—understandable protection, horrible solution. Repeated exposure to the repressed memories eventually does away with embarrassment. It's just something you have to put up with in the first part of remembering. Do you know what the result of all this editing is?"

"I suppose I'll be freed up to start where Aaron is and get on with a productive solution to the lying."

"You will, Carl. Here's what you can expect. With this awareness you'll be able to stop your current behavior and use more of your parental love to change your behavior. This new behavior becomes your new video. By the way, when you do a good edit or make a new video, this new video will be available for viewing in future parent-child problem situations. Be aware, for a while the old video will switch on when the next parent-child conflict occurs; you might want to put an 'adult block' on this old video in your mind-computer. For a while you'll need to make a special effort to pull up the new video you made. Within a short period of time, less than ten successful attempts, the new video will increasingly be available, and you'll be well on your way to instilling solid beliefs in Aaron in ways that will help him grow to be all you hope for him. Thanks, Carl, for all your courage. The dividends of the initial very hard work will be abundant."

> You will know your unconscious belief is playing a part in the problem when the following is occurring: Your emotions are excessive, your response is rigid and repetitive like the Energizer Bunny constantly beating a drum, and what you're doing continually doesn't work.

# Unstuck in Four Steps

Let's summarize the four essential steps to getting unstuck in your parenting:

1. Stop your behavior and take time to understand the part you play in a repetitive parent-child problem. You will know your unconscious belief is playing a part in the problem when the following is occurring: Your emotions are excessive, your response is rigid and repetitive like the Energizer Bunny constantly beating a drum, and what you're doing continually doesn't work. Know where the switch is; turn it off as soon as possible.

2. Talk with someone who is open to your feelings, or write about the beliefs you're trying to understand. Review all aspects of your childhood memories: the event and what your parent(s) and you said, did, and felt.

3. Understand why the uncovered beliefs are causing intense emotion as you relate to your child. Reread Carl's situation above for clarity about how this understanding occurs. Hidden beliefs are powerful. Uncovered beliefs will not have the excessive emotional impact on the current problem in parent-child conflicts. You will be able to think in a clearer and healthier manner about parent-child solutions.

4. Produce a new belief video or edit the old belief based on the new uncovered information. Then store it in your belief video library. Put an adult block on the old video. Archive the old movie; it will always be a part of your belief video library, but you will diminish its power significantly by not using it.

Keep in mind the new video will not switch on automatically when a parent-child conflict occurs. You will need to search for it. The video will increasingly be available after repeated viewings. Use all parental-love requirements as the basis of the new or edited video.

These will be the foundation for your revised passionate parental belief.

# Unproductive Parental Behaviors

Before we conclude this chapter, let's look briefly at several common, unproductive parental behaviors all grounded in the parental belief system.

## Fathers Nurturing Less Than Mothers

Fathers need to be sure they focus as much on emotions as behavior, a trend we're seeing in our society. The majority of fathers tend to focus more on behavior than on emotions. Conversely, mothers tend to focus more on emotions and struggle at times with setting adequate limits on behavior. Sometimes, fathers are negative toward the mothers' focus on emotions and feelings. Fathers, be careful with your criticism. If you explore your unconscious beliefs, you may find that you did not receive adequate emotional nurturing from your parents. Not enough nurturing causes us to feel uncomfortable, and we've learned that unconscious uncomfortable feelings can cause negative reactions in a person's day-to-day life.

Some of you men may think, *No way. It's not possible that my lack of nurturing would cause me to feel uncomfortable when I see my son nurtured by my wife.* Most men were not nurtured to the degree that they needed to be during their childhoods. If you are overly critical of your wife's nurturing, look at how much nurturing you received as a child. If this shoe fits, consider changing your behavior: Uncover the emotions about your childhood belief related to nurturing; feel the hurt about it; don't let the hurt cause you to be uncomfortable about how much nurturing your child is receiving; and then work to be happy that your wife is nurturing your child.

A father may see his child's mother setting inadequate limits on behavior, which may be true. Mothers may set inconsistent, inadequate limits, especially if nurturing is lacking from the child's father:

*Becky's dad does not nurture her enough and is too rough on her. I'll make up for it by nurturing her a lot and not setting such strong limits.* Dads, deal with this lack of limit-setting by encouraging Mom to set firmer behavioral limits, not to decrease her emotional nurturing. Clear, firm, consistent limit-setting is essential; plenty of emotional nurturing is even more important.

Some mothers do not set adequate limits because of their conscious or unconscious belief created from their childhood experiences of aggressive limit-setting by their father or mother. When these aggressive limit-setting memories are unconscious, the mother will react to these memories by parenting in a manner the opposite of the way she was raised. She will go too far in the other direction and set inadequate limits. (Of course, this process applies equally to fathers.) Mothers, if your limit-setting is not adequate, become fully aware of your limit-setting beliefs and make the necessary parental adjustments.

## Defending Your Parents' Behavior

Unproductive or even destructive parental behavior occurs from time to time with all parents. This behavior is rooted in your unconscious beliefs derived from how you were parented. Make sure you candidly put the responsibility where it belongs, usually with your parents. Remember, the primary source of your parental beliefs is your parents' responses, which you have integrated into your belief system. Minimizing your parents' poor behavior when you discover how they behaved with you in various parent-child conflicts is normal. The purpose of awareness is not to condemn your parents but to clarify why you are behaving unproductively with your child. Candor about where your unproductive parenting behavior came from is essential in order to change your current parenting behavior.

## Parenting Opposite of How Your Parents Parented You

This type of parenting is called "undoing" when done excessively.

An example of undoing would be a father who is excessively lenient in setting limits with his child. This behavior comes from the father's parental belief system derived from his parent(s) being too strict; thus, he thinks, *I'm not going to be as strict as my parents. It hurts too much.* In this situation, some reduction of strictness is healthy, but excessive father-child leniency in limit-setting would be a case of undoing and not healthy.

Another example of undoing would be a mother who excessively protects her child from any feelings of failure. This behavior comes from a mother's parental belief system derived from her parent(s) being too critical, resulting in the mother continually feeling "I'm bad" as a child. She thinks, *My child will never go through what I went through.* Too much maternal or paternal protection against failure keeps a child from developing skills to cope with failure. Self-confidence will not develop adequately.

If you've seen yourself reflected in any of the above descriptions of unproductive parenting habits, take the time to review the four steps to getting unstuck. Look for those hidden beliefs and deal with them appropriately.

## Summary

Let's now summarize this chapter, starting with our definition of parental beliefs:

> Parental beliefs are a set of logically based, passionate, emotional convictions—specific morals, principles of good behavior, and values—that are essential for a child to be a "good" person. Parents want their children to share and practice these beliefs.

These convictions have been cemented into your identity from emotional experiences between your parents and you. The most critical ingredients in the cement are (1) the behavior needed to feel "I'm good" and (2) the intense emotions occurring during the engagement between you and your parents. Intense emotions served as the hardening ingredient of the cement. These experiences are the basis of your belief system and your convictions about how life is to be lived. Your parental responses are derived from this belief system.

Since the belief system is mostly unconscious, your parental responses are mostly automatic, without any thought about how the beliefs were formed or what is contained within the beliefs. If the parental responses come from an internal belief of "I'm good," your child will acquire a positive belief system. If the parental responses come from "I'm bad," your child will be at risk to acquire a negative belief system.

In this chapter you've learned how to manage your parental responses in the very best way possible: stopping unproductive parenting, becoming aware of your parental beliefs, changing beliefs that are unhealthy, and imparting new healthy beliefs to your child through parental love. These revised or changed healthy beliefs are integrated within your child and experienced within your child as "I'm good." A healthy belief system is now established from which your child can live a fulfilling life.

Now that you've learned how to manage your parental belief system effectively, let's turn to the subject of our next chapter: temperament traits and how best to match your traits with your child's—in other words, goodness of fit.

### CHAPTER 4

# Temperament Traits, Part 1: Understanding Goodness of Fit

"I DON'T UNDERSTAND WHY my six-year-old, Jennifer, is so difficult. Emily, our ten-year-old, is so easy. Jennifer is unbelievably cranky when she wakes up; it takes forever to get her out of bed; and the whole family's angry by the time she's up. She ought to be able to jump out of bed and work on having a positive mood instead of ruining everyone's morning! And when anything even minor disappoints her, her emotions go crazy; she cries or gets really mad at the slightest provocation, stomping around and slamming things down. Then, when something good happens, she gets almost giddy—she skips and jumps, pinballing from one person to the other. Wish the giddy happened more often. Not only that, every time she has to change activities or move from, say, the living room to the kitchen, it's an emotional hurricane. Emily never acts that way.

> Most of the problem is not parenting; rather, it has to do with your child's inborn and unique personality characteristics—her temperament traits.

"When Emily was Jennifer's age, she would get up, and with only a little encouragement, get herself ready for the bus every morning. And unless there was a big problem, she just rolled with the punches; we could tell her to turn off the TV and come to the dinner table, and she'd just do it.

Even now, she only cries and raises her voice if something is really serious; she's much less emotional than Jennifer.

"My husband and I have tried everything with Jennifer—nothing works. I hate to say it, but we almost dread every morning; it's such a struggle with her. Why is she so difficult and Emily so easy? It's got to be our parenting. Help!"

I've heard this type of scenario countless times in my office, and perhaps you've had similar thoughts and concerns within your family as well. Let me put your mind and heart at rest: Most of the problem is not parenting; rather, it has to do with your child's inborn and unique personality characteristics—her temperament traits. Again, when problems like those in Jennifer's family occur, the core problem is typically difficult temperament traits, not primarily what parents are doing. Parents play a part in it, but the child's difficulty is primarily caused by several temperament traits that are not easy for most of us to handle. Determining the part difficult temperament traits play in your child's problem behaviors and what part you play is the subject of this chapter. And, of course, I'll also equip you with the understanding and skills you need to better deal with this type of problem. Let's dig in.

## What Are Temperament Traits?

Everybody has nine temperament traits, and each trait can be expressed along a continuum of intensity.[1] Here's a list of the temperament traits and how each one can vary. I call the specific variations of a trait "trait characteristics." (Feel free to circle numbers for both your child and yourself. You'll find the comparison enlightening, and you'll use the information a bit later.)

1. **Activity Level**: Your child is either more active or more quiet.

| | Quiet | | | | Active |
|---|---|---|---|---|---|
| Child/Parent | 1 | 2 | 3 | 4 | 5 |

2. **Regularity**: Your child's behavior is regular (predictable) or irregular (unpredictable) related to physical functions: eating, sleeping, etc.

|  | Regular |  |  |  | Irregular |
|---|---|---|---|---|---|
| Child/Parent | 1 | 2 | 3 | 4 | 5 |

3. **Adaptability**: Your child shifts from one thing to another easily or with great difficulty.

|  | Quick to adapt |  |  |  | Slow to adapt |
|---|---|---|---|---|---|
| Child/Parent | 1 | 2 | 3 | 4 | 5 |

4. **Approach/Withdrawal**: Your child approaches new situations easily, with confidence, or is more uncertain and withdrawn.

|  | Initial approach |  |  |  | Initial withdrawal |
|---|---|---|---|---|---|
| Child/Parent | 1 | 2 | 3 | 4 | 5 |

5. **Physical Sensitivity**: Your child tolerates physical sensations well or is highly sensitive regarding taste, sight, hearing, smell, touch.

|  | Low sensitivity |  |  |  | High sensitivity |
|---|---|---|---|---|---|
| Child/Parent | 1 | 2 | 3 | 4 | 5 |

6. **Intensity of Reaction**: Your child's emotional reactions to events, either internal or external, are experienced somewhere on a continuum from mild reactions to high intensity.

|  | Mild reaction |  |  |  | Intense reaction |
|---|---|---|---|---|---|
| Child/Parent | 1 | 2 | 3 | 4 | 5 |

7. **Distractibility**: Your child experiences distractibility somewhere on a continuum from very distractible to not distractible.

| | Not distractible | | | | Very distractible |
|---|---|---|---|---|---|
| Child/Parent | 1 | 2 | 3 | 4 | 5 |

8. **Positive or Negative Mood**: Your child's mood is experienced on a continuum from positive to negative.

| | Positive mood | | | | Negative mood |
|---|---|---|---|---|---|
| Child/Parent | 1 | 2 | 3 | 4 | 5 |

9. **Persistence**: Your child can sustain his or her attention, effort, and energy for long periods or falls somewhere along a continuum toward weak persistence.

| | Strong persistence | | | | Weak persistence |
|---|---|---|---|---|---|
| Child/Parent | 1 | 2 | 3 | 4 | 5 |

Your child's one-of-a kind personality is made of up these nine uniquely expressed temperament traits. Now, if you're feeling that all this sounds a tad complicated, you're not alone. It does sound complicated at first, but like everything else, once you get a little more information, it will make a lot of sense. Let's start by applying this list to Jennifer's and Emily's personalities.

Based on Mom's description, we know Jennifer cries easily. What temperament trait does this relate to? Several, but mostly trait 6: intensity of reaction. Crying easily is Jennifer's unique expression (trait characteristic) of this trait. Her level of intensity is high. What is Emily's unique expression of this trait? Her level of intensity is low; she "rolls with the punches." There are other unique differences, but we don't need to go into any more detail for now. Emily's personality is different than Jennifer's; each child's nine traits are expressed differently.

Unfortunately, some personalities are fun to be with and others are not. Since the not-so-fun kids cause a lot of heartache, let's press into the problem a little further before we look at the solution.

## Easy and Difficult Children

Mom labeled Emily "easy" and Jennifer "difficult." Little did she know she was using labels psychologists identified more than thirty years ago to describe children who are difficult (about 10 percent of children) and children who are easy (about 40 percent).[2] Let's see what the temperament traits look like for both of these:

*Easy Child*
   Activity Level: moderate
   Regularity: regular with most physical functions
   Adaptability: most of the time
   Approach/Withdrawal: mostly approaches new events easily
   Mood: mostly positive

*Difficult Child*
   Activity Level: high
   Regularity: unpredictable
   Approach/Withdrawal: withdraws from most situations
   Adaptability: almost never
   Intensity: elevated emotional responses
   Mood: mostly negative

You will notice all nine temperament traits are not listed in either the easy child or the difficult child list. Only certain traits out of the nine are prominent for the easy child and the difficult child.

With an easy child, such as Emily (and Michael in chapter 1), everyone is happy. The personalities are pleasant, and most of the nine traits are not noticed; they are taken for granted. Jennifer's mom noticed just one out of the nine, adaptability: "She rolls with the punches." It's a different story with the difficult child. Parents of these children almost always volunteer descriptions of behavior that fit all six of a difficult child's traits.

Have you been mentally assessing your child's trait characteristics as you've been reading? Good! Knowing your child's unique trait characteristics is essential for turbo-boosting your parental love. Shortly, I will show you how you can determine your child's specific trait characteristics as well as your own, but let's first cover a very important point: "goodness of fit."[3]

## What Is Goodness of Fit?

To understand goodness of fit, you need to know not only your child's unique trait expressions but also yours. Why? (Starting to sound like too much work? It is some work at the front end, but stick with me; I think you'll find the "work" will pay big dividends.) You need to know your temperament traits because most of the time some of your traits and your child's are different; they don't fit very well. Goodness of fit is the term psychologists use to measure these temperament differences. For example, if you're a 5 on the activity level scale and your child is a 2, your goodness of fit in this trait would be low. If you're both 3s, your goodness of fit would be high.

> To understand goodness of fit, you need to know not only your child's unique trait expressions but also yours.

When your traits and your child's traits do not fit well, as in Jennifer and Mom's case (we'll talk about this in more detail shortly), conflict occurs, and the "B" word pops up: Both parent and child feel "bad." To avoid feeling bad, you need to know all of your trait characteristics as well as your child's and then find a way to fit them together better. The first step is yours—fitting your traits into your child's traits. There it is again: Start where your child is, not where you are.

*Okay,* you may be thinking, *this looks great on paper, but how in the world do you get Jennifer to get up in the morning and not be cranky?* Good question. Let's walk through it.

First, let's see whether we can understand which of Mom's traits don't fit with Jennifer's. The lack of fit signifi-

> When your traits and your child's traits do not fit well, conflict occurs, and the "B" word pops up: Both parent and child feel "bad."

cantly affects Mom's expectations. Once Mom understands the differences between her traits and Jennifer's, she will be able to modify her expectations to fit better with where Jennifer is starting. From what Mom said, at least two traits are involved: adaptability and mood. "She ought to be able to get right out of bed in the morning" was Mom's first comment. That's related to the adaptability trait (trait 3). The "ought" shows us that Mom is adaptable—Jennifer *ought* to be able to get up—she's using herself as the reference point. Okay, that's one trait that doesn't fit. What about Mom's comment about Jennifer's needing to "work on having a positive mood" (trait 9)? "Work on" means Mom believes if Jennifer just tried, she would be able to have a positive mood. Again, Mom's reference point is herself; therefore, she must have a more positive mood than Jennifer does. This is another trait that doesn't fit well with her daughter's temperament. Mom's comment at the beginning of this chapter—"I don't understand why my six-year-old, Jennifer, is so difficult"—represents an attempt to force-fit the traits. This approach never works, but it's the default for all parents until they understand more about temperament traits. Now is a good time to learn about how to achieve goodness of fit.

# Goodness-of-Fit Steps

Mom needs to use the following goodness-of-fit steps to fit her expectations into Jennifer's difficult trait characteristics:

1. Identify both her temperament traits and Jennifer's and understand which traits are problems for both of them.

2. Accept Jennifer's problem trait(s) for now.

3. Stop what she's doing that doesn't work with Jennifer. Understand her own temperament traits and the part they play in the problem.

4. Start new parental behaviors that fit better within Jennifer's problem traits.

> Someone purposefully choosing to do something that aggravates us—especially if the person isn't trying and doesn't care—activates the frustration button every time!

Let's apply the steps. The result of step 1 is that Mom now sees Jennifer can't just get out of bed as Mom can. Since Mom read the previous chapter and has an edited video, she realizes she was unconsciously projecting her way of doing things—based on her trait characteristics—onto Jennifer and expecting her daughter to be just like her. She was also responding to Jennifer as if she were purposefully resisting getting out of bed—that is, if she really wanted to get out of bed, she could.

No wonder Mom was getting so upset! Someone purposefully choosing to do something that aggravates us—especially if the person isn't trying and doesn't care—activates the frustration button every time! The whole picture has changed now: Mom understands that Jennifer's problem is inborn; she's different from her mother, and Mom has accepted all of this for now; step 2 has been accomplished. (Note: There is always a portion of a child's response that is manipulative, but in this situation the majority of the problem is caused by Jennifer's adaptability problem. In these first steps, always decide what to do next based on the temperament problem, not the manipulation part; that comes later.)

Now Mom's ready for the editing. She has realized that nagging, yelling, and threatening don't work to get Jennifer out of bed. She's deleting that part of her behavior (step 3) and replacing it with new expectations and new behaviors (step 4). She's determined to use parental-love requirements to start new or modified parental behaviors that fit better within Jennifer's problem trait of low adaptability—trouble shifting from being asleep to being awake—and her cranky moodiness.

Here's how Mom found an option that worked:

"Jennifer, what do you think about the way I handle getting you up in the morning?"

Jennifer's back stiffened, she stuck out her chin, focused her gaze as far from Mom as possible, crossed her arms, and said, "You're mean!"

Mom gulped down her old responses and remembered "emotions first." "It's upsetting, isn't it?"

Jennifer relaxed a bit. "Yeah, you yell at me in the morning." Mom caught Jennifer's quick, darting glance at her.

"How about we change things a bit, and I start waking you up with your favorite Hannah Montana music?"

"Really? You would do that, Mom?" Mom hadn't heard that tone of voice for a long time, and she knew Jennifer's full eye contact meant something positive was happening. She'd forgotten what the glimmering of hope felt like.

"I'll come back after about five minutes and ask you to sit up in your bed so I can give you a cup of your favorite pineapple juice—"

Jennifer jumped up and into her mom's lap in one movement. "Mommy!" The hug felt like they were one. For a moment they both felt hope's warmth and comfort, like sitting by a blazing fire after a day of ice skating.

Does this type of parental behavior work right away every time? No. It's not magic. Sometimes, however, it does work right away.

And for those times when it doesn't, hang in there. Eventually, it will always work if—and it all hinges on this *if*—you remember to do the following: Fit your parental behavior into your child's problem temperament trait. You've tried it the other way, and it hasn't worked. (That's why you're still reading!) Then, always remember the two steps in starting where the child is: Be at the center of your child as much as possible, and start with a plan that will be 98 percent successful.

In this situation Mom may need to make several modifications before the fit (her modified parental behavior) is adequate to deliver the desired result: Jennifer getting out of bed and dressing without being excessively cranky. The basic shifting problem, the adaptability trait, will always be there, but significant modification can be expected because her parents are starting this early in her life.

It may take a week or two for Jennifer to shift out of her old getting-out-of-bed habits based on her mom's new behaviors. Look at figure 4.1. The different lines represent differences between Mom and Jennifer. Note that Mom's differences fit into Jennifer's; they are underneath Jennifer's differences. The result: checkered lines representing Jennifer's new behavior influenced by her mom's parental behavior.

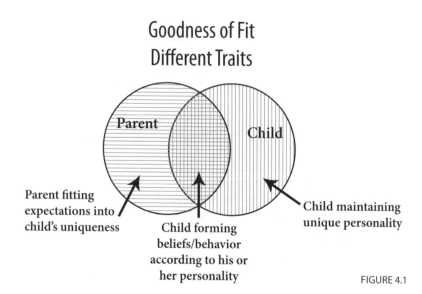

## Goodness of Fit
## Different Traits

Parent

Child

Parent fitting expectations into child's uniqueness

Child forming beliefs/behavior according to his or her personality

Child maintaining unique personality

FIGURE 4.1

Are you wondering how to make this temperament information work for you? In just a little bit I'll give you an example of how you can determine both your and your child's temperament trait profile and how to establish a better fit between them. Before we get to that, though, I need to share several more points about goodness of fit.

The easiest goodness of fit occurs when your and your child's predominant temperament traits are substantially similar and mostly positive. In figure 4.2 both the child's and parent's similar traits are represented by horizontal lines, the child's lines a little thicker than the parent's. Notice how the parent's traits fit into the child's by being underneath them but still affecting them. Michael's and his dad's predominantly similar traits are a good example of an easy goodness of fit.

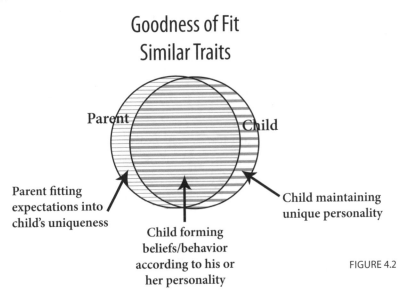

## Goodness of Fit
## Similar Traits

Parent

Child

Parent fitting
expectations into
child's uniqueness

Child forming
beliefs/behavior
according to his or
her personality

Child maintaining
unique personality

FIGURE 4.2

The worst fit occurs in two situations: (1) when a parent's expectations are continually resisted by the child and (2) when the parent's expectations do not adequately consider the child's uniqueness and the child does not resist.

There's another typical temperament-trait fit problem: when you have
a predominant negative trait that is the
same as your child's predominant negative trait. Here's an example: Both you
and your child have a predominant trait
of excessive emotional intensity, which
happens often. There are two ways a
parent can respond to this situation.

> The easiest
> goodness of
> fit occurs when
> your and your child's
> predominant temperament
> traits are substantially
> similar and mostly positive.

The first and most common reaction is anger: increasing frustration with the child's excessive emotional expressions. Negative
emotional intensity from anyone is frustrating, no doubt about it,
and detrimental if left unchecked. Continual anger from the parent makes matters worse. If you are in a similar situation, follow the
goodness-of-fit steps outlined above. Step 3 is the key for solving this
problem, particularly related to your anger: Stop what you're doing
and understand your child's temperament traits and the part they
play in the problem. Chapter 8 will help you deal with anger and
frustration effectively.

The other way a parent can respond to a shared predominant
negative trait is to be empathetic. Usually this means the parent has
successfully done the goodness-of-fit steps.

One last point: Your child's basic trait characteristic, the unique
way the child expresses a trait, cannot be totally changed, but it can
be modified. At first this may sound discouraging, but as you work
through this reality, you will actually start to feel encouraged. Here's
why. Accepting the basic trait expression means you will no longer
fight it and try to change it. More loving energy will be available to
your child to modify the difficult trait characteristic.

We've all experienced this ourselves. How many of us have perfect personalities and perfect physical features? Show of hands? Of
course, no hands. It took me years to accept having red hair and
freckles. What a relief when I finally did! It took a beautiful woman,
inside and out (my wife), to tell me repeatedly I was a decent-looking

man for me to accept these physical features completely.

How does this acceptance work for your child? Let's look at the trait of approach/withdrawal. If the trait characteristic is avoidance of all stressful situations, you can train your child to improve to some degree his or her ability to approach difficult situations. You'll see improvement, but the overall orientation of the child will be toward avoidance. Let's say seven-year-old Tyler always responds to the challenges of a new task with tears and gives up. Typical encouragement will not work; the repeated comments of "You can do this" usually turn into "Why can't you just try instead of always giving up?" In this situation we have a choice: We can repeat the same failed efforts over and over, or we can apply parental-love knowledge about temperament trait differences. Let's choose to reprogram the bunny to deal effectively with the avoidance trait.

> Your child's basic trait characteristic, the unique way the child expresses a trait, cannot be totally changed, but it can be modified.

We'll begin our reprogramming efforts by reducing previous big steps into baby steps. Instead of "I know you can do it," start by saying, "I know this is really hard." After some 75 percent listening conversation (75/25 rule), you start the action part.

Let's say Tyler is trying out a new Wii game with a friend for the first time and within minutes runs to his room, crying. First, find the level of involvement Tyler finds easy. Take all the baby steps you need to teach Tyler the game before he tries it with a friend; you may need to crawl at first. If frustration occurs with either you or your child, you know what to do. As Tyler experiences mastery with new activities, his ability to approach new activities will improve. Every chance you have to modify your child's temperament trait, take it. Make sure the starting point results in mastery as many times as possible. The trait will be noticeably modified over time but not completely changed.

# Wrapping Up

Let's summarize before we do some personal application in the next chapter. Temperament traits are the parts of the personality we are born with. Each child will express characteristics of these traits in a unique way. When your child's predominant negative traits are substantially different than yours, goodness of fit will be lacking, and conflict will more than likely occur.

When this happens, identify which temperament traits are involved (both the parent's and the child's) and accept that for now this is the best your child can do. Pay attention to unconscious projection and correct it when necessary.

> Instead of "I know you can do it," start by saying, "I know this is really hard."

Then, develop a plan for fitting expectations more effectively into your child's temperament trait system using parental-love requirements. The closer the plan can start at the center of the child and result in 98 percent success, the sooner goodness of fit will be achieved. Keep modifying expectations until you get to a consistent 98 percent success rate. Be patient. Plan on about three weeks to get the plan running smoothly.

Remember Karen from chapter 1—the girl who said she didn't care anymore? Her mom and dad had just gone through an ugly divorce, and Mom (Joan) felt like a complete failure and left my office, saying, "I'm not doing a very good job of parenting. I need a lot of help from Gary."

Well, since that first interview, Joan has made significant improvement. She's worked especially hard on understanding temperament traits and then putting that knowledge to work in her relationship with her daughter. Keep in mind as we share this experience together: It's not the exact outcome and how well Joan parented that matters; what matters is her (and your) persistent efforts to engage her love for her daughter, which resulted in noticeable improvement in Karen. Chapter 5 gets into the nitty-gritty of just how Joan and Karen turned things around—and you'll see how you can do the same.

CHAPTER 5

# Temperament Traits, Part 2: Establishing Goodness of Fit

JOAN BEGAN HER JOURNEY by determining the fit between her temperament trait characteristics and Karen's. To do so, she filled out the Temperament Trait Characteristics: Comparison and Goodness of Fit Plan. I'll summarize the results so you can get an idea how to do it yourself if you choose to. (See appendix B for a blank Temperament Trait Characteristics form you can use to evaluate yourself and your child.)

## Temperament Trait Characteristics: Comparison and Goodness of Fit Plan

1. **Activity Level:** Your child is either more active or more quiet.

|  | Quiet |  |  |  | Active |
|---|---|---|---|---|---|
| Karen | ① | 2 | 3 | 4 | 5 |
| Joan | 1 | 2 | 3 | ④ | 5 |

2. **Regularity:** Your child's behavior is regular (predictable) or irregular (unpredictable) related to physical functions: eating, sleeping, etc.

|  | Regular |  |  |  | Irregular |
|---|---|---|---|---|---|
| Karen | 1 | 2 | 3 | 4 | ⑤ |
| Joan | 1 | 2 | 3 | ④ | 5 |

3. **Adaptability:** Your child shifts from one thing to another easily or with great difficulty.

|  | Quick to adapt |  |  |  | Slow to adapt |
|---|---|---|---|---|---|
| Karen | 1 | 2 | 3 | 4 | ⑤ |
| Joan | 1 | 2 | 3 | ④ | 5 |

4. **Approach/Withdrawal:** Your child approaches new situations easily with confidence or somewhere on the continuum toward fearful withdrawal.

|  | Initial approach |  |  | Initial withdrawal |  |
|---|---|---|---|---|---|
| Karen | 1 | 2 | 3 | 4 | ⑤ |
| Joan | 1 | ② | 3 | 4 | 5 |

5. **Physical Sensitivity:** Your child tolerates physical sensations well or is highly sensitive regarding taste, sight, hearing, smell, touch.

|  | Low sensitivity |  |  | High sensitivity |  |
|---|---|---|---|---|---|
| Karen | 1 | 2 | 3 | ④ | 5 |
| Joan | 1 | 2 | ③ | 4 | 5 |

6. **Intensity of Reaction:** Your child's emotional reactions to events, either internal or external, are experienced somewhere on a continuum from mild reactions to high intensity.

|  | Mild reaction |  |  | Intense reaction |  |
|---|---|---|---|---|---|
| Karen | 1 | 2 | ③ | 4 | 5 |
| Joan | 1 | ② | 3 | 4 | 5 |

7. **Distractibility:** Your child experiences distractibility somewhere on a continuum from very distractible to not distractible.

|  | Not distractible |  |  | Very distractible |  |
|---|---|---|---|---|---|
| Karen | 1 | 2 | ③ | 4 | 5 |
| Joan | 1 | 2 | ③ | 4 | 5 |

8. **Positive or Negative Mood:** Your child's mood is experienced on a continuum from positive to negative.

|  | Positive mood | | | | Negative mood |
|---|---|---|---|---|---|
| Karen | 1 | 2 | 3 | 4 | ⑤ |
| Joan | 1 | ② | 3 | 4 | 5 |

9. **Persistence:** Your child can sustain his or her attention, effort, and energy for long periods or falls somewhere along a continuum toward weak persistence.

|  | Strong persistence | | | | Weak persistence |
|---|---|---|---|---|---|
| Karen | 1 | 2 | ③ | 4 | 5 |
| Joan | 1 | 2 | ③ | 4 | 5 |

# Plan Results

After doing this comparison, Joan filled out the second section: the Goodness of Fit Plan.

Here's a summary of her plan.

The biggest temperament trait characteristic differences were found in activity level, approach/withdrawal, and mood. Kind of a full plate for a mom, isn't it? Joan was completely unaware of how similar she and Karen were in regard to adaptability and how different they were in the way they approached or withdrew from various situations. She was always really angry about these traits, particularly adaptability. Joan was spanked by her dad when she couldn't change from one activity to another fast enough. No wonder she put that video as deep in her unconscious video library as possible!

Joan chose the adaptability and mood trait characteristics as her focus. After all, even the best parental love has its limits, and nobody can change everything at the same time. She decided to keep her eye on the other two traits but put them on the back burner to simmer. Focusing on all four traits was too much. (Joan was applying the "stretch but doable" approach to herself. Excellent!)

Her next step in the plan was to share the comparison section with Karen. It didn't go over well. When Karen first saw it, she said, "So?" and that was it. It would be nice to sing "We Are the World" in perfect harmony on the first try, but I wouldn't warm up the band just yet. However, please don't close the book. This type of response is totally normal at the beginning of problem solving. Fortunately, Joan remembered this from her therapy sessions. She swallowed hard and said to her daughter, "Just wanted to let you know what I'm trying to do to be a better mom." (Joan got to skip the next quiz in the Psych 102 class for her extra credit response.)

Now Joan was ready to apply all this new temperament-trait and goodness-of-fit information to the biggest problem facing her and Karen: poor school performance. Karen had prepared well for this battle. Now halfway into the second quarter, Karen had logged four or five missing assignments every week. Her progress report showed three Ds, one F, and two Cs. (Remember, last year she was a solid B student.) Since homework is always the main problem related to a low grade, homework became Joan's and Karen's focus.

Here's how Joan described the problem to me: *Karen spends a half hour on one of those MySpace or Facebook or whatever websites after school for down time. I set a timer to signal when she's supposed to log off, but she never obeys. I am so angry that this happens all the time. I have to remind her at least five or six times, and each time I get louder and more intense.*

Hopelessness is the biggest obstacle we face in solving problems, and it's often what keeps us from being successful.

*Karen ends up yelling and swearing at me. After at least ten minutes of yelling, she will finally start her work. My evening is usually ruined after these yelling spats, and we can hardly talk with each other. We have an agreement that I can check her homework for completeness when she's done. Ninety percent of the time this check ends up in a shouting match. She does the absolute minimum on every assignment. There is not one element of parental love in our exchanges! I feel like a total failure. But I'm not giving up!*

"Surrender? No way!" was Joan's battle cry. Even though she hadn't yet implemented the principles, Joan had established enough confidence in using parental-love tactics, including a strategy for fitting her temperament traits into Karen's existing traits, resulting in a win-win, at least on paper. And you'll see in the following pages that she was right! Before we go into this family's story, however, I'd like to share several important points that will help you to appreciate fully what Joan did.

First, perhaps you're thinking, *Well, sure she succeeded. She had a therapist right next to her for the whole thing! I already feel pretty overwhelmed, and I sure don't have that kind of money. How could I ever do this on my own?* Your feelings of hopelessness are the reason I wrote this book. Hopelessness is the biggest obstacle we face in solving problems, and it's often what keeps us from being successful. Try to put that feeling aside for the next several paragraphs as you read what Joan did. I think your confidence will build as you see the principles unfold. Remember, you don't need to do everything the way Joan did or have the same outcome. Use the overall approach Joan used, and you too will see noticeable improvement in your child's behavior.

> The parental-love approach meets an inborn need we all have—validation that we are good but that our behavior at times needs improvement.

Here's an interesting and encouraging part about what we're learning together: All parents (yes, every one) I have been involved with have ended up wishing their parents had used this parental-love approach with them. If you were raised this way, you're the exception. Some of you experienced a lot of validation as a child and now as an adult; some of you did not experience this at all; and most of us are somewhere in-between. The parental-love approach meets an inborn need we all have—validation that we are good but that our behavior at times needs improvement. We all thrive on validation. Doesn't it feel good to know from within yourself that this parental-love approach is not just some unproven theory? Rather, it's what we all need, and it's possible to give it to our children.

Back to the hopeless feeling for a moment. Most of you will not need a counselor, either because your situation is not overwhelming enough or because the information in this book will fit your situation adequately so that you can solve the problem independently. Support, though, is essential for change to happen. Utilize your relationships for this support. If you cannot get adequate support, do not hesitate to utilize the help of a licensed counselor or therapist.

One key thing to remember when you're feeling hopeless: For most recurring parent-child problems, you'll need to use this approach for at least three weeks before you see your child's behavior begin to change. The first week is especially hard; the child may actually get worse. Children will resist validation at first. Because they're not used to it, it doesn't soak in right away; it's too new. Prior to your using the parental-love approach, the child's experience has been "I'm bad." It takes time to believe "I'm good." Chapters 6 and 7 will give you a lot of information on change—how it happens and how to make it happen in the best way possible.

> For most recurring parent-child problems, you'll need to use this approach for at least three weeks before you see your child's behavior begin to change.

For example, when we decide to plant a garden in an area that's full of weeds and hasn't been watered for a while, we need to prepare the soil before the plants can have even a chance of growing. When you begin to use the parental-love approach to problem solving, you'll spend the first week preparing the soil of your child's heart with plenty of validation and being at the center of your child's world. No plants at first, just soiled hands. Usually within the second week you will see the signs of growth—more smiles, a kinder tone of voice, less resistance, and more participation in problem solving. Don't give up. Keep the validation going; it's sinking in, even though at first you will see no evidence of it. Look out for your old parenting weeds; pull them out by the roots as soon as you see them.

If you persist in demonstrating parental love, you can expect to see a couple of major results. First, your child will establish trust with you. I think you will be impressed with how Karen's self-confidence improved.

Then, as a result of increasing trust, you and your child will begin to work together to tackle other weeds in the garden, as Joan and Karen did. The most frequent feedback I get from clients is that when they use this approach with their children, a bond of trust is established and maintained, not perfectly, but far better than it had been in the past.

> The most frequent feedback I get from clients is that when they use this approach with their children, a bond of trust is established and maintained, not perfectly, but far better than it had been in the past.

One last point before we look at Joan and Karen. Your success does *not* depend on your completing the detailed plan (appendix B) Joan did as summarized above. We all march to a different drummer, and some of us do not like drums at all! For some of you, reading the information is plenty. For others of you, filling out the plan will be useful.

Now for the long-awaited presentation of Joan's performance. Feel free to take a minute to refill your popcorn bowl before reading on.

## Joan and Karen at Work

The homework plan involved four parts, and each part took into full consideration Karen's adapting and mood trait problems:

1. Set grade goals mutually with Karen.

2. Set up a mutually determined study schedule that includes free time on the computer.

3. Establish a monitoring system for missing homework and grades.

4. Identify motivators to encourage change and eliminate barriers that keep change from happening. (We'll talk a lot more about this in chapter 6.) Joan remembered my one-liner: Maximize motivators; minimize barriers.

To make sure she always used the parental-love approach, Joan copied the parental-love requirements (appendix C) to keep by her side as she worked through the issue. Before dealing with the homework problem, Joan and Karen worked out grade expectations that reflected starting where Karen was. Remember the two important parental-love battle tactics:

1. Be in the center of where your child is: emotions first, then behavior.

2. Encourage behavior that's a bit of a stretch but still doable for a child gradually moving up from unacceptable to improved behavior, that is, apply the 98 percent success rule.

They started with the worst grades: three Ds and one F. (The Cs were accepted as part of the final plan.) Previous to this discussion, Joan had spent two weeks working hard to validate Karen's feelings, preparing the soil. Karen was starting to participate, and her tone was a little less harsh—a good sign that Karen was feeling heard and the validation was sinking in. For the first time in months, Joan was starting to feel hope.

"Karen, I want to support you to find a way that works for you to deal with the Ds and the one F. Is it okay to start with the three Ds?" (Being specific about what to discuss is essential.)

Joan leaned forward to hear Karen's response. Her daughter sat with her head down and turned as far away from her mother as possible. "Why talk about it? I know they have to be all Bs."

"Actually, no."

Karen's look from the window to Joan surely must have caused whiplash, and Joan had not seen such wide eyes since Karen's birthday last year when they surprised her with an iPod.

"I think all Bs is too big a step. Let's talk about what you think you can do for the rest of this quarter."

"What do you mean?" Whatever was outside the window was obviously of no interest now.

"I looked at your grade percent in each subject. Biology—I know you hate that class—is 61 percent, language arts is 64 percent, and history is 69. Do you think you can bring any of these up to a C?"

"Well, I like history; I know I can bring that up to a C."

Joan was really feeling stronger now. Karen was acting like her old self: seeming to care and giving a little bit of detail in her responses. This was a far cry from the previous months' comments of "Who cares" and "I don't know."

"Okay, what about biology?"

"Mom, that teacher hates me!" Joan listened for at least five minutes to the details. (Fortunately, Joan had inserted the "bite-your-tongue gauze" I give all clients—guaranteed to reduce the pain of keeping your mouth shut at times like these.)

After adequate validation, Joan responded. "What do you think about replacing this class with a correspondence biology course?" Joan caught Karen's startled look. "I checked with the school, and they'll support this option."

Trying to keep from smiling (kids are very cautious about feeling good when they feel bad most of the time; it hurts too much to get their hopes up and then be disappointed), Karen muttered, "That would help."

"What do you think you can do with the language arts class?"

"I kind of like the teacher, but I don't see how I can get that one up to a B or C with only five weeks left in the quarter."

"What about shooting for a 68 or 69 percent?"

The old Karen smile couldn't be held back any longer. "I think I can do that."

Joan could hardly keep back her tears. That feeling of warmth from hope was almost overwhelming.

"And the F in German. Let's drop that class for now."

Karen's face reddened slightly as she tried to get in an undetected shocked look at Mom.

"I checked with the school, and you are really okay with your credits. We can make up this dropped class in your sophomore or junior year."

Karen couldn't keep the tears in. She quickly brushed them away as Mom touched her shoulder and said, "I love you." Karen burst out crying and raced out of the room. Mom gave her a couple of minutes and then went to her side, with enough tissues to handle both their tears.

"We're going to get through this. I know we can do it. Let's do something fun. How about going to McDonald's for fries and a shake?"

What do you think? Is Joan too lenient? That's what 95 percent of parents feel before they actually experience for themselves how parental love touches a child's heart.

When the heart is touched, big things happen. It's like what realtors say about the three most important things for selling a house— location, location, location. The same is true for making changes in your child's behavior—validation, validation, validation. (We'll refer to this trio of validations as the 3 Vs, which could even double for victory.)

> When the heart is touched, big things happen.

Joan told me, through tears of joy, that Karen talked more to her at McDonald's than she had for two months. Remember what we said about joy, one of the five core emotions: When joy flourishes, the other four emotions—fear, disgust, sadness, and anger—wilt like they've been sprayed with weed killer.

Let's stop for a moment and connect the homework scenario with Karen's problem temperament-trait characteristics of adaptation and mood. The mood problem is not particularly complicated, so we'll start there.

When a moody person is in an emotional hole, he or she feels it's impossible to get out. Remember, we are in the center of Karen. She feels no optimism, zilch. She knows no such word as "hope." That's the default spot for a moody person. What's the remedy? The adult's responsibility is to impose a melody of hope and optimism through action and to create harmony with a few well-placed words of encouragement. You know how kids love music.

That's exactly what Joan did. The typical and natural parent response to the poor grades, however, would be, "You're capable of Bs. Let's find some ways to make it happen." The melody and words coming from this chorus sound good, but it's the wrong music for this occasion. After we've sung ourselves hoarse for a few weeks, we move to another song: "I wish you would be more responsible. Why can't you show as much interest in your schoolwork as you do in your computer time?" We all know this song will never make the top forty.

Joan pulled the right tune out of her new playlist, and it was from the "easy duet" book. Singing this song together resulted in grades Karen thought she could manage. "Let's drop the F subject" really struck a chord with Karen. Through all of Joan's validating actions, Karen's negative mood trait was improved.

Can you always do things with a moody child that maintain positive feelings all the time? No. There will be ups and downs. But you can minimize the negative feelings. Experiencing positive feelings is central for a moody person to learn how to cope with moodiness. Joan was providing the training Karen needed.

What about the adaptation temperament trait? Remember, adaptation is the ability to stop one activity and start another, also known as shifting. Some people can do this with ease, whereas others, such as Karen, find it much more difficult. People who adapt easily move from one activity to another the way a car turns a corner—fast or slow, sharp or soft. People who are slow to adapt, however, turn more like a sailboat. With a sailboat, a sharp turn is impossible. The adaptation (shifting) characteristic of a sailboat turn is "easy as she goes"—it takes more time and distance. Slower-to-adapt people need time and space to move from one activity to another.

Joan understood and accepted that Karen could not adapt or shift easily. Though Karen had several shifting problems, the biggest one was shifting from her computer time to homework. Of course, we all struggle a bit with shifting from something fun to something boring. (You'll see later in the chapter how Joan handled this.) With an adaptation problem, however, the shift is much harder.

Another shifting problem involved Karen changing her strong "hate" feelings about the biology teacher (which made it impossible for her to learn the subject material) to "tolerating" feelings and putting this new energy into learning her biology material. After evaluating the situation, Joan quickly concluded that Karen was not ready to shift in this situation. The solution: Cut your losses (one productive thing she learned from her dad) and take a correspondence course.

Karen did show her potential for shifting with her history grade, currently a C, when she said, "Well, I like history; I know I can bring that up to a B." Joan knew this shift was possible because of the "I like history" motivator. (We'll talk a lot more about using motivators in chapters 6 and 7.)

The takeaway here is something you've read before, but it bears repeating: At the beginning of problem solving, adjust your expectations until they match what your child can do 98 percent of the time. When this happens, you'll have proof you are at the center of your child. The evidence? Mastery and the accompanying joy. Joan demonstrated how this works. She put her feelings and thoughts aside temporarily, which allowed her to start where Karen was. The result: goodness of fit, success for both Karen and Joan, and the beginnings of reestablishing the bond between mother and child.

## Karen's Homework and Monitoring Plan

Joan had two more parts of the plan to accomplish: a homework plan that took into account the importance of online time and a monitoring system to ensure ongoing successes. What actually happened between the two of them would take another chapter to tell, so I'll summarize.

Two big barriers existed with the homework: (1) Karen hated homework, and (2) she loved her half hour online after school. These inclinations are fairly typical for a teenager but really a problem when you have temperament traits like Karen's. Joan used the same parental-love principles she had used to arrive at the mutually agreed upon grades above:

- She started where Karen was.
- She accommodated for the mood and adaptation trait difficulties.
- She validated Karen.
- She used Karen's ideas whenever possible within general non-negotiable limits.
- She set mutually determined realistic expectations (98 percent successful).
- She maximized the motivators and minimized the barriers (two key components of effective change).
- She kept the parental-love requirements ready at a moment's notice.

Here were the tougher issues Joan faced: how to get Karen to end her time online and start her homework and how to avoid the emotional minefield when she checked Karen's homework.

Here's what Joan did. First, she set the nonnegotiable limit that all homework needed to be done by eight o'clock. Both Joan and Karen determined the length of time it took Karen to do her homework, typically one to two hours. Then, within that deadline of eight o'clock, Karen was allowed to make choices: when to start her homework and how much transition time she would take between the computer and her homework. Joan was prepared with some surprises (motivators to shoot down the barriers) to help with shifting from the computer to homework: more online time, special snacks, extra time to switch from computer to homework, and a special reward for complying with the nightly plan. Not bad, Joan!

After a lot of validating, listening, and using plenty of ideas from Karen, mom and daughter established a plan. Karen chose to get all of her homework done by dinner instead of using the eight o'clock deadline. They both agreed that if either one of them started to yell or be disrespectful, the discussion would stop, and one of them would leave and then come back to talk later. Here's the rest of the plan:

- Karen's online time was increased to one hour (2:30–3:30). The shock value of a thirty-minute time increase was a huge motivator. They decided to do away with the timer; Karen "hated" timers. Karen asked her mom to remind her once to turn off the computer, and if she did not turn it off within five minutes, she would lose computer privileges for twenty-four hours. Perhaps you're thinking, *No way; not realistic.* It wasn't realistic before all the progress had occurred, but it had become definitely possible with how good Karen was feeling. During the very first experiences with problem solving this would not have happened. Remember: Joan had already been practicing parental love several weeks before this plan, and she had successfully worked out the grade issues. When children are given a lot of decision-making power and plenty of validation, they invariably, with coaching and encouragement from parents, come up with good ideas.

- Transition time to homework would be fifteen minutes, spiced up by Karen's getting any snack she wanted from a list approved by Joan. (Yes, there were some unhealthy items included.)

- Mom would check her daily homework only for completion, not correctness. The requirement was that Karen would not moan and complain through the checking exercise. Joan

> When children are given a lot of decision-making power and plenty of validation, they invariably, with coaching and encouragement from parents, come up with good ideas.

had decided to deal only with Karen handing in all assigned work for the first week or so. First things first, right? They both decided they would review grade performance after three weeks of little to no missing homework. Checking only for completion was a huge motivator for Karen. Prior to this plan, Joan required Karen to get Bs or better on her homework. If the work was not B level, Karen would need to redo it. Now Joan realized that hunting rabbits with hand grenades was overkill. Diplomacy was the better tactic.

- A weekly CD reward (with a preset monetary limit) was added for three weeks of following this plan successfully. The success requirements went like this: first week, three out of five days successfully following the plan; second week, four out of five days; and third week, five out of five days. (Three out of five days for the first week was considered the "stretch but doable" result. Her compliance to behaviors similar to the plan had not occurred once in the last month.) Karen accepted an important point about motivators: She really shouldn't be rewarded forever for the plan's requirements; this is the way kids should act anyway. But as Joan explained to Karen, Karen was in a deep hole and needed extra rope and pulleys to get out. Once she was out, the rope and pulleys could be stored. The reward for three weeks was to put a little fun into the whole thing, after which the reward would stop.

So, how did the implementation go? Well, the parental love truck hit the road with Karen as the driver and Joan the navigator. (Joan had an emergency brake on the navigator side and an emergency steering wheel available at a moment's notice.) The first week was bumpy. Joan needed to brake and grab the emergency steering, but she did it all with plenty of validation. Karen did pull off the first week's requirement and got her CD. The second week she did not meet the requirement. But the third week she again received her CD reward.

Now Karen had two weeks left in the quarter. Joan decided to extend the CD reward period for the last two weeks of the quarter, letting Karen know not to expect this type of reward for the next quarter. (Reward warning: Continued progress after the first three weeks may require you to continue a reward for several additional weeks.)

Monitoring the plan was the last part of the overall parenting plan. After the first three weeks of the quarter described above, Joan started monitoring in earnest. Joan set up two nonnegotiable requirements for the remaining two weeks of the current quarter and the following quarter: Joan would need to know without a doubt what Karen's weekly grades were and the weekly status of missing homework. After considering several plans, such as grade checks (which never worked), they agreed to review Karen's grades and missing homework online every Monday night. After two weeks of working the bugs out—there were some pretty severe bites—this online plan worked well. Karen had only one missing homework assignment during the fourth week and no missing assignments during the fifth week.

By the end of the quarter Karen's grades looked like this: history, 72 percent (up from 69 percent); language arts, 69 percent (up from 64 percent); and the other two C subjects were maintained at a C level. Karen was not able to start the biology correspondence course during the quarter but was set up for the next quarter.

Besides improved grades, Karen and Joan accomplished several important things: (1) They established successful problem-solving experiences through parental love that could be applied to future issues; (2) they reestablished the parent-child bond; (3) Karen experienced success and mastery, a critical self-confidence builder; and (4) the biggest success was Karen feeling lovable, valued by her mother, and most of all "I'm good."

> Some problems are more difficult and some easier, but the same theme is present in all of the problems: The parent has not adequately started where the child is.

This result is typical and consistent with parents who use the parental-love approach that Joan demonstrated so well.

After reading this hard-fought struggle, maybe you're thinking, *Who has the time to put this much effort into so many problems?* or *This sounds too perfect; I can't imagine planning something this good and it working out so well. I'm more discouraged now than I was before!* It does sound overwhelming, but taking it step by step will make it possible for you to experience success.

Of course, not every one of my clients' efforts turns out this well; most do eventually, and the vast majority of situations result in noticeable, satisfying change. Some problems are more difficult and some easier, but the same theme is present in all of the problems: The parent has not adequately started where the child is. There is always noticeable improvement when this step is achieved through validation.

One more point: The actual outcome of Karen's situation is not as important as how Joan focused on validating Karen and Karen's responses. That's where the gold is. Just like new shoes feel a little uncomfortable at first and you wonder whether they'll ever fit, so it is with validating your child's feelings. It doesn't feel just right at first (there may even be blisters), but with ongoing validation, your child will always feel more comfortable and increase the feeling of "I'm good." Pretty soon the parental-love shoe feels so comfortable that you don't even know you're wearing it; the validation just happens automatically. Keep trying; you will get comfortable validating your child.

Now let's answer some of the questions you may have rolling around in your mind.

# FAQs

*I have two children—my daughter, who's an easy child, and my son, who's definitely difficult. My son and I fight all the time. With him, I can now see that we have several significantly different temperament-trait characteristics. I've been expecting him to be just like me, and when he wasn't, I've become really upset. This makes me feel guilty and bad that our conflicts are my fault, which they are. When I read information like this, I'm struck by how unprepared we are as parents for the most important job of our lives and how much damage an unprepared parent can do to a child. How can I get over how bad I was as a parent?*

First of all, your difficult child is lucky to have you as a parent. I know looking at our past mistakes is painful. I've been there in my own parenting, and I see the pain in my clients every day when they realize how much they didn't know. Your child is fortunate because of the immense

**Mistakes are part of the parenting journey.**

love you have for him. If you didn't really love him, you wouldn't care about being aware of your part in the problem.

Be careful not to allow shame to enter into your admission of your parenting mistakes. Almost all my clients use the term "damage" like you did when they first face their issues head on. This word has a shameful meaning to it—as though what you did permanently injured your child and as though you knew what you were doing and did it purposely. You and I both know better! Load that garbage onto the next truck and send it to the landfill.

Mistakes are part of the parenting journey. Like bumps or potholes developing on a road, you can keep hurting your car by running over them at full speed, or you can fix the bumps and holes, restoring the road for a smooth drive. Here's what it sounds like to fix the psychological bumps without shame: *I didn't know it at the time, but now I can see that what I did contributed to my child's current problems. I acknowledge my mistakes and now, with new awareness and appropriate parenting tools, I will move forward to help my child improve.* This kind of repair job results in what feelings from you and your child? Yes, I can almost hear you: "I'm good." I know, not right now, but eventually with this type of realistic thinking, you won't struggle with the past that much—especially as you see the results of your parental love unfold.

One last word of encouragement on this temperament issue: Take the time to fill out the Temperament Trait Characteristics Plan in appendix B. Pick the trait with which you have the biggest problem. (Watch out! No shame.) Remember the next critical step: accepting for now your child's problem trait(s) and yours. Now you're ready to set aside your differences and develop a goodness-of-fit plan: you fitting into the center of your child in order to start the successes.

*I'm impressed with this temperament information. Karen's school problems are almost identical to my son's difficulties. I do have a huge problem with Joan settling for Ds and Cs, though. And I definitely do not see how dropping a class would work. I don't teach my child to give up! With all due respect, how can you support this kind of parental behavior? If Karen had not had any experience with correspondence courses, how would she ever do this on her own? I think a lot of your stuff is pretty good, but this is going too far. I think Joan is making "starting where the child is," as you say, way too easy.*

> If a child experiences too much failure, life starts to feel like a toxic waste dumpsite.

Most parents have the same initial response; this type of plan is "enabling" or "teaching irresponsibility" or "not making the child face his lack of effort" or "not helping her to be a responsible adult." If I had a dollar for all the times I've heard these comments, I could have retired ten years ago. Thank goodness I didn't; I would have missed out on all these great experiences.

Here's the bottom line: When a student has Karen's kind of grade history for more than a quarter, expecting a child or adolescent to do any better than the improvements worked out with Joan is unrealistic. It results in failure and feelings of "I'm bad," and the problem gets worse. If a child experiences too much failure, life starts to feel like a toxic waste dumpsite.

None of us wants our child's workday to be a failure. School is the child's day job. Your child derives most of his or her self-worth, value, and "I'm good" or "I'm bad" feelings from school. When the performance is predominantly poor, self-confidence plummets, like bathwater after you pull the plug. Without water, you can't get clean. Without self-confidence, you can't perform.

Put yourself in your child's shoes: Do you do better at work if the bar for success is continually out of reach? Sometimes, maybe—after all, challenges are stimulating. But *always* out of reach? Of course not. Often when we apply what our child is going through to our own lives, we really get the point.

Now, perhaps, this seemingly "way-too-easy" plan is making a little more sense, especially considering Karen's temperament-trait problems: negative mood, slow to adapt, irregular, quiet, and initial withdrawal. When Joan got to the center of Karen's trait problems, accepting and validating them, she developed a plan that fit into these trait problems better.

> Your goal for your child will be reached faster and with a lot more self-confidence building within your child when you set the bar using parental love rather than when you set it out of reach.

On the surface, dropping a class and accepting two Ds seem ridiculous. Looking deeper, to the center of Karen (putting aside your unconscious projections), the plan ingredients are essential to ensure successes. We want Karen to be as pleased with her successes as Goldilocks was with Baby Bear's porridge: It was just right, so she ate every drop, without thinking twice about it. Well, none of us can get it that perfect, but you get the point.

Keep in mind that success and mastery are critical motivators. They're great at destroying barriers—and they don't cost a cent. Well, maybe a CD here or there, but that's a small price to pay. Also, you can continually raise the bar as long as the new position of the bar is (all together now) a stretch but doable and offers a 98 percent chance of success for the first series of goals. I've got a guarantee for you: Your goal for your child will be reached faster and with a lot more self-confidence building within your child when you set the bar using parental love rather than when you set it out of reach.

Your question related to dropping the course with an F was a good one. This again sounds like taking the easy way out. On the surface, you're right. But sometimes the easy way is a good way. From the center of Karen, Joan could see that Karen had given up and knew it was impossible to raise the grade. (Perspective is a wonderful thing, isn't it?) Joan cut her losses and dropped the F in a supportive, non-shaming way. She could have said, "This grade is because of your irresponsibility..." and on and on. Instead, she took the battery out of the bunny!

What about the correspondence course? I agree with you that the correspondence course was a risk for successful follow-through. Correspondence courses require a lot of self-initiative. If the proper structure is provided by the parent, though, a correspondence course can be an excellent way to get school credits. With Karen's increased hopefulness, her input into choosing to do a correspondence course, and Joan's supervision and love, Karen passed the course. Plans like this actually work most of the time.

## Wrapping Up

Almost across the board, when you are having difficulty with your child, it's a temperament-trait goodness-of-fit problem; several specific temperament-trait characteristics are clashing between you and your child.

Here are the five steps to establishing goodness of fit:

1. Become aware of the differences between you and your child's temperament-trait characteristics. (Use the Temperament Trait

Characteristics Comparison and Goodness of Fit Plan form for assistance.)

2. Accept your child's problem traits for now.

3. Stop doing what doesn't work (poor goodness of fit).

4. Plan and start modified parental behaviors and expectations that will fit within your child's problem trait characteristics. (If helpful, use the Goodness of Fit Plan found in the Temperament Trait Characteristics Comparison and Goodness of Fit Plan sheet, appendix B.) Develop a plan to get as close as possible to the 98 percent success rule. Keep modifying expectations until you achieve this level.

5. Monitor success for at least three to four weeks and then maintain monitoring for at least several months for continued success. Remember that success and mastery combine for the best fuel for change.

Now that we have finished the temperament material, what's next on our parental-love menu? Change. Change has been a continual underlying theme for both parent and child throughout this book—changing your parenting beliefs and thinking, and changing your child's behavior. We need to understand it well and know how to make change happen in the best way possible. Let's learn about change in the next chapter.

CHAPTER 6

# Go for the Gold—
# Invest in Change

AS THE RUBBER MEETS the road on your journey to upgrade your parental love, I'm sure you've thought, somewhere along the way, *I don't know if I can do this.* I've witnessed hundreds of parents voice that very thought and then proceed to make significant positive changes in the way they interact with their children. Of course, you can expect barriers; they're part of the initial landscape as we journey from the old to the new. This chapter will help you navigate through or around these barriers successfully.

Maybe the first roadblock to change is that huge surge of unrealistic excitement about the idea of change before we make the first change steps: *This new diet will definitely work* or *This new anger management program is going to eliminate my problems with my temper.* Change is transforming, so we jump in with both feet. Then come those first steps: giving up the old, comfortable sneakers and making the commitment to walk in a new pair of pumps (or wingtips, as the case may be). The first actual steps don't feel very comfortable; we wobble a bit or slip on those new leather soles; we move forward with uncertainty, looking back at our old Nikes that seem to be calling out to us. *I've not dropped any weight in a week, and I've worked so hard; I did everything the instructor said, and I still lost my temper with my wife.* We become discouraged, and all too often we give up changing our behavior and go back to our comfort zone.

How, then, can we maintain our courage to make it through those first steps? We need to understand the dynamics of change, know what to expect, learn how to navigate those first unexpected curves, and, finally, determine the best way to reach our destination.

With the right road map and full knowledge of what needs to be done, we then create our own expectations around the 98 percent success rule: Maybe you can follow the diet three days a week rather than seven; perhaps you can focus on one or two concepts from your anger management class rather than all ten.

You also include plenty of motivators to overcome the barriers or resistance: Buy a book or DVD after a week or two of success. In the context of your family, you have a long-term motivator: your child's increased self-confidence and joy; that's the gold. Let's dig into what makes change work the best.

First, we'll look at how change happens; there are actually stages of change, five of them. Then we'll uncover two tried-and-tested tricks to make these stages work in the best way possible: (1) behavior modification, and (2) knowing when and when not to use reasoning. Let's start with the five stages of change.

## Five Stages of Change

The "Stages of Change Model" was developed in the late 1970s and early 1980s by James Prochaska and Carlo DiClemente at the University of Rhode Island when they were studying how smokers were able to quit. I've modified the wording of these stages and put them into two categories:

*Thinking*
 1. unwilling to think
 2. willing to think

*Doing*
 3. planning (98 percent successful)
 4. action
 5. monitoring

Most of us do our parenting in this way: "You have to pick up your room before we go to the park" or "Will you please stop calling your sister names!" or "Don't you ever learn that when you come in past curfew you lose privileges? Now you're grounded." All are examples of action (stage 4), including none of the other stages; there is no engaging your child in the thinking or planning stages. And you know one thing for sure: Too many times your child is stuck at stage 1, unwilling to think about change. Starting at the action stage is a lot like putting the cart before the horse and then trying to push it uphill while the horse grazes in the ditch!

No wonder we rarely see change in our children! We're missing three important change stages: helping the child to think about the problem (stage 2) and then jointly developing a plan (stage 3) that fits best into the child's temperament traits. Seldom have teachers or parents heard about these stages. Once they get this information, however, I see smiles and nods of understanding. Everyone has an aha! moment. The concept makes sense instantly and ends up being extremely useful for achieving effective change.

## Change Factors

Three specific factors of change can make or break your efforts if you're not prepared for them. Let's start with an overarching feature of change: relapse. It's the part that's so discouraging—you yelled at the officer who gave you a speeding ticket on the way home from anger management class; you ate a bowl of ice cream four days into your diet. Expect relapse; then it will not take you by surprise. You probably won't be happy, but the disappointment won't be as strong.

Relapse isn't insurmountable, but if you don't see it as part of change, you're more likely to simply give up and stop trying.

Fortunately, there's an answer to relapse: Modify your plan to make it more realistic. Instead of expecting yourself to be Little Miss Sunshine after one session of anger management, you might try for three blowups a day instead of five. Instead of attempting to eliminate sugar from your diet in one afternoon, maybe allow yourself a spoonful of ice cream (rather than a pint) after dinner. In just a little bit we will get into more detail about how this all works.

Two other critical ingredients determine the success or failure of these change stages: motivators and barriers. Adequate motivation or enthusiasm throughout each stage is essential. And you're the only one who can determine what "adequate" means in this case. Your future health may not be an adequate motivator at this point for you to lose weight. The person who's "pre-diabetic," however, might find health to be more than adequate as a push for change.

> Relapse isn't insurmountable, but if you don't see it as part of change, you're more likely to simply give up and stop trying.

Motivators include both external rewards (candy, money) or deprivations (no TV) and internal rewards. When you begin a weight-loss program, you may need to reward yourself with new clothes, concert tickets, or a massage for every five pounds you lose. But eventually, there will come a time when your rewards shift. You realize you feel better, look better, and have more energy, and those become your internal motivators for maintaining the change you worked so hard for. For your child to change, you may need to begin with rewards of cash, movie tickets, or gift cards, but eventually your child's motivators will also shift from external to internal. Your child's feeling of being valued by your acknowledging or using the child's idea for a solution to a problem will propel him or her toward change. The internal rewards are where the gold is; that's the nutrient that has the most effect on "I'm good" taking root in your child's heart and soul.

What about barriers? They are a given. And if they're not addressed, failure is assured. Harsh but true. For example, if you plan (stage 3) to lose three pounds a week or never become angry again, you're likely setting up insurmountable barriers, in the form of unrealistic expectations, for yourself. Reduce the barrier, and your plan will work if reduced to the point of regular success.

With your child, you may face barriers such as unhealthy habits (whining, complaining), an inadequate relationship between the two of you, or no interest in school. Your plan will need to outline baby steps to deal with each one of these barriers so that each barrier is gradually dismantled. Since you are still involved in the action (stage 4) of reading this book, you are demonstrating a good combination of enough enthusiasm and minimal barriers to continue to improve your parental love. This is why you are succeeding in changing your parental love so far. Way to go! Your child is so fortunate to have you as a loving parent, one who's willing to consider seriously new ways to make your son or daughter feel as good about him- or herself as possible, even though sometimes it feels too hard.

> For your child to change, you may need to begin with rewards of cash, movie tickets, or gift cards, but eventually your child's motivators will also shift from external to internal.

Do you know the main reason you're continuing with this fourth stage of change? *Of course, I know, Gary. I'm just an awesome parent; let's face it.* I agree—but that's not the primary reason. You have successfully achieved the first three stages. When you first saw this book at your favorite bookstore or website, perhaps you browsed through it and decided it wasn't for you. You were in stage 1, not willing to think about the issues facing your family; there were more barriers than motivators: *I don't have time to read a book; I know I love my child. How could there be anything that new about love?* Result, the book was out of your mind while you went about your multiple parental duties for another week.

Sometime during the second week you found yourself starting to think about the idea of parental love; at that point there were as least as many motivators as barriers. You didn't know it, but you were in stage 2. You thought something like, *Maybe there are some things I don't know about how to love my children.* Translating your love into improved parental behaviors was feeling more and more interesting. As you thought about this book, the motivators were gradually overtaking the barriers. *Yes, I really want to learn more about parental love; I want the best for my child; maybe I can find something useful in the book; I'm going to get the book tomorrow.* A plan (stage 3) emerged, and all of a sudden you found yourself ready for the action stage. Tomorrow comes, and your car's in the parking lot of your favorite bookstore. Within minutes you have the book in the bag and you're on your way home, anxious to begin reading as soon as possible.

Did you know you've been in the monitoring stage (stage 5) since reading this book? To keep the action going, you've needed to keep the motivation higher than the barriers. Maybe you felt the temperament information with Joan and Karen didn't apply to you. Your interest waned, and that's a barrier. But as you monitored your feelings, you decided you would read that chapter anyway and not let this barrier stop you. You didn't know it, but you were doing the monitoring stage well: paying close attention to when you started to get bored with the material (identifying barriers) and doing something about it (identifying motivators that work). Most of us don't monitor the motivators and barriers well during change; we quit, not knowing that we need to identify the barriers, reduce them, and increase the motivators.

> Most of us don't monitor the motivators and barriers well during change; we quit, not knowing that we need to identify the barriers, reduce them, and increase the motivators.

You may have relapsed. It's normal; you may have stopped reading the book for a week or so because you felt overwhelmed by the task ahead of you. But now you're reading again because you've realized you're up to the challenge and your child's need to feel "I'm good" overcame your hesitance. Good for you!

Now, let's mine these stages to see how they apply to parental love and make change more successful.

## Parental Love and the Stages of Change

Here's a typical scenario involving sibling rivalry between fourteen-year-old Alex and his eight-year-old sister, Maggie. For the last two years Alex has been increasingly using mean words and putdowns, yelling, and sometimes hitting his sister. Mom has tried everything she knows: reasoning, grounding, taking game systems away. Nothing has worked, and the problem is getting worse.

She decided to try counseling. At the second parent counseling session, Mom brought Alex and Maggie with her because of some scheduling conflicts. They sat in the waiting room while I began the session with Mom. After she told me about the sibling problem, I briefly went over the five change stages, including the points about motivation and barriers, then asked, "What do you think?"

"I think I've already been through the getting-Alex-to-think part. I've told Alex, I don't know how many times, that—"

From the waiting room the yelling started. "You brat! Give me that magazine. You've had it long enough. Give it to me now, or I'll bash your head...."

Mom rushed out of the office. "Alexander James—"

"Mom, she's being a jerk. It's my—"

"Alex, give me that magazine." Mom grabbed the magazine, now in two parts. "Sit over here and behave."

Now I was in the waiting room. Alex sat in the chair, smoldering, while Mom put her arm around Maggie. "Sweetie, I'm sorry he's so mean to you."

As Mom comforted her daughter, I spent a little time with Alex. "Sounds like things are pretty rough for you and Maggie. Come over here a sec. I've got a new PS3 game you might be interested in."

Alex gave a quick glance toward me and moved over to the TV while I started up the game.

With Alex now enthusiastically playing, I invited Mom back into the session. After commiserating a bit with her, I restarted our discussion and asked what stage of change she thought Alex was in.

"He's got to be in stage 2, the thinking stage. I've told him over and over how his meanness is not acceptable in our house. He just doesn't listen."

Most parents assume that when they're lecturing, the child is thinking.

"How effective are your lectures for helping Alex to think?"

"I always thought they were pretty effective, but I guess he really can't think about the problem if I'm telling him what to think. Come to think about it [Mom's just entered stage 2], Alex says all the time, 'I don't care.' That must mean he's not willing to think about what I'm saying or about the fighting problem with his sister."

"On the surface, it seemed he must have been thinking. What else could be happening when you were lecturing? Now that you're looking below the surface, you're seeing something else. The 'I don't care' comment is caused by his self-talk, which goes something like this: *No one really cares about me; Mom always sides with Maggie; no one ever listens to my side of the story; I give up.* A lot of children who say 'I don't care' eventually share what they're thinking, similar to the self-talk I just mentioned. Alex will eventually share his specific thoughts. Children in Alex's situation are actually in stage 1, not willing to think about problem solving but thinking a lot about why he dislikes his sister. Only when Alex feels validated will he— Here's a tissue. What's the sadness about?"

"How am I supposed to care what he's thinking when he's beating up his sister? He just needs to stop.... I'm sorry; give me a second." Mom wiped more tears away, sat back, and exhaled heavily. "Okay, I think I'm starting to get it. I guess if I'm always chewing him out, after a while he's got to feel I don't care."

"You're making headway. You're giving yourself a chance to reflect and think from Alex's point of view, and you're beginning to feel what he feels. This is so hard to do, especially when his behavior is totally unacceptable."

"Then tell me how to get him to think. If you can do that, I'll sure feel a lot better."

Let's fast forward. Here's a summary of how Mom used the stages of change to make the necessary adjustments to help Alex solve the problem. Every stage we went through focused on the three "Vs": validation, validation, validation.

## Stage 1: Not Willing to Think about the Problem

Mom learned the key for this one. First, she needed to talk very little and listen a lot. When talking, she learned to validate without defending (I call it validation listening). Here's the lesson Mom learned: If a child is in this stage and the parent is talking way too much, the parent needs to get out of the hurricane protection center (protecting your ideas, staying away from the child's storm) and move into the eye of the storm (the center of your child; it's calmer in the center anyway). Let's listen in on how well Mom learned this lesson.

"Mom, you don't care."

*Of course I do*, she thinks, but instead says kindly, gauze firmly inserted over tongue, "That's got to be horrible. Tell me what I do to make you feel that way" [validation listening; validating Alex's emotion; Mom not defending her point].

"Uh, I...I don't...you just don't care." Alex is just beginning to think. He's not quite able to articulate his feelings.

Being in the center, looking out at the fury of the storm, Mom picks up an object on the radar: "Seems like I'm always picking on you and never on Maggie...."

"That's it. You're always on Maggie's side."

Heart beating faster and taking a deep, hopefully undetectable, breath, she continues. "You're right. I hardly ever [have to be a little truthful, after all] pick on Maggie."

Their conversation continued, but that's enough to see how Mom got Alex to take the first step out of "not willing to think" toward "willing to think." What was the motivator for Alex? Validation of his feelings. And a big barrier was starting to be dismantled: *Mom is not disagreeing with everything I say.* Of course, he didn't say it; that would be too easy. But I guarantee he was starting to feel it.

## Stage 2: Willing to Think

Mom learned the key for this one as well: Validate your child's feelings and thoughts, and start to think together with your child, focusing on how to maximize the motivators and minimize the barriers. She worked hard during this thinking stage to talk little and listen a lot (75/25 rule).

As a result, she discovered several of Alex's barriers: Mom picked on Alex too much and Maggie too little; she wasn't accepting what Maggie was doing to make Alex angry; and she wasn't finding a way that worked for Alex to deal with his anger. These barriers are Alex's words and experiences. Remember that you need to be in the eye of your child's storm looking out. That's where the gold is.

Now, what about Alex's motivators? At this stage, internal motivators are the best. Over multiple validations, Alex became convinced that Mom understood and accepted the above-mentioned barriers; now that's motivating. She learned the lesson well: Through parental action, you can convince your child that the barriers can be almost completely eliminated.

Another internal motivator is taking your child's initial ideas seriously about how to reduce the barriers and increase the motivators. This is done in stage 3 planning. As adults we experience the same feeling when a supervisor or loved one takes our ideas seriously. It's empowering, and there's nothing like feeling valued and good. Now we know what James Taylor meant when he sang, "How sweet it is to be loved by you." Well, maybe he wasn't talking about parental love, but it all comes down to the same thing: Feeling valued and good is a joyful experience.

> Validate your child's feelings and thoughts, and start to think together with your child, focusing on how to maximize the motivators and minimize the barriers.

## Stage 3: Planning (98 Percent Successful)

At this stage, Mom learned to transform the discussion about maximizing motivators and minimizing barriers into action steps. The plan must maintain high levels of motivation and guard against old as well as new barriers developing. Here are some guidelines Mom followed:

- Set nonnegotiable parameters right away: No hitting, inappropriate yelling, or name-calling in the home. Within these parameters Mom used Alex's ideas about how to deal with his upset effectively, including rewards (with a monetary limit set by Mom). She agreed with one reward suggested by Alex: a rental video game each week if he performed according to the plan.

- Plan for at least a month for the new behaviors to become established and at least an extra month of daily monitoring to ensure the solutions stick.[1] The first two weeks are heavily oriented toward making sure the plan is 98 percent successful. The remaining two weeks and the next month are more focused on monitoring to make sure the behavior is being sustained.

- Always use internal motivators as your plan's foundation: validation, validation, validation.

- Use external motivators—rewards and/or deprivations—to supplement internal motivation. The motivators need to be chosen by your child within a monetary limit you set. Don't automatically think your motivator is going to work. Here's the rule: The reward must motivate your child to do what you want him or her to do more than what the child wants to do.

Just a brief comment on how rewards work best. The tougher the problem, the closer you place the reward to the behavior you want to happen. If you have gone from a weekly reward to a daily reward and the behavior still hasn't stopped, add a deprivation. Alex was mean to Maggie two or three times a day. The weekly video reward was not enough. During the first week the reward requirement was the following: No more than one mean exchange per day for five out of seven days and no hitting. If Alex was mean more than once daily or hit his sister, he lost his game system for twenty-four hours. (The next section on behavior

> The tougher the problem, the closer you place the reward to the behavior you want to happen.

modification will give you more details about how to use rewards and deprivation.)

- Success during the first week must be 98 percent. Plan carefully for it. Be ready to adjust right away, after the first day if necessary, reduce the barriers, and increase the motivation. Mom planned for two possible adjustments if needed, which you'll read about shortly.

- Throughout these first three change stages, Mom worked hard to use the parental-love approach, especially the validation part, validating the emotions under the harsh attitude and mean words. The toughest part is always at the beginning of problem solving, when the storm is the worst. Alex blasted Mom: "You don't care about me; you always side with Maggie; you never discipline her; I wish she wasn't even my sister." Be prepared. The child's comments and behavior at the beginning of problem solving feel next to impossible to handle. Mom knew she loved Alex and could give him at least ten reasons why she did. She also knew she disciplined Maggie, and she wanted so badly to tell Alex, "Didn't you see when I disciplined Maggie yesterday?" but she held back. What's extra hard is to validate feelings when the words and attitude are so mean: "I wish Maggie wasn't my sister" or "She's such a jerk."

Here's the plan summary: All the agreements were written on a sheet of paper with a chart attached to keep track of the daily requirements. Mom then posted it on the kitchen bulletin board. At

Alex's request the parents tracked daily the times they used validation listening. Alex and his parents signed the plan agreements.

The chart tracked four areas:

1. The number of negative episodes per day

2. The number of days during which Alex met his goal

3. The number of times Alex appropriately left a conflict with Maggie before it turned sour, and then shared his feelings with his parents

4. The number of times a day the parents used validation listening

Five out of seven days of no more than one negative episode per day would win Alex a video game rental. The parents agreed that every time Alex stopped a conflict appropriately and shared his feelings with them, he'd get a checkmark. For every ten checks, he got an hour of video-game playing added to his two-hour limit on Saturday (maximum hours added were two). When his parents floated that part of the plan to him, he launched out of his chair, with fist almost hitting the ceiling, "Yesss!"

## Stage 4: Action

The focus of the first week is implementing the plan. Once the first week or two is done and you can see the action is working, the primary focus turns to monitoring (stage 5). Of course, you're monitoring throughout all the stages to make sure the plan is working. As I've said before, during the first week or two, 98 percent success is essential. Make sure the motivators are high enough and the barriers are low enough.

Here's what happened with Alex by the end of the fourth day. Two out of the first four days, Alex met his goal of no more than one negative episode a day. With only three days left in the week, Mom realized the requirement of five out of seven days needed to be changed to four out of seven days (98 percent success rule).

He left conflicts with Maggie to express the problem to his parents eight times. Leaving Maggie during a conflict was huge—he had rarely done that before—and Alex seemed to be enjoying the high fives.

The parents added a very creative option to help him achieve his four-out-of-seven-days goal. If he had a second negative episode in a day, he could erase it by apologizing to Maggie and doing something nice for her. Mom and Alex agreed on two options for "something nice," not taking more than five minutes, that Alex could choose from.

Alex stopping his conflict with Maggie before a fight broke out really worked well; he did it thirteen times by the seventh day. Each time he reported a problem, the parents discussed the problem with Maggie and realized they were not noticing how much she was contributing to the struggle. They disciplined Maggie appropriately and made sure Alex knew about it. Alex could hardly control his smile. The action by the parents really made Alex feel better; more than once he commented, "Now you see what I've been telling you."

The parents were amazed at how little they used validation listening: the first day not at all (they lectured); the second day one time; and after that they used validation listening at least five times daily. They had never really used validation listening before. It was kind of a hassle to keep track of it, but the tracking helped them to try harder—especially since Alex was the scorekeeper. It paid off.

> Parental love evaluates success from inside the child out, not from outside the child in.

End of first week: gold medal. Alex met his goals, got his video rental, and was able to add one more hour onto his Saturday video game playing. But is it fool's gold, making it too easy? Yes, if you look at it from outside in. You might be thinking *the parents practically gave it to him by making all the adjustments.* No, if you look at it from inside Alex out: The goal is Alex experiencing noticeable change and Alex feeling successful. Remember, feeling successful is the same as "I'm good," the source of self-confidence. Parental love evaluates success from inside the child out, not from outside the child in.

Cue the music. Alex is on the stand, ready to receive his medal. Congratulations, Alex. The room is filled with smiles, even a few tears of joy—quite a difference from all the grim faces that filled the house during the previous weeks.

In the second week, Mom and Alex decided to go back to the requirement of no more than one negative interaction for five out of seven days. They kept the apologize-and-do-something-nice program. By the end of the second week, Alex met his goal of five out of seven days, and he left a conflict with Maggie eleven times. He got one extra hour of game time on Saturday and his rental video game. The parents used validation listening more than 50 percent of the time.

Mom is now ready for the next stage, focusing primarily on monitoring. The wrinkles have been mostly ironed out, and everyone is feeling pretty comfortable. Since wrinkles have a tendency to come back or even to pop up in new places, she'll keep all plan aspects ready for action just in case something needs to be ironed out.

## Stage 5: Monitoring

The task at this stage is for Alex and his family to maintain the new behaviors. The tendency is to stop paying attention to the new behavior when things are starting to go well. Focus on this monitoring activity for at least two months and fairly intensely during the first month because you know what's coming: relapse.

Relapse means your child has fallen back to stage 1, 2, or 3. Immediately go back to doing whatever is necessary with motivators to get out of this stage and back into the action stage as soon as possible. At

> Focus on this monitoring activity for at least two months and fairly intensely during the first month because you know what's coming: relapse.

this point, you may not only have to think outside the box; you may need to think outside the warehouse. But remember what we said about relapse: Expect it. Don't let it surprise you or set you back. Also, you can significantly reduce the likelihood and consequences of relapse by making sure the motivators stay high and the barriers remain very low.

Deal with relapse immediately. If relapse happens many times, the new behaviors won't have a chance to take root. Your child is much like a young plant. You pay close attention to that plant—you protect it from pests, bad weather, and so forth—until you see clear evidence that the roots are taking hold. That done, you can expect a robust plant over time. If you don't, it's gone.

> Deal with relapse immediately. If relapse happens many times, the new behaviors won't have a chance to take root.

Let's check back in with Alex and his family. In the third week the parents added one day to the no-more-than-one-negative-exchange requirement, from five days to six out of seven. Everything else stayed the same. Alex didn't make it. He only achieved the old goal, five days. Mom dealt with this by continuing to encourage him for his progress and reminding him that sometimes we just don't meet our goals. Alex understood and felt that the increase from five to six days had been fair, so they decided to maintain the plan. His response showed Mom he hadn't reverted to a lower stage; he was still supportive of the plan and was ready to continue the action stage. Mom felt the motivation of encouragement was enough to overcome the barriers. (In some situations, a higher reward would be needed or the goal would need to be modified.)

In the fourth week, Alex met his six-out-of-seven days goal of no-more-than-one-negative-exchange-per-day requirement. And for the fourth week in a row he got his one hour additional game time on Saturday. He hit Maggie only once in the four-week period.

During the sixth week, Alex met all of his goals! The behavior was becoming well rooted. When this happens, you know you're getting good at maximizing motivators and minimizing barriers.

By the eighth week Alex rarely fought with his sister and was continually leaving conflict situations. Now he often just ignored Maggie when there was a problem and didn't even bother to report it to his parents. As long as Alex continued with this great behavior, he and his mom decided the following rewards would be permanent: a video game rental every month and increasing his game time on Saturday from two to three hours if the goals continued to be reached. Alex was a happy camper. Of course, this made the other campers in the family happy too.

Scenarios like that of Alex's family aren't impossible dreams. Our parental-love approach is a great fit with the five stages of change, and the chances of victory for you and your child are significantly improved when you follow the principles we've just discussed. Now you can more accurately know where to start with your child. You can find the center of your child more easily by knowing the stage he or she is in. A real turbo boost for victory is maximizing motivators and minimizing barriers. Stick with this approach to change, and within several weeks you will see some great victories for you and your child. Go for the gold; it's within reach.

Now let's cover another effective tool for our parental-love efforts: behavior modification.

CHAPTER 7

# Change from the Inside Out

ONE OF THE BEST tried-and-tested tools to make change happen in the best way possible is behavior modification.[1] It's always useful in any change you are going through with your child. (I know "always" and "never" are not supposed to be used, but this tool actually *is* always useful. You be the judge after using it for yourself.) Let's take a couple of minutes to understand it first before learning how to use it with your child.

Throughout the five stages of change we learned that motivation is at the heart of change—maximize motivation, minimize barriers. Behavior modification gives us a manual about how motivation happens and how to use it in the most effective way possible. Some therapists use this approach exclusively and call themselves behaviorists. I use it as part of my therapist tool bag but not exclusively. I've come up with the following definition of behavior modification:

> Your child's behavior is shaped by the events and behavior that happen outside your child and the thoughts and beliefs that happen inside your child.

In other words, kids learn their behaviors from two sources: what happens externally to them and what happens internally.

# External Events

What do I mean by "outside" them? A parent smiling and talking happily to a baby is an example of an event happening outside a child. The baby responds to the parent's smile by smiling, wiggling with excitement, and maybe even verbalizing with those precious baby sounds. Be assured the baby notices the excitement we all feel and express at these responses, and he or she learns two things: (1) what behavior makes Mommy and Daddy happy, and (2) that smiling is the right response to someone smiling and talking happily to her.

Besides other biological and psychological causes, a significant reason for a child's response is what a parent has done. If parents repeat their behavior over and over again, the child repeats her response over and over. The child's response is being set in concrete (reinforced) by the parents. Remember Carl in the chapter on beliefs: "No matter how often I explain why lying is wrong, he continues to lie." The lying was set in concrete, and the behavior modification manual would call this lying a "conditioned response"—the child's behavior has become ingrained because of what the parents say and do over and over again. The short version: Repeated parent behavior causes repeated child behavior, whether good or not so good.

If you are ingraining or reinforcing good behavior, that's great; if it's negative behavior, that's not so great. Who wants to reinforce negative behavior? No hands. But when we look at the behavior modification manual to understand how to change our child's negative behavior, we can see that our parenting behavior is a major cause of our child's negative behavior. Ouch, that stings! Nobody reinforces negative behavior on purpose.

*If you stop doing what isn't working and start a better parenting behavior, you can expect your child to stop the negative behavior and start better behavior—usually within days and sometimes right away.*

There is tremendous good news, though: If you stop doing what isn't working and start a better parenting behavior, you can expect your child to stop the negative behavior and start better behavior— usually within days and sometimes right away. Our changed positive behavior results in the child's new positive behavior. That's what Alex's mom did; she stopped repeating her old behaviors, started repeating many new positive behaviors, and Alex gradually stopped repeating his old negative behaviors and started repeating his new ones. That's the gold about using the behavior modification concept. Now you know why you get so stuck: Your repeated behavior is actually reinforcing your child's repeated negative behavior.

> Now you know why you get so stuck: Your repeated behavior is actually reinforcing your child's repeated negative behavior.

You've actually witnessed the effectiveness of behavior modification throughout this book. Excessive parent lecturing causes a child to disagree, feel bad, and stay stuck in negative behavior. Remember Karen and Joan from the temperament chapter: "I set a timer to signal when she's supposed to log off, but she never obeys. I am so angry that this happens all the time. I have to remind her at least five or six times, and each time I get louder and more intense."

When Joan stopped this behavior and started repeated validation behaviors, Karen's actions and responses increasingly became more positive. And, as she increasingly repeated these positive behaviors, she repeatedly felt "I'm good." Repeated validation causes repeated positive behavior and continually reinforces "I'm good." You've probably noticed the word *repeated* repeated several times already in this chapter. The behavior modification manual makes it clear, and my experience bears this out: Repeated judgmental lectures result in repeated negative behavior; repeated parental love results in gradually repeated positive behavior. Take-home lesson: Repeating good stuff is a must; repeating negative stuff is a dead end.

So, in just a couple of pages, here's what we've learned: Your child's negative behavior is largely determined by your behavior. Stop repeating behavior that doesn't work and replace it with a repeating behavior that meets your child's needs better. Here's a tip: Radical and abrupt positive behaviors get the fastest results. For example, stop talking and start listening (the 75/25 rule, or maybe you increase it to the 90/10 rule), ask questions, reflect, validate, and radically change your expectations to ensure success 98 percent of the time. Karen's mother did this in one fell swoop: "Let's drop the class with the F." That was radical and was a significant contributor to Karen's changed behavior.

## Internal Events

In our plain English definition of behavior modification, I said children's behavior is not only learned by what happens outside them but inside them. Let's see how this inside business works. A great but disheartening example is how lying gets established. Remember Aaron in the chapter on beliefs, the child whose lying upset his dad so much? Let's see how that problem was resolved using our new information on stages of change and behavior modification.

First, let's get a little more background about Aaron. Ten-year-old Aaron has attention deficit/hyperactivity disorder; impulsive responses, both verbal and behavioral, are a big problem. His biggest lying problem was about homework. He's had trouble doing homework since the second grade. He's now in fourth grade in his second semester. Aaron didn't fill out his planner all year long and has at least four missing assignments a week. Every night his parents ask about homework, but Aaron seldom brings homework home. "I don't have homework tonight" or "I did it at school" are the chronic responses. You can imagine what the parents are doing—lecturing, imposing consequences that don't work, and labeling his behavior "irresponsible" and "lazy."

From a behavior modification perspective you can see what is happening: The parents' repeated behavior inadvertently ingrains

Aaron's lying. The angrier they get, the more Aaron has to lie. Aaron's internal logic goes like this: *If I lie, maybe I won't get caught and Dad won't get angry.* I know it doesn't make sense—unless you're in the center of your child's hurricane, hearing what makes your child's behavior tick. This is where internal reinforcement—what we say to ourselves—enters the picture.

Our self-talk is what sense we make out of a current situation based on our past experiences. We use our self-talk as a basis for what we believe and how we behave. And it almost always differs from the way other people would describe events that happen to us. I call it "emotional logic," logic heavily affected by our emotions. Just like a parent's repeated behavior reinforces a child's behavior—good or not so good—so it is with our internal self-talk; repeated self-talk reinforces our behavior and beliefs and keeps them going, regardless of whether they're good or not so good. *Doesn't have to make sense to parents or teachers as long as it makes sense to me.*

> Our self-talk is what sense we make out of a current situation based on our past experiences.

## Lying Works?

Regarding his homework, here's another sample of Aaron's self-talk: "I need to lie just to stop them from being so mad. And besides, when I lie, most of the time I don't need to do my homework. I hate homework. It's too hard, and I can never finish it."

How do I know a child like Aaron has self-talk like this? No, I'm not a mind-reader. The majority of children I work with eventually tell me and their parents about these internal thoughts.

Let me give you another tip: When you first hear these thoughts, do not correct them. Remember, start with emotions, not behavior. Correct the thoughts, and you are cementing into place more reason for your child to lie. Let the thoughts go by you and focus your attention on the center of your child, looking out. Validate, validate, validate the emotions causing the lying. With your repeated validation listening, your child will learn that you will listen and understand where he or she is at the moment. Since you are reinforcing your child's feelings (and does your child ever purr when you do that), your child will tell you who he or she is. Keep your attention on your child's feelings, not the lying behavior. A child like Aaron will in time start to tell the truth with repeated valuation from parents. Validation is gold. Your investment will yield significant returns.

Let's go back to Aaron's very real self-talk: "When I lie, most of the time I don't need to do my homework." Remember, it's emotional logic; it's not what *you* see, but it's at the center of Aaron's hurricane. You are in the center, right there with him, so you believe him, for now. Don't you?

> Validation is gold. Your investment will yield significant returns.

Children like Aaron tell me their lies work "most of the time." When pressed, children typically tell me lying works for them 30 to 40 percent of the time. These children will continue to lie because they think each time they lie, it just might be within their "lucky" range.

Here's the behavior modification explanation: Repeated self-talk messages teach the child what to do. Said another way, we learn what the best personal behavior is from our repeated self-talk. Equating lying with "best personal behavior" sounds weird from the outside. Inside the child, it's the best behavior because it produces the desired outcome more often than any other single behavior—in Aaron's case *maybe I will not have to do my homework.* Let's look at Aaron's other self-talk comment: *I need to lie just to stop them from being so mad.* Children tell me lying often reduces the length of their parents' lectures, questions, and the accompanying yelling. When the parents don't know for sure, they often stop nagging; at least that's what most kids say. That works enough of the time for them to continue their lying. Here's how Aaron's lying problem typically starts out about homework. Watch for how his parents' response inadvertently teaches Aaron that lying works. Still sounds weird, doesn't it? But, remember, we're reading from the behavior modification manual.

Upon arriving home from school, Aaron opens the door as quietly as he can; he's been waiting all day to play his new video game.

"Aaron, is that you? Aaron Edward, is that you?"

*She heard me. I know what she's going to—*

"Don't start the game. You know our agreement...."

Trying to match her volume, he says, "I got all my homework done at school."

By now Mom has caught up to him. *Why does Mom have to make me look in her eyes?*

"Are you sure you did your homework?" Her face looks pretty scary close up.

Trying hard to make his voice as strong as possible, Aaron says, "Yeah, I'm sure."

The silent three-second wait for Mom's answer seems to take forever. *She always does that when she's mad.* "Okay, I hope you're telling me the truth." Mom turns and goes back to fixing dinner.

*Whew, I don't have to do homework tonight. Yahoo! Now I can play my game.*

After three weeks of more of the same, Mom raises the white flag and passes the baton. The bugle sounds, the big guns are now loaded. Dad is in charge, and the battle shifts to the courtroom. Let's listen in to Dad's prosecutorial approach.

*He always talks in a slow, serious voice when there's trouble.* "I checked your grades and homework completion online, and you're missing 50 percent of your homework in math." *Dad always says everything so perfect.*

Aaron scowls and looks sideways at Dad, trying not let his voice shake. "I handed the work in, but that stupid teacher lost it."

"That's what you always say. If I find out when I talk to your teacher that what you're saying isn't true, you'll get two weeks of no video games instead of one week taken away like I did last time."

*I know I'm really in trouble when Dad starts his checking-with-the-teacher stuff. He means it when he tells me he'll take things away. And his face, it's scary. I wish this would stop....*

"Why can't you just tell me the truth?"

*I'm busting inside. Here it comes. Yelling's going to pop out of me....* "Please don't take my game system away again. I know I handed in all of that work." *Tears are coming; keep them in, keep them in. Now Dad's busting out, oh no.*

"Aaron, if you would only tell the truth, I could help you get all your work done. It's not right to lie. I can't believe you do this with me."

*This is awful. Please, Dad, stop. What am I going to do?*

"You know our family does not tolerate lying. I can't even trust you anymore. Can't you see that in the end getting your work done would make it easier for—"

*Keep the tears in, keep them in. Don't let him see the tears.* "Dad, I'm telling the truth."

This exchange went on for several minutes more, but I think you get the idea. Everyone involved feels horrible. And now Dad grabs the white flag and readily raises it. Aaron is confused; all he knows is that he needs to keep lying, but it hurts so much to see Dad so disappointed in him. Remember Aaron's self-talk: "I can get away with not doing my homework sometimes, and I want my parents to stop getting mad." This was the state of affairs when the family decided to try counseling.

What needs to happen to get out of this mess? You already have the answer, don't you? From a behavior modification point of view, the parents need to stop repeating what they're doing—Mom had used "the look" and Dad had made "the speech" hundreds of times—and they need to start new behaviors that will reinforce Aaron's telling the truth. But what can possibly work?

# Think Out of the Warehouse

The parents need to stop the yelling and lecturing and start validating and valuing. They need to find a completely different way to motivate Aaron to do his homework and tell the truth. Use "out of the warehouse" thinking. Don't even consider out of the box; it will not work. Here are some important ground rules to get you thinking:

> Use "out of the warehouse" thinking. Don't even consider out of the box; it will not work.

- First steps cannot include deprivations such as grounding and no video games; deprivations at this point reinforce "I'm bad." You'll need to discard parenting behaviors that cause "I'm bad" and start behaviors that cause "I'm good."

- Validate, validate, validate. Remember, center and emotion: "I know you hate homework. It's way worse than I thought. I should never have bugged you the way I did. No wonder you lie. I probably would too if I hated something like homework as much as you do." Don't panic: This is reflecting Aaron's center; it's starting where he is. You're setting aside your center, so you should feel uncomfortable; it's a new place. Aaron will appreciate you far more when he knows you are in the middle of his storm with him.

- Use external motivators determined by Aaron.

- Use internal motivators to the max. You'll make a lot of headway in getting Aaron to start thinking (change stage 2).

- Find ways that reinforce telling the truth about homework, from Aaron's point of view. What are his thoughts and feelings? (Are you sitting down and strapped in?) "Aaron, I'll do several things. I'm not going to get mad at you or give you a consequence if you tell me you do have homework and didn't bring it home. If I do get mad, I'll give you a dollar. I'll ask the teachers to reduce all your homework for a while and to allow full credit for homework that's up to one week late. We will have two out of four days of the week where you do no homework but get two hours of video time." You'll find these ideas are outside the warehouse, and when you begin using them, you'll need to repeat, repeat, and repeat some more. (Warning: It will take at least one or two weeks of repeating before you see results. Guarantee is invalid if repeating does not occur.)

Here's a summary of Dad's two-part plan.

### Part 1: Changing Dad's Behaviors and Thinking
During the first three weeks:

a. In the first week, there should be no anger and no consequences when Aaron tells the truth or lies about homework; it's an amnesty period of sorts. If Dad thinks Aaron is lying, Dad could say (without emotion) something like, "I'm not sure about that." No additional talking, though. No consequences means that homework would not need to be done for that night if Aaron says there is homework and did not want to do it.

b. If Dad is sure Aaron is lying, Dad would not meet him at school the next day to get his homework. (Are you starting to wonder which warehouse I'm looking in? This is what Dad did before—check with the teacher to verify what Aaron told him. You need to stop everything you were doing before. Everything! Remember, we are talking about the next several weeks, not the next ten years. If you repeat it, the lying will continue. Remember, repeated parent behavior means repeated kid behavior.) Instead, Dad will acknowledge the lying based on Aaron's self-talk: "I guess it's still too hard to tell the truth. I think something else happened other than what you said, and I hope you eventually feel safe enough to tell me the truth." (Remember, this is just for one week or so to see how much progress can be made.)

c. Dad determined to follow the rule he had written on a 4 x 5 card and placed on his bathroom mirror: "Stop all past behavior; start all new, mostly radical, behavior, and repeat, repeat, and repeat."

d. Dad would listen carefully to Aaron's barriers and motivators. He remembered the five stages of change directions about moving from stage 1 to stage 2: Do what's necessary to get Aaron to think. He'd push the mute button on his own stuff and plug in to the center of Aaron: Listen then validate; listen then validate; listen then validate.

> Stop all past behavior; start all new, mostly radical, behavior, and repeat, repeat, and repeat.

e. By the end of the first week, Dad needs to craft a motivator plan, with a lot of input from Aaron, that starts where Aaron is and ensures 98 percent success while taking into account the concept of thinking out of the warehouse.

## Part 2: The Plan—Mutually Determined with Most of the Ideas Coming from Aaron

After thoroughly validating Aaron's hatred for homework, Dad agreed with his son that homework was awful a lot of the time. (He skipped the "necessary part" that he always used to say.) This is the beginning of the "setting overall parameters" part, with adequate buy-in from Aaron, of course. (If you are interested in the specifics, refer back to what Joan did in the first part of her problem solving with Karen in chapter 5.)

Here were the mutually agreed upon outcomes:

a. Aaron would work toward maintaining a C average, with no more than one D, with specific dates for the C average to come later. (Before the plan, the requirement was no grade under a B.) At the start of the plan, he had two Cs, one D, and one F. He agreed to go to an after-school study hall program. No more homework at home. (Dad checked the program out, and the teacher assured him all homework would be adequately monitored to ensure completion.) Improving the grades was not the task at hand; telling the truth and facing homework was the essential first task. Improving grades would come later.

b. Every Monday night both Dad and Aaron would monitor the missing homework on the school website that identified missing homework. The rule for Dad: When reviewing the website for missing homework, look; don't speak unless validating; always find something to validate. The purpose for looking was to validate something positive and to see where the plan wasn't working so that modifications could be made right away, but away from Aaron. By looking at the school performance together, both Dad and Aaron were seeing the truth in black and white with no negatives.

Dad and Aaron chose an external motivator. Aaron was a very good baseball player and loved baseball cards. He really wanted a twenty-dollar card set. Dad determined the goal for each week, a stretch but doable. For six weeks before the plan, Aaron was averaging six missing homework assignments weekly. This was the starting point, and a goal needed to be set that was a stretch but doable and was going to be 98 percent successful. So, for the first week, the mutually agreed upon goal was no more than four missing assignments; the second week, three; and the fourth week, two. The pack had twenty-four cards in it, and Dad divided it into four groups of six cards. Aaron could receive six cards every time he met his goal for the week. Aaron was thrilled! The pack was placed on the kitchen table for extra motivation.

I've been involved in hundreds of plans similar to this one, and they all work to almost eliminate lying. I say "almost" because once lying gets ingrained with its barriers and motivators, it takes weeks to eliminate. You will see gradual, noticeable improvement over a three-to-four-week period. Relapse will be frequent during the first six weeks and will occur less frequently over a period of two to three months. That's the bad news. The good news is this: A relapse simply means there are more barriers than motivators; lying behavior has some heavy-duty barriers for telling the truth and minimal motivators. Aggressively deal with eliminating these barriers and increasing the motivators. Expect lying to be history if you can be vigilant about repeating parental behaviors that reinforce and motivate your child to tell the truth and eliminate barriers. Chronic lying takes longer to eliminate, but eventually you will see progress.

Let's summarize this section.

Behavior modification theory explains the nitty-gritty about how behavior is established, how it becomes ingrained. You establish your child's behavior by repeating your behavior, whether good or not so good.

Your job as a parent is to identify your repeating behaviors that teach your child to behave in a negative way. I hope this doesn't sound as weird as it did when we first started this discussion. Your behavior modification plan maximizes motivators and minimizes barriers. You and your child join hands at the eye of the hurricane and walk through the storm together until the weather clears. More times than not a rainbow appears, and you will be assured that all your hard work was worthwhile.

> Your job as a parent is to identify your repeating behaviors that teach your child to behave in a negative way.

We've got one more trick that really works to make change work well.

## Emotions + Logic = Change

Emotions and logic are the two essential human ingredients contained in a successful recipe for changing your child's behavior. Finding the right amount of each and mixing them together in a way that works for your child will bring the best results. Remember, when you are validating your child, he or she is purring. Being perfect is not a requirement for living. We've learned that too much talking doesn't work—that's the logic or reasoning part of the mix. Doesn't taste good to your child. Let's dig in to the best mix of emotion and logic.

Any amount of lecturing with no attention to the child's emotions at the beginning of a problem means that a parent is using logic, thinking, or reasoning as the only way to help the child change. It doesn't work (as you already know). Here's a central take-home tip on the mixture issue: Add your reasoning to your child's emotions, not the other way around. I'll show you how to do that in this section, so put on your parental-love chef's hat, and let's go to work.

Remember Joan and Karen and the big problem Karen had with school performance? Before Joan learned the parental-love approach, she did the same thing every parent reports to me before his or her first counseling session: She used logic with hardly any attention to her child's emotions. Joan learned that her logic mixed with Karen's emotions about as well as oil mixes with water. Here's the logic and reasoning approach Joan used when she found Karen's report card stuffed under her bed. Remember, Karen had three Fs, and Joan was plenty frustrated.

"Karen, where is your midterm report card?"

Karen felt like putting headphones over her ears, and she could hardly bear to look into her mom's glaring eyes. It was all she could do to answer. "Uh, I don't know...."

Waving the crumpled report card just inches from Karen's face, Mom's voice went up a few decibels. "This is 'I don't know'?"

It seemed like hours before Karen could get anything out. Finally, she forced out a whimper. "I can never do anything right for you." *Where are my headphones?*

"All you have to do is ask for help. I've said that to you so many times. Don't you know that...."

Let's not listen in any longer. I can assure you, Joan tried to reason with Karen for several more minutes—reason after reason with none of Karen's emotions considered. Seems obvious reading this, but in the heat of battle our default mechanism for trying to change our child's behavior is to use only reasoning. Does this sound familiar? Every parent who seeks counseling from me reports this type of approach.

Why is this reasoning approach doomed from the get-go? Here's what happens during a conflict. The higher the intensity of emotion, the lower the thinking ability available to solve the problem. Reasoning simply doesn't work when emotions are elevated.

Here's an analogy I use in my practice to help parents understand why reasoning alone is useless during the first highly emotional stages of problem solving.

> The higher the intensity of emotion, the lower the thinking ability available to solve the problem. Reasoning simply doesn't work when emotions are elevated.

Imagine a bucket that's full of water. (See figure 7.1.) The water represents a person's potential thinking capacity. In a conflict, emotion, represented by sand, and thinking share the same bucket. As conflict escalates, "emotion" sand pours in and pushes the "thinking" water out; emotions become more dominant, and thinking ability decreases. (See figure 7.2.) When the emotion decreases, the emotion sand empties from the bucket, leaving room for the thinking water to fill the thinking bucket again. (See figure 7.2.)

## Thinking/Emotion Bucket

FIGURE 7.1

Applied to parenting, as your child's emotion increases, his or her thinking ability decreases. That's why you simply cannot start with reasoning when there's a lot of emotion; you must temporarily set aside your emotions and thinking and start with your child's emotions—where the child is. Only after the emotion has decreased significantly can you start to mix in reasoning with your child's emotions—but always season with parental-love dialogue requirements.

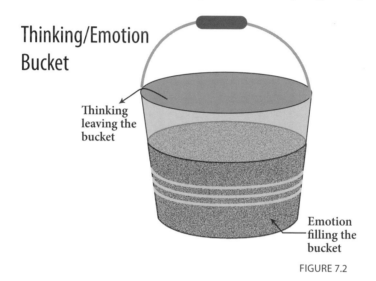

## Thinking/Emotion Bucket

Thinking leaving the bucket

Emotion filling the bucket

FIGURE 7.2

## The Frustration Tolerance Scale

At the beginning of this section I mentioned that we need to measure emotions and thinking, making sure we have the right amount of each. I've developed the Frustration Tolerance Scale (FTS) as a tool to measure and communicate these emotional levels. (See figure 7.3.) The critical measurement is at level 5. That's when there is as much thinking as emotion in the thinking-emotion bucket. When 5.5 is reached, parents need to stop reasoning and immediately do one of two things: Encourage the child to vent his or her emotions, which often results in less emotional pressure, or take a break and come back later when the emotional level is lower.

## Frustration Tolerance Scale

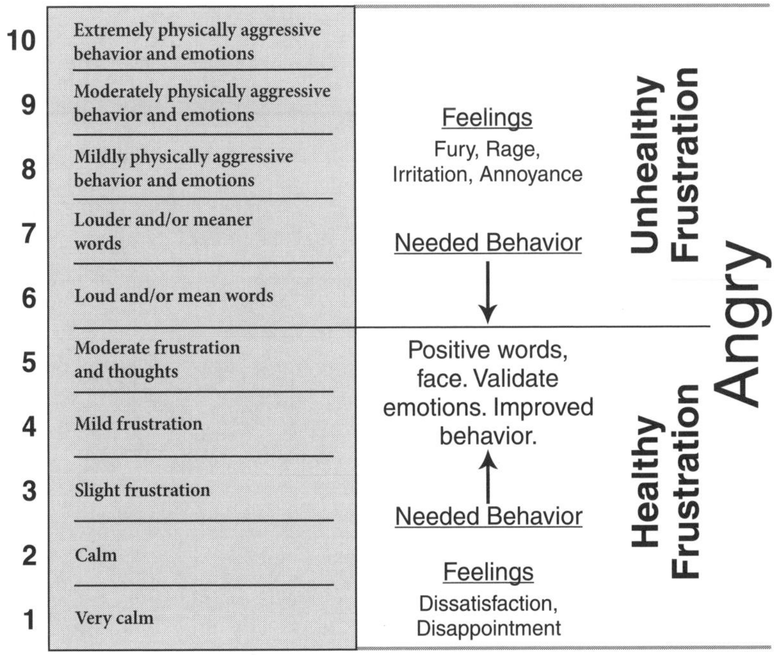

| | | |
|---|---|---|
| **10** | Extremely physically aggressive behavior and emotions | |
| **9** | Moderately physically aggressive behavior and emotions | |
| **8** | Mildly physically aggressive behavior and emotions | |
| **7** | Louder and/or meaner words | |
| **6** | Loud and/or mean words | |
| **5** | Moderate frustration and thoughts | |
| **4** | Mild frustration | |
| **3** | Slight frustration | |
| **2** | Calm | |
| **1** | Very calm | |

Feelings
Fury, Rage,
Irritation, Annoyance

Needed Behavior
↓

Positive words,
face. Validate
emotions. Improved
behavior.
↑
Needed Behavior

Feelings
Dissatisfaction,
Disappointment

Unhealthy Frustration

Healthy Frustration

Angry

FIGURE 7.3

Let's go back to the report-card exchange we just witnessed between Joan and Karen. Hiding a report card is common when grades deteriorate and parents are not adequately supportive. Here's how another parent, Liz, handled a similar situation with her twelve-year-old daughter, Madison.

"Hi, Madison. How was your day?"

*Mom used to be so cheery, but she's seemed really down these last few weeks. I wonder what's going on.* "Okay."

"I have something I need to go over with you."

*Uh-oh. I know trouble's brewing when Mom tilts her head and puts her hand on my shoulder. Shield up; try to act calm.* "What's the problem now?"

"School has been getting tougher, hasn't it?" *Over the first hurdle, started with emotions first, not my lecture, this is a piece of...*

*Oh no, the stay-calm button isn't working.* "Mom, not again. I'm doing fine. Leave me alone."

*Quick, frustration tolerance. She's at a 5.5. What am I supposed to do? Give her a piece of my mind? No, validate.* "I know in the past I've not understood at all how hard school is for you and—"

*I don't care. She deserves the popping-out stuff.* "You don't understand me, and you never will." *I can hardly keep from running to my room, but I've got to stay.*

*Quick! Where am I? The 5.3 alarm is ringing. Should I leave or stay? Stay, and validate...brief comments...make it my fault.* "You're right. I haven't understood you at all. I have to do a lot better." *I don't know if I can keep this up.*

*What's happening? I'm crying, and I can't stop.* "Mom, I've got three Fs." *I can't even talk; everything is coming out.* "I know you're going to ground me for a month like you always do." *There she goes, touching my arm. Don't pull away. I don't know what to do.... Why did I pull away?*

*Madison's at a 6.5. I'm supposed to stop; I was at a 6 when she pulled away, but I'm sad for her hurt; wow, my level dropped to a 5; I'll keep trying. Think radical.* "No, there will be no grounding. I'm going to try to do something that works better for you." Liz caught Madison's wide-eyed glance. *I can't believe I just said that. Maybe it's a big mistake.*

*What's Mom doing? She never talks like this. Keep the shield up.* "I'll bet you won't."

*Hey, she's at a 5.5. It's working. I'm on a roll. Okay, think validation.* "You and I will find a way to help you improve your grades other than grounding. Grounding will not be used anymore. Let's you and I go down to the Dairy Queen and get your favorite Blizzard."

*Now I'm totally confused. But the Blizzard idea is great.* "Okay. Let's go. Can I have the double Snickers bar with whipped cream?"

"Why not? You can have the cherry on top if you want."

Liz should be writing this book. That's parental love at its best. Liz used the FTS measurement tool well and mixed in reasoning just right. I can see the frown on your face; who would ever remember all these numbers during a heated exchange, let alone use numbers to calm down? That's what all parents feel when first introduced to the FTS. With disciplined awareness and at least three weeks of practice, using the FTS becomes easier and easier. The noticeable reduction in your and your child's anger will be a big motivation for continuing to use the FTS.

How did you like Liz's gutsy statement about no more grounding for bad grades? That grounding rule was useless anyway. And the shock value of her statement on a scale of 1 to 10 was a 12. A huge barrier in Liz's and Madison's relationship was Madison's feelings of "You don't understand me, and you never will." But Liz's words and actions in the scenario above began to weld a new belief into place: *Maybe Mom does understand me. And to go for ice cream and allow a double Snickers? Wow!* In the past Liz had tried to control Madison's food choices in an effort to manage her daughter's weight and would never have given her permission for such a treat. But now her focus has switched to demolishing barriers and building motivators in the relationship. (And my prediction is that when the relationship is healthy, overeating won't be such a problem for Madison.) She used behavior modification: She stopped the old, worn-out grounding and started refreshing behaviors that were motivators for Madison.

In summary, trying to change your child's behavior by reasoning is useless if emotions are too high. Reasoning is useful and necessary when you mix your reasoning with your child's emotions, but only if the emotion is low enough—level 5 or lower on the FTS.

Now you know about behavior modification and how to apply that knowledge to your child. Start where your child is by progressing through the stages of change at your child's pace; always play motivation high and barriers low; and reserve your reasoning for just the right time and the right place. Do this, and you'll begin to see the best possible changes in your child—from the inside out.

There's one more very important consideration for change to work well: harnessing the power of anger and fear, the subject of our next chapter.

CHAPTER 8

# Good Anger? Good Fear? Good Grief!

TOO MUCH TABASCO SAUCE burns the tongue, the stomach, and everything in between; but just the right amount and the food tastes extra good. The right amount, though, is different for each person. So it is with anger; too much results in your child feeling "I'm bad." Just the right amount mixed in with parental love and your child will feel valued, respected, and "I'm good," even when you are disappointed and dissatisfied with your child.

Everyone experiences anger; it's normal, natural, and potentially a great motivator and energy source for change. It's the way anger is managed that needs special attention. Expressing anger in the healthiest way possible is essential as your child's behavior is changing from unacceptable to acceptable.

> Expressing anger in the healthiest way possible is essential as your child's behavior is changing from unacceptable to acceptable.

## Anger Can Be a Problem

Anger is an intense emotional signal to yourself or to someone else that you are upset about something important that is happening or has happened. The purpose of anger is to stop what is making

131

you upset. Anger can stay inside or be expressed outside; either way, it can be a problem. Expressing intense anger through yelling and mean facial expressions and words is a problem. This type of anger needs to be kept inside until you have a chance to work it through—maybe discussing it with a friend, exercising, or journaling.

Keeping intense anger inside without working it through is also a problem. Usually, when we harbor anger toward ourselves, our self-talk turns into something like this: "How could you be so stupid? That was the dumbest thing you ever did!" Unresolved anger toward others will likewise result in a negative internal dialogue: "She's always undermining me! That makes me so mad! If she really cared about me, she'd quit doing that. Hey, maybe I'm not worth caring about." Not working these feelings out will eventually harm your relationship with this person.

As a parent, an anger signal means you are upset about your child's unacceptable behavior. Showing anger toward your child is designed to stop the unacceptable behavior. Throughout this book you've read about parents' healthy and unhealthy anger in response to their children who lie, don't do homework, or fight with their siblings. We saw in chapter 3 how Carl handled his anger (before learning the parental-love approach) by spanking and yelling at Aaron, but later he learned how to express his anger in a healthy way: He stopped interacting with Aaron until his anger was reduced enough that he could validate Aaron's emotions.

## The Benefits of Healthy Anger

There are three significant benefits to expressing your anger in a healthy way. First, appropriately expressed anger can result in your child's stopping his or her unacceptable behavior in the best way possible. Second—and probably the biggest benefit of all—your child maintains a fundamental experience of "I'm good"—most of the time—throughout the change from unacceptable behavior to acceptable behavior. Third, your child learns and takes in from you the healthiest way to deal with anger. After all, you want your child to be recording the best video clips possible on how to handle and express anger well.

Consider Liz and Madison in the last chapter. When Liz said, "School has been getting tougher, hasn't it?" Madison responded, "Mom, not again. I'm doing fine. Leave me alone." Mom headed off both her own and Madison's escalating frustration and stopped it at level 4 on the FTS by saying, "I know in the past I've not understood at all how hard school is for you."

The anger signal was there, but Liz regulated it well. At the same time Madison was going to school on how anger is supposed to be expressed. Once stored in her "How to Be Angry" video library, this video, along with many others, will be a great resource for future reference when she becomes angry at herself or someone else. We know what the scene would have been like if Liz had yelled or lectured. No one would have felt good.

What did Madison learn from Mom's response? She learned that when there is a conflict, at least three things can happen: (1) You can stay calm; (2) you can be caring to yourself and the other person; and (3) it's possible to feel valued and acknowledged even when you are faced with unacceptable behavior. Now that's an Oscar-winning video!

If Mom would have allowed her anger to go too high, which all of us do more times than we'd like, Madison would have learned the opposite: When I do something wrong, people will yell and say mean things; I'll be scared; I'll feel "I'm bad"; and I'll need to defend my point by either attacking or withdrawing. Too many of these feelings and thoughts diminish self-confidence and cause what I call excessive shameful guilt.

## Guilt 101

Guilt. Let's delve into it for a little bit. Guilt is our internal judge and jury system for determining whether we are right or wrong and what the punishment should be. If a parent's anger is too strong when a child makes a mistake, the child will learn to be extra-mean and harsh to himself—and to others, for that matter— when he does something wrong. His self-talk will go something like this: "I'm so terrible for doing that. I don't know how anybody could ever love me. I'm worthless." This is shameful guilt. If, however, parents use just the right anger, the child's internalized judge-and-jury system will give a respectful, caring verdict, some-thing along these lines: "I really hate disappointing Mom. I messed up here, but it's not the end of the world. I can tell she still loves me even though I did something wrong. Next time I'll do better." This type of judge-and-jury system is so important that I've dedicated the next chapter to guilt.

> If a parent's anger is too strong when a child makes a mistake, the child will learn to be extra-mean and harsh to himself—and to others, for that matter—when he does something wrong.

This is sounding like pretty heavy stuff, isn't it? I wish there were an easy way around anger, but there isn't. The best we can do is un-derstand it fully and learn how to manage it in the best way possible. Let's continue.

## Anger 101

Let's do just a little classroom work on understanding the nuts and bolts of anger. (I'll set the timer; no more than five minutes!) When you read the chapter title, did you wonder what fear had to do with anger? Fear is actually the root cause of anger. And getting angry is one way we attempt to stop the fear.

Sometimes these fears can be intense, as when we narrowly miss hitting a pedestrian who appears seemingly from nowhere and cross-es the road in front of us. Sometimes these fears can be almost unno-ticeable, appearing in the form of an uncomfortable feeling, as when in a restaurant our food is delivered to our table cold. Occasionally, the fear we feel seems irrational on the surface. Remember Carl in chapter 3: "What if he grows up to be a liar?"; "I'm really afraid"; and "Lying is a big deal to me." Seems at first to be a little exaggerated, but not when we understand Carl's childhood experiences with lying.

The stronger the underlying fear, the stronger the expression of anger. Typically the two are proportionate to each other. In the examples above, the person steps out in front of you, fear skyrockets, and you swerve to avoid hitting him or her. Now it's your anger's turn to blast off. You start to feel angry about how careless the person was, and you might even be tempted to turn around and go back to give the individual a good verbal thrashing. That's a lot of fear, and it results in a lot of unhealthy anger. When your first bite of pasta primavera isn't piping hot, however, most likely you'll simply call your server over and ask him or her to take your plate back to the kitchen. You probably won't feel the need to lecture the server on the meaning of quality and customer service. That's a small amount of fear causing just a little bit of anger. How could there be fear in this situation? On the surface this seems to be annoyance, plain and simple. It is mild annoyance, but unconsciously mild fear triggers the annoyance: "I'm fearful I will not have warm pasta; I need warm pasta." I know this all sounds petty, but that's what goes on unconsciously within us.

> The stronger the underlying fear, the stronger the expression of anger.

As we are seeing, anger is a natural reflex of both the mind and body to control or stop a threat or fear. Our thoughts race with possible responses, our cheeks may flush, our hearts beat faster, and we can feel the adrenaline rush. Of course, the higher the threat, the more fear—and the more possibility of expressing it in unhealthy ways. Also, our immediate and unconscious response to threat and fear is helplessness. That's really uncomfortable, and this feeling fuels our desire to stop the threat through anger. No wonder Carl did so many angry things; he was feeling helpless and fearful. For him there was a real threat that his son would become a chronic liar; he felt that nothing could be done about it; and he knew from his past how dangerous lying was.

Simply put, we feel uncomfortable (threat and fear) when what we want is in danger of not happening. Anger is our natural reaction, designed to stop whatever is causing us to feel uncomfortable. The higher the threat and accompanying fear, the more helpless we feel, and the more likely we are to express unhealthy anger.

As I mentioned before, anger can be a signal of an internal threat, when we feel we are losing control of something important like an essential belief. The lying behavior from Carl's son threatened Carl's internal belief about lying: *Lying can never happen, or else.* Carl needed to stop the lying immediately. Unhealthy frustration was the result.

> The higher the threat and accompanying fear, the more helpless we feel, and the more likely we are to express unhealthy anger.

Carl allowed his natural instincts to flow, angrily defending and attacking—the two most common signs of anger whether expressed outwardly or kept inside. (Some people withdraw and bury their threat, but most attack and defend.) This defending and attacking can be physical, but in Carl's case the response was verbal. The hurt Aaron felt from Carl's attacks, however, was as painful as a physical attack. A child receives these attacks as hurt, sadness, and the parent feeling disgusted with the child. These emotions plus the others we've mentioned are heavy-duty: hurt, sadness, disgust, anger, and fear.

Remember, everything you teach becomes part of your child. If attacks become a pattern, your child gets hurt a lot, and the hurt remains a video clip at the child's core.

A cautionary note: Please be gentle on yourself. We all have been caught in the unhealthy frustration range. If you find yourself there only occasionally, it's not a problem. If it's a pattern, read on; you'll find out how to reduce this natural but unhealthy tendency. You do not want unhealthy frustration to be a regular occurrence because of the hurt it will cause your child.

At the deepest part of your child's being, he or she is always seeking your confirmation of his or her worth. Every time you find a way to correct your child through validation of emotions first and then deal with the behavior in a supportive but firm manner, your child grows stronger and self-confidence flourishes.

Anger sure is a complicated emotion. And here's a tricky twist: Untamed, unhealthy frustration often stops your child's unacceptable behavior, but the cost is enormous. This route to change behavior is a hurtful path, for the Tabasco sauce may start to burn the stomach's lining.

Let's summarize the benefits of healthy anger. Tamed anger, or healthy frustration, is just the right amount of spice. Your child handles your disappointment by changing unacceptable behavior and at the same time feeling valued and respected. Your child learns that when an unacceptable behavior occurs, it's possible to deal with the mistake by changing the behavior and at the same time feeling "I'm good."

> At the deepest part of your child's being, he or she is always seeking your confirmation of his or her worth.

Before we leave our classroom work and get into some real-world examples, we need to look briefly at one more aspect of anger: the thinking component, which psychologists call "cognition." I'd like to give you a brief summary of what sense I have made out of the research on this complicated subject after many years of seeing it firsthand in my own life as well as those of my clients.

Using our thinking tools to the max is essential to cope effectively with the fear causing the anger. We have three essential thinking tools at our disposal to cope effectively with anger: an emotion regulator, an emotion and thinking separator, and a monitor for accurately observing what part you play in a conflict and what part the other person plays. I've simplified these three thinking tool descriptions to three "or" words: "regulator," "separator," and "monitor." (They're easier to remember this way. Technically, these tools are called "executive functions." There are more of them, but I find these three to be the most central for dealing with anger. If you want to learn more about executive functions, there's plenty of information available online and in books.[1])

We are born with the potential for developing these thinking tools to sophisticated levels; they naturally develop from birth into adulthood and are fully developed by age twenty-two. The degree of growth is determined by our temperament traits, heredity, and how well our parents train us to use these tools. (You'll learn more about how to train your child to use these tools throughout this chapter. It's never too late to increase your child's—or even your own—skills in using these tools.)

That's it for the classroom work. Now let's apply this information to you and your child. The next section will help you acquire two essential abilities: (1) manage your anger in the best way possible so that it does not escalate into the unhealthy frustration zone, and (2) teach your child how to do the same. The most important tool for learning to stay within the healthy frustration zone is the FTS. We've looked at it before, but let's get some in-depth training on how to use this tool.

## The Frustration Tolerance Scale (FTS)

As we all know, anger can be expressed in healthy or unhealthy ways. The FTS (figure 8.1) explains these two anger (frustration) levels. Healthy frustration—just the right amount—is when we feel dissatisfied, disappointed. Here's what it looks and sounds like:

With a slightly firm but normal tone of voice and an "I'm serious" look on her face, Mom says, "Josh, I'm frustrated that you don't do the dishes right away when I ask you. Next time I ask, I'll count to three and then turn the TV off." That's a level 4.5. Anything from 5 and below is within the healthy frustration zone.

## Frustration Tolerance Scale

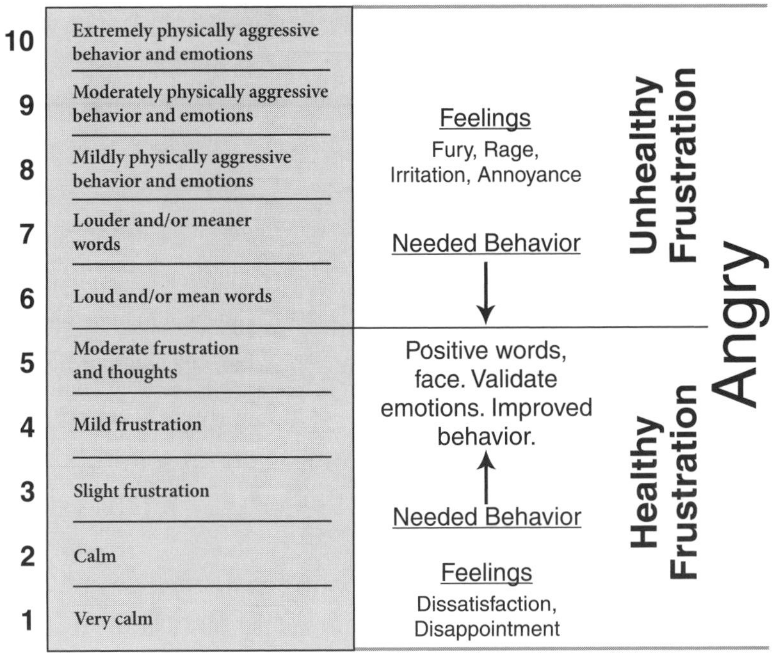

| | | | |
|---|---|---|---|
| 10 | Extremely physically aggressive behavior and emotions | | |
| 9 | Moderately physically aggressive behavior and emotions | **Feelings** | **Unhealthy Frustration** |
| 8 | Mildly physically aggressive behavior and emotions | Fury, Rage, Irritation, Annoyance | |
| 7 | Louder and/or meaner words | Needed Behavior | |
| 6 | Loud and/or mean words | ↓ | |
| 5 | Moderate frustration and thoughts | Positive words, face. Validate emotions. Improved behavior. | |
| 4 | Mild frustration | | **Healthy Frustration** |
| 3 | Slight frustration | ↑ Needed Behavior | |
| 2 | Calm | Feelings | |
| 1 | Very calm | Dissatisfaction, Disappointment | |

**Angry**

FIGURE 8.1

Showing these signs of frustration (tone of voice, facial expression, words used) to your children is essential for healthy change to occur in them. A parent's expression of healthy frustration generates a certain amount of low-level fear within a child, which creates an energy source, a motivation for the child to grow and become a better person. Thus, when we express healthy frustration, our children feel valued and "I'm good" as they are guided through changing their behavior.

Unhealthy frustration is another story, however, and occurs when we feel moderate to severe anger—from annoyance, irritation, and disgust all the way up to fury and rage. Unhealthy frustration generates an unhealthy level of fear within your child, that is, feelings of "I'm bad."

Before Carl and Joan learned the parental-love approach, they got into this unhealthy frustration zone—yelling, spanking, lecturing, labeling—and as a result their children became fearful and responded negatively rather than positively to them.

Here's an illustration of the various FTS levels that certainly would test anyone's capacity to stay in the healthy frustration level, but the scenario isn't uncommon.

For more than two months, seventeen-year-old Sophia has consistently broken her midnight curfew; she often comes in thirty to sixty minutes late. Dad has tried everything—grounding, lecturing, taking the car away. Nothing works, and Dad has found his anger escalating from irritation (levels 5 and below) to fury (levels 7 and 8).

> A parent's expression of healthy frustration generates a certain amount of low-level fear within a child, which creates an energy source, a motivation for the child to grow and become a better person.

Last Saturday, Dad got into a shouting match with Sophia, saying, "You're the most irresponsible person I know, and I'm sick to death of you and your disrespect for me and the rules of this house!" (level 6 to 7). Sophia was pretty angry herself and called her dad a stupid b——. Dad lost it and slapped Sophia (level 8 and above).

Now that you're a little more familiar with the levels and terminology of the FTS, I need to make one note of exception to the FTS. Some people are adept at showing their anger by making embarrassing or demeaning comments in a quiet voice, with no visible signs of frustration on their face or in other body language, seemingly below a level 5. This sarcastic and cruel expression of anger—often portrayed on TV as "funny"—has absolutely no place in a parent's behavior toward a child. These mixed signals—body language that says everything's fine and words that cut and belittle—are devastating to a child's self-confidence and ability to trust.

All of us have experienced the various levels on the FTS. Maybe you haven't crossed into the physical levels, but you've probably flirted with them. It's our natural orientation to allow our frustration to go too high, but we must remember that when we express unhealthy frustration, our children feel disrespected, devalued, and humiliated. The words I hear children use the most are "hurt" and "sad." The good news is that we can develop skills to keep our frustration within healthy limits.

## Handling Anger Like an Adult

Now that we have a good idea about how to use the FTS to measure our frustration, we need to learn how to handle frustration. That's where the thinking tools come in: the regulator for adjusting your emotional levels, the separator for extracting your emotions from your thinking so you can think straight, and the monitor for accurately observing what you are doing and feeling and what your child is doing and feeling. Parental love works at the highest level when these skills are well developed.

> When we express unhealthy frustration, our children feel disrespected, devalued, and humiliated.

Very few parents use their regulators, separators, and monitors to the fullest extent, but when they do, they are usually quite pleased with the results. Most parents experience noticeable success with these tools after only three or four weeks of practice. To achieve this, you'll need to follow four guidelines carefully regarding awareness, planning, and monitoring during this three-to-four-week period.

1. Before the next conflict occurs, study the FTS and become aware of what your behavior is like when your anger goes above level 5: voice level, facial expression, and words and phrases you typically use. Write down these descriptions. Then identify the percentage of time in a given week that you reach a 5+ when you're frustrated with your child.

2. When frustration occurs in the next conflict, monitor when your frustration level is moving close to the 5+ zone: loud voice, mean

words and facial expression. When you are close to this 5+ level, stop what you are doing. If you can continue the dialogue at a level below 5, shift to validating your child's emotions and asking questions. If you can't get below a level 5, follow step 3.

3. When frustration is above 5, immediately stop the interaction and leave your child.

4. After you've left your child and the frustration is reduced to level 4 or below, plan a different approach to the conflict, using as many parental-love requirements as possible. If you can't go back and deal with the problem in a different way, wait until later when you are prepared with a different approach that will be presented below a level 5. (In the next several paragraphs you'll witness how this is done.)

Remember, look for noticeable improvement, not perfection. Expect a steep learning curve at first. Especially during the first week, you'll fail more than you'll succeed, but keep trying. Remember the big bonus: As you get good at this, you are automatically teaching your child the same skills. And the mother lode of all bonuses: Your child will be feeling "I'm good" even when the two of you are experiencing conflict.

Let's get into the trenches and see how these skills are developed in real life. Seven-year-old Ethan is experiencing anger problems. Here's how his mom, Kendra, described their problems to me.

### Kendra and Ethan

"Ethan throws at least a ten-minute temper tantrum every time his dad and I say no, and this might happen three or four times a day. Like today, we were at the store, and he said nicely, 'Mommy, I want this Lego set.' I knew what was next. I gently said no, and he started yelling and then collapsed on the floor, flailing his arms and kicking. And, of course, everyone was looking. I felt like I was on stage with the Department of Social Services reps watching my every move. I don't want to go into the rest of it, but it was ugly.

"That night, another tantrum happened when I asked him nicely to turn off his video game to go to bed. Of course, I was dead tired by then and, frankly, sick and tired of his disobedience. I know I respond in the same way every time. I try not to, but I always do. I go from stern talking to bargaining to begging to threatening—and then yelling. Finally, I just pick him up and dump him into bed, turn out the light and slam the door shut—both of us still screaming at each other—and he cries himself to sleep. I feel awful, and pretty soon I'm crying too. I can't take it anymore. What should we do?"

"Wow, Kendra," I said. "I tense up just hearing the story. I don't see how you can keep going. I don't blame you for feeling hopeless. Who—"

"It *is* hopeless. I've tried everything I know."

"Let's both take a deep breath and start by identifying your level of frustration. On the Frustration Tolerance Scale over there on the wall, what do you think your level is during the bedtime problem?"

Carefully reviewing the different behaviors listed on the FTS, she finally said, "Most of the time it's at a 7, but I'm always fearful I'll get into the 8 and above range. That's bad, isn't it?"

"It's the level anyone would get to without effective ways to handle Ethan's temper tantrums. What's great is that you're now doing something about it."

"Yeah, but I really don't feel that great, and I won't until I can fix it."

"Here's what we're going to do. When you sense that you're at level 5.5, leave Ethan. I know, this sounds like giving in. It is, on the surface, but from the parental-love approach it's not. Unhealthy frustration must be avoided as much as possible. Don't come back until you can stay below a 5 on the scale. The sooner you stop, when you get to that level, the better you'll be able to solve Ethan's anger problem. By leaving, you switch on your regulator, and frustration is turned down from a 5.5 to maybe a 4."

"I've done that a couple of times. It doesn't work. He yells and screams louder and follows me wherever I go. Have you ever known a kid like Ethan to act like this?"

"Many. What percent of the time have you left right away when you start to go above a 5?"

"None. Yeah, I guess none. I always have to say something to him, like 'Don't act like that to me,' 'When will you ever learn?' and a couple of other bad phrases I seem to use all the time. That's when I leave, after trying to convince him to stop. I leave, and he follows me."

"Consider this. If you would stop right away and leave the minute you are at a 5, the length of Ethan's anger episodes will likely gradually decrease by the end of a week, especially with a seven-year-old. Would you feel successful if this happened?"

"How would I know? It's never happened! I guess it could…but what do I do about him following me?"

"Leave him right away and don't talk as he follows you. He's trying to keep you engaged. This may sound weird, but staying with him when you are above a 5 and yelling answers back to his questions—that actually reinforces his anger, keeps his anger engine revved up. Remember what we said about behavior modification. If Ethan keeps up his behavior, it means you're doing something to keep it going. Stopping what you're doing will eventually reduce his behavior."

"That does make sense. I never thought about my behavior causing him to be angry in the way you just said it. Reinforcing—that's just the opposite of what I want. Now I'm really feeling stupid." Tears drop down onto her blouse before she can find the Kleenex box. "I'm sorry. I promised myself I wouldn't cry."

You've probably felt the same thing Kendra did. Acknowledging the part you play in your child's problems often feels unbearable. I wish there were a way to skip this task, but it's essential to face our part before we move on to solving the problem.

"This is the hardest part," I said to Kendra. "But I promise you, you are going to get answers that really work, and we'll stick with this until you have it fixed. Now, back to Ethan. He *will* follow you, but don't talk to him. Lock yourself in the bedroom or bathroom if you need to. As long as Ethan is not destructive, stay there until he is below a level 5."

"I think I can do that." Kendra's tears stopped, and I could see she was feeling a little less helpless. "But what do I do with him when he's calmed down?"

"First of all, I want to point out several things. This next week you will be able to use your monitoring ability to identify when both Ethan's and your frustration levels reach 5. Don't expect perfection. You might identify these levels after a problem or sometimes during a problem. Expect to use your regulator sometimes; that's when you'll stop—when your frustration level is above 5—and walk away. When you do this, the separator is ready for action—separating the emotions enough from the thinking so the thinking can take charge. Remember the emotions-thinking bucket? When there's less emotion, more thinking is available. By doing all of this, you are automatically teaching Ethan the basics; he's got his video camera running. Best of all, Ethan is experiencing what it's like to reduce his 5 to at least a 4, eventually, and thinking, *Mom still loves me even though she's angry with me*—and that's a good thing. With multiple video clips like this, pretty soon he'll be able to noticeably regulate his frustration in other situations."

> Acknowledging the part you play in your child's problems often feels unbearable...but it's essential.

"Sounds like you're making this really complicated, but as I think about it, I can see what you're saying. Monitoring myself better is really important so I can regulate my emotions more effectively. I know I need to do that better."

"Great. I know it sounds kind of technical, but it works. Does it all make sense to you?"

"I like the idea that the separator skill almost happens automatically when I regulate and reduce my emotions. I think I've got it. Now, what do I do with Ethan now that we're both at a 4 on your scale?"

"You do have it down. One thing to keep in mind. This new skill takes about three weeks to become almost automatic. At first you will find yourself going above a 5; that's just habit. Just remember to turn on the monitor; watch yourself and Ethan, and start to regulate and separate.

"Now, to answer your question about what to do with Ethan, let's not deal with him just yet. This week, just practice your monitoring, regulating, and separating emotions from thinking. The big steps to concentrate on are stopping what you're doing and leaving the situation so that both you and Ethan get below a 5."

"I'm kind of disappointed that we can't solve the whole enchilada, but one thing at a time, right?"

### Bedtime Blues

At the next session, Kendra smiled as she walked into the room, and before she sat down she said, "I'm really getting good at keeping my frustration below a 5."

"That's great! Is that what's got you so happy, or is there more?"

"I guess I'm feeling pretty good about myself. I have not once gone above a 6—at least not for more than thirty seconds. None of this works for bedtime, but other times I'm making headway. I want to deal with bedtime during this session. But going back to me not going above a 6…not bad compared to where I was—especially considering how the week started. Ethan's tantrums got longer and wilder the first time I locked myself in my room. You didn't tell me that would happen. But after I separated from him several times, his flare-up lasted only two or three minutes. And the next time he didn't follow me. I was amazed.

"Now he tries to stop me from leaving. But I only stop if he's below a 5. All this works fine. The problem comes when I try to talk to him about his anger. Most of the time he gets right back to a 5.5 or higher. What am I doing wrong? I'm staying below a 5. I must admit, I have to force myself to talk slower, and I kind of stumble around for words to stay there. I've even had to leave the room several times and come back. I kind of feel stupid sometimes not knowing how to say this stuff."

"It's really hard not to talk too much. Remember the 75/25…"

Shaking her head slowly and with her eyes cast down, Kendra said quietly, "Yeah, I keep thinking I have to do the talking. Do you have a tip?"

"When you go back to him, briefly validate his basic feeling. Say something like, 'I know this makes you upset; it's so hard.' Then say, 'I can't stay here if you handle your upset by yelling.' If his frustration level stays below 5, ask him a question instead of giving a mini-lecture: 'What do I do that makes you so frustrated?' There's more to it, but this would be a good start."

With those words, I got up and walked over to where she was sitting on the couch. With raised hands I said, "You've really made a lot of headway this week. Talking about fives, give me two." (Therapists don't have to stay in their chairs all the time, you know.) "You're making great progress. Ethan's learning a lot from you about regulating his emotions. Now let's help Ethan deal with his anger."

"How do we do that? Isn't there someplace on the Internet where we can just buy a regulator, separator, and monitor for him?" (Thank goodness for humor.)

"I wish…. Here's the first point to understand. Ethan's repeated experiences of reducing his frustration are caused by your repeated action of leaving. Remember the behavior mod stuff we talked about? He has no audience, and without an audience, there's no reward for throwing a tantrum. Enough of these video clips, and he starts to reduce frustration on his own."

"Okay, Gary, I get it. What do I do?"

"I can see I'd better get to it now, or you're going to move to a 5.5. Let's role-play. I'll be you; you be Ethan. Tell me the situation first."

"I'd like to focus on the bedtime temper tantrums. Those are as bad as ever. Here are the highlights. His bedtime is 8:30. He's supposed to put his pajamas on at 8:00, brush his teeth, and go to the bathroom. We used to have a problem with that, but we said he could have twenty minutes of video time before bed if he did the eight o'clock routine first. That part works now without a temper tantrum.

"At 8:20, when I ask him nicely to turn off the video game, he says, 'I will, Mom.' I tell him I'll give him five more minutes. After five minutes, I tell him to stop, and if he doesn't, I'll turn off the game system. Then all you-know-what breaks loose. He throws himself down, pounds on the floor, and yells, 'You're so mean! You never let me play!' Now I don't yell; I just unplug the system. Then he really throws a fit—at least a 7 on the scale."

"Okay, here's the plan, and then we'll role-play it. Ethan feels threatened when you turn off the game. He tries to control you by attacking with tantrums. The first thing we need him to do is to think about the problem in order for his behavior to change. Change stage 2, remember? Then, as soon as possible, we need to get him to label his feelings instead of show them with his tantrum. But first things first. What do you need to do to get him to think about the problem?"

"Yeah, I got it. Give him enough motivation to stop so that he doesn't have to play his game 24/7 and can give it up. Good luck! You'd better pull your genie out for this one."

"Do you remember what the biggest motivator is—internal or external?"

"Okay, Gary, I'm paying you for the answers, just give it to me."

"Internal. We involve him in the plan, make him feel important, empower him, make him feel 'I'm good.' Here are the basics. First, we need to change the video time to before he puts his pajamas on. Video time just before bedtime isn't a good idea. He's getting too revved up to shift from video to nighty-night. Instead, we'll start the video game time at 7:45. Then at 8:15, PJs on and bathroom stuff. If he can stop his video playing without a temper tantrum, he can have thirty minutes of video time the next night. If he can't, he gets his regular time of twenty minutes the next night. Now, here's the procedure for stopping: You give ten- and five-minute warnings and a 1-2-3 count at the point of shutting down his game. If he follows this procedure, he gets thirty minutes the next night. Sound okay?"

"Sure. Let's get started."

"Before we get into the role-playing, let's talk about why anger is happening with both of you. I've talked to you before about how anger happens, that anger is caused by feeling threatened, the threat triggers fear, and anger happens as a way to stop the threat. So, what are you feeling threatened about and want to stop?"

"That's easy. During this bedtime fiasco, I'm fearing failure—that I can't control my kid. To me, that's a sure sign of a 'bad' parent. That's threatening. In the past it's been a vicious cycle: The more he disobeys, the more I'm threatened—as you put it—with failure. Then I get angrier, and the failure just gets worse."

"Great, you've got it. What do you think the fear is in Ethan?"

"That's easy, too. His fun time is being threatened; he's fearful he'll have to stop, and he's right. He's getting angry in an attempt to get rid of the threat, which is me. I guess he's fearful, at that time, that he will never get to play again for the rest of his life. I can't wait to see how you're going to help me stop his video game without him feeling a big-time threat."

"Excellent. You get an A+ for your analysis. There's just one more thing. Throughout this role-playing I'll use the word *upset* to identify his feeling causing the temper tantrum. Labeling feelings and understanding how they work is a key regulator skill. Later in the role-play I'll demonstrate how to teach him to say the feeling. Eventually, by saying what he feels, he won't need to show it through unhealthy frustration. Sound good?"

Kendra nodded, and after some fine tuning and minor changes, we started the role-playing.

*Dress Rehearsal*

*Mom (a.k.a. Gary)*: You be Ethan, and I'll be you. Talk with Ethan when he is calm, 4.5 or below. Here goes. I want to talk to you about what happens when you're playing your video game and it's time to go to bed.

*Ethan (a.k.a. Kendra)*: You never let me play enough video games. I never have enough fun. [The monitor reads 6.5.]

*Mom* (dialing her own regulator from a 5.1 to about a 4.5): You really like them, don't you? I'm so happy it's so much fun. And stopping playing is really upsetting. It should be. When we have to stop something we like, it's upsetting. It makes us afraid we'll—

*Ethan*: Yeah, I wish I could play them forever. [Now at a 5.1, Ethan is starting to think; the separator is starting to kick in.]

*Mom*: Do you remember how long you get to play them?

*Ethan*: Yeah, twenty minutes. It's not long enough. Dumb, stupid bedtime. I should get to stay up until nine.

*Mom* (starting the change stage 3, planning for 98 percent success with a motivator): Here's what we're going to do: We're going to increase your game time to thirty minutes.

*Ethan*: Can we start it tonight, Mom? Please? Please?

*Mom*: Actually, we're going to change the video time to before you put on your pajamas.

*Ethan*: Okay, can we start it tonight?

*Mom*: Yes, but can you first listen to the rules?

*Ethan*: Okay. What are they?

*Mom*: We'll start your video games at 7:45, and you can play until 8:15. I'm going to use a timer with a ten-minute and five-minute warning for when to turn off the computer. What do you think so far?

*Ethan*: Yeah, I can do that.

*Mom*: Okay, here's the biggie. You'll need to turn the computer off when the five-minute warning rings without showing you're upset by yelling and kicking. [Mom is introducing how upset feelings cause the yelling and kicking.]

*Ethan*: Mom, I can, I can. Can we start tonight?

*Mom*: Yes, but first, do you know what upset means? [Mom is encouraging more thinking.]

*Ethan*: Yeah, I...uh...yell.

*Mom*: Do you also kick and say mean things when you're upset?

*Ethan* (looking down, almost whispering): Yeah, I do.

As Ethan is thinking, he is starting to learn the monitoring skill by looking at his behavior and what is happening inside him to cause the temper tantrum. (I know it's basic, but it's where we need to start.) By regulating his emotion to stay below a 5, Mom's making it happen, but Ethan's experiencing it. He's thinking and talking about the problem without so much emotion—there's the separator—and another valuable video clip is taking shape. Trying to explain the threat and fear part of anger in detail is too complicated for this part of the teaching experience; introducing how the emotion is connected to the angry behavior is plenty. Ethan is a little too young to grasp the fear point.

Back to seeing how the plan works.

*Mom*: It's upsetting to stop, I know, but if you don't stop the game or if you start kicking and yelling as a way to handle your upset, the next night you only get twenty minutes. I'll help you to—

*Ethan*: I don't care; it's not fair. [Ethan's frustration hits 5.5 and is rising rapidly. The threat barrier needs to be decreased. The dump-the-emotion alarm is sounding.]

*Mom*: I know it seems like it's not fair, but I'll help you to not handle your upset by yelling and kicking. I know together we can make it happen.

*Ethan*: How? [Whew, back to 4.9.]

*Mom*: We'll set a timer like I said—first for ten minutes and then for five minutes so you have time to prepare for stopping and can think about handling your upset in an acceptable way. During that time you can think about how you'll get to play thirty minutes the next night. Then you won't be so afraid that you won't get enough video time.

*Ethan*: Yeah, and then what?

*Mom*: If you still haven't turned off your game, I'll count to three and then turn it off if you can't.

*Ethan*: No, I don't like that. [There goes the level to a 5.8.]

*Mom*: I'll help you. Upset feelings are hard to handle. [Mom reaches out to touch Ethan's shoulder gently.] It will be hard at first, but I know you can eventually do it. It might take a few times to get used to it. But I'll help you.

Hear all the loving support? That's the good, heavy-duty internal motivation we've talked about.

*Mom*: Tell me what the rule is so I'm sure you understand it.

Here Mom is using an important technique: repetition. By repeating the expectation, Ethan is adding his own words and voice to his video clip so that when he refers to this clip in the future, it will be his words and voice. Mom is also setting important expectations: "It might take a few times." When the "few times" happen—and they will—Ethan will have some recognition of this and not feel so disappointed. This preparation video is an essential part of making regulation in the future conflict a little easier. Talking it through is kind of like a trial run. Ethan has some familiarity with what will happen.

*Ethan*: We'll use a timer, and then you'll say one-two-three and turn the game off if I don't…. But, Mom, don't do that. [The preparation exercise is working. He's putting himself into the future situation and feeling how stopping is not what he wants.]

*Mom*: You don't have to worry. I'll help you. We'll do it together. [Ethan's at a level 4.5; regulation is working.]

That's the textbook plan (change stage 3) for helping Ethan begin to acquire regulator, separator, and monitor skills and the typical way you set expectations with a seven-year-old. I say textbook because I was the mom, giving the most therapeutic way to train her child while I sat in a comfortable chair, getting paid to do it right. You will find your own way, which is the best anyway, to do what I demonstrated. Remember, noticeable change is great progress. The result is what counts, and the result you're looking for is you and your child remaining as much as possible in the healthy frustration zone.

Enough of the regulator, separator, monitor stuff; let's look at the action stage of this plan and see what happened in the first several weeks. But first I want to share with you how Mom helped Ethan label his upset feelings and connect these labels to frustration behaviors.

Every time she saw an opportunity, Mom helped Ethan label his upset feelings and experience the connection between being upset and his yelling and screaming. She helped him to learn how to leave the room if his upset feelings were too much. Here's the typical way this is stated when your child is calmer, below level 5. When you watch for these opportunities, you'll find plenty to work with. You may need to break the following example up into several sessions with your child. As I have said before, introducing the fear aspect is a little too complicated for this age range. Connecting feeling and behavior is the first major step. Later, you can introduce the fear part in more detail.

When she had the opportunity, here's what Kendra said: "Sometimes [don't say 'all the time'—too threatening] you're handling your upset feelings by yelling and screaming, Ethan. I yell sometimes when I'm upset, too. That's not acceptable. Instead, I want to help you to say you are upset or leave the room instead of yelling and screaming."

Mom is preparing Ethan for handling his feelings appropriately in the healthy frustration zone and the unhealthy frustration zone. When in the unhealthy zone, you leave the room. When in the healthy zone, you say your feelings. Mom tried to connect feelings with behavior every time she could—both happy and negative feelings. (I ask parents to do this at least several times a day for three to four weeks and keep it up to a lesser frequency throughout the child's life.)

Here's the typical statement: "I notice you're frowning; are you feeling upset?" Or: "You're smiling; what are you happy about?"

Now, let's go back and see how Kendra's plan worked.

### Raise the Curtain

As you probably guessed, the first week was rocky. The first night, it didn't work at all; Ethan blew up like he usually did, but Mom stayed at a 5. That night, right after Ethan put his pajamas on and was calmer, Mom prepared him for the next day with a lot of support; the video time would not be increased the next day. Ethan expressed some frustration, but he didn't throw a tantrum. During breakfast the next morning she gently prepared him for the twenty-minute video time he would get that evening. Supportive preparation for a future frustration is an essential regulation requirement.

That second evening Ethan barely made it, but the progress was noticeable. He was told he'd get thirty minutes the next night. Because regulating his anger was so difficult for him, Mom added a motivator the rest of the week: If he stopped his video game when asked and did it at a level 5 or below, he'd get a checkmark. Three checkmarks (three out of five nights) equaled a game rental on the weekend. For the rest of the week the plan worked; he got his game rental.

For the second week he had to get four checks (four out of five nights) for the video rental. He got his video game with a lot of support from Mom. When he started to get into the 5 zone, she touched his shoulder gently and said, "Let's make sure to get your check tonight so you'll get your game." In addition to implementing the plan, she started using the motivator and regulator ideas on other problems with quite a bit of success. Mom could see a noticeable difference in Ethan's mood; he seemed to feel good about himself more. Kids really feel good when they can regulate their upset, because people are not mad at them nearly as much—a huge internal motivator.

Except for a few minor relapses, the plan was successful. By the end of the fourth week, Ethan rarely had a temper tantrum, turned off the computer 90 percent of the time, and was able to start using the "upset" label to talk some about his feelings. Mom gave him a lot of support to achieve this.

> The more frequently and longer a child feels "I'm bad," the more you can expect diminished self-esteem and self-confidence.

One more point and probably the most important one: Mom's management of her frustration was key to Ethan's increased regulation ability and the resulting feeling of "I'm good." If Kendra would have continued with her unhealthy frustration, Ethan's potential for learning the regulation skill would have significantly declined, and, worse yet, his experience of "I'm bad" would have intensified. The more frequently and longer a child feels "I'm bad," the more you can expect diminished self-esteem and self-confidence. This slide can develop into serious situations such as depression, anxiety, oppositional/defiant behavior, and possibly delinquency. Don't let this happen.

# The Plan at Your House

Now that you see how this approach can work, what should your expectations be for your family?

If you have an "easy" child (remember this type of child from the temperament chapter), the results of your training should be similar to what Ethan's mom accomplished. If you have a child somewhere between "easy" and "difficult," expect the results to take longer to achieve and possibly not be as complete. Do count on your child's regulator, separator, and monitor skills to improve noticeably, however.

A "difficult" child will require significant reduction in your expectations from what happened in Ethan's situation. Don't be discouraged; you can still expect your child to make headway in acquiring these thinking skills; you will simply be starting at a place where your child can experience success according to the 98 percent success rule. That starting point will not be the same as it is with an easy child.

Here's an example of a realistic expectation for a difficult child, using the scenario from Kendra and Ethan. You would change the video time to before dinner. Regulating something your difficult child loves most of all just before bed is a strategy doomed to fail. Powerful motivators are essential. Eating is more than likely a big motivator, so that's why you would have the video time before dinner. The main idea here is to set expectations that match your child's starting point for success.

Above all, be patient with yourself. You may find it cumbersome at first to connect feelings and behavior as easily as Ethan's mom did. It really is like a different language for most parents. Be satisfied with some improvement, not Ethan's and Kendra's exact results. Don't forget it takes about three weeks for any change to be established. And the first week usually feels like nothing will ever get better. Don't stop your efforts. Once those first three to four weeks go by, keep up the monitoring stage for at least a month or so.

Are you feeling uncomfortable about how often you've been engaged in unhealthy frustration? As we take inventory, it's easy to wonder, "Is my child ruined?" Unhealthy frustration has happened and will happen again to all of us. Unhealthy frustration is a natural instinct. But we can train ourselves to mange it. Because of our unique temperament traits, the management will be harder for some of us and very easy for others. Be gentle with yourself! As I've said before, if unhealthy frustration happens occasionally, it's not a big deal.

If it happens regularly, don't let it continue. I've seen the results in children and adults. I've heard the self-talk these children and adults have learned from their parents when unhealthy frustration was the dominant parenting response. The biggest and most devastating result is children turning their parents' anger on themselves. Here's the way children and adults describe their self-talk when even a minor mistake happens (single quotes are directly from parents): "How could I be so 'stupid'? I'm so 'irresponsible.'" What's even worse is when these messages are unconscious, and all the child or adult feels is unmanageable shame.

This chapter has given you the necessary information to avoid unhealthy frustration. It's never too late to stop unhealthy frustration. If you can't do it by yourself, seek professional counseling. It will be worth it.

> When your regulator, separator, and monitor are working well, you are teaching your child these skills.

## Wrapping Up

You now have a guide for how to recognize and stop unhealthy frustration and achieve healthy frustration, for both you and your child. Regulating, separating, and monitoring are the essential skills for both of you to acquire. When your regulator, separator, and monitor are working well, you are teaching your child these skills.

When these skills are developed to a noticeable level in your child, the result is increased self-confidence and improved relationships all the way from childhood to adolescence and into adulthood—in the workplace as well as at home.

Let's summarize this section with a to-do list:

1. Be aware of your and your child's frustration levels and what is causing you to feel uncomfortable; maybe an important belief is being challenged, or maybe you are just tired of failing with your child. Through your awareness, reduce your discomfort level well within the healthy frustration zone before reengaging with your child.

2. Stop all talking when your or your child's frustration is above level 5. This means getting away from each other.

3. Teach your child to label feelings and connect feelings to behaviors. Then help your child talk about these feelings. Find every opportunity to show this connection: TV shows, news articles, other kids, you, and of course your child. Labeling and talking about feelings are the two essential ingredients for developing the three thinking skills: regulating, separating, and monitoring, particularly regulating and separating. When regulation occurs and feelings are level 5 and below, separation of emotion from thinking is highly possible. You need to support your child's regulator actively during a conflict. Don't let the emotions get above a 5 for too long; otherwise, the wrong video will be taken.

4. Teach your child the connection between anger and fear after he or she has learned that emotions cause behavior and when developmentally he or she can understand the connection between fear and anger, typically around eight to ten years of age. Of course, start whenever you think this issue will make sense to your child. Here are the main points about the fear and anger connection. When something happens that we don't like, we feel threatened and afraid the situation will not stop. We respond by

getting angry as an attempt to control our circumstances and stop feeling the threat and fear, or we may withdraw and get away.

5. Teach monitoring skills. This skill deals with accurately observing the part you play in a conflict and the part the other person plays. As a teacher, it's most important for you to acknowledge and admit your part in a conflict. By admitting your part, you can change the whole situation faster, and your child will learn the value of owning his or her part in a problem. Talk openly about feelings as much as possible. This is the grease needed for your and your child's regulator to work at top capacity.

That's it for this chapter. The next chapter deals with what happens when a parent slips too many times into unhealthy frustration: shameful guilt, the type of guilt we want to avoid as much as possible.

### CHAPTER 9

# Yes, Virginia, Guilt Can Be Good

HAVE YOU EVER LAIN awake until the wee hours because you suddenly realized a mistake you'd made? Maybe you misspelled a colleague's name on a company report. *How will I ever explain this to my boss? Is there some excuse.... No, shall I just wait? Maybe no one will notice.... How could I be so stupid? Maybe everyone will notice....* If you've lost sleep or worried like this about a mistake, you know all about shameful guilt. You most likely picked up this practice from your parents, and unless you become aware of your shameful guilt, you'll pass this way of handling mistakes on to your children.

But don't despair; there's hope. You actually can choose which type of guilt your child ends up with: healthy guilt that helps us deal with mistakes in a caring way or shameful guilt that plagues us when we make a mistake and fail to meet others' expectations. Shameful guilt always results in "I'm bad" and repeated self-talk that "proves" how bad you are and how others will feel the same way about you.

> You actually can choose which type of guilt your child ends up with: healthy guilt that helps us deal with mistakes in a caring way or shameful guilt that plagues us when we make a mistake and fail to meet others' expectations.

Who would ever choose that? It sounds downright ugly. And it is. Of course, you want your child to have healthy guilt, the kind of guilt that is at the very heart of parental love. Healthy guilt always results in your child feeling "I'm good." This chapter is a crash course on how to teach healthy guilt to your child and avoid shameful guilt. Are you tensing up? No need. Take a deep breath and relax. This is a tough subject, one that can generate a great amount of fear, but you will feel more comfortable as you read on.

## Shameful Guilt

What is shameful guilt? It's a label I use to describe what happens when the excessive harshness of unhealthy frustration is used to deal with being wrong. It's the fastest and easiest way to correct wrong; it does stop behavior fast, most of the time. The downside: It always results in diminished self-confidence. It's a sure bet for establishing feelings of "I'm bad."

Unfortunately, shameful guilt is what everyone uses to some degree for dealing with being wrong. It's unavoidable. The good news: No matter at what age you start—including adulthood—you can help your child develop healthy guilt and minimize shameful guilt.

## The Purpose of Guilt

Guilt helps us do two very important things. First, it helps us know what is right and wrong; and second, it helps us to handle being wrong. The first part is fairly easy for your child to learn; the second part is really tricky. Eight-year-old Cooper knocks over a glass of milk and runs to his room crying after his mother says (at an FTS level 6), "If you wouldn't rush so much, you wouldn't knock over so many things." Mom runs after him and finds him on the floor sobbing, hitting his head with his fist, and screaming, "I'm so dumb. You ought to get rid of me. I always mess up." That's the harshness of unhealthy frustration; that's shameful guilt.

After reading this example, maybe you're feeling something like *That sounds just like me,* or *That's what my kid does; I'm such a bad parent.* I'm sure you love your child so much, you expect yourself to always do the right thing. The "always" part is impossible, so be gentle with yourself.

Maybe you use a lot of healthy guilt with your child, as Ava's dad did. Here's the situation: Nine-year-old Ava sneaks four gummy bears into her school lunch when she's only allowed two.

> Guilt helps us do two very important things. First, it helps us know what is right and wrong; and second, it helps us to handle being wrong.

She comes bouncing into the family room after school. "Hi, Dad." She loves how her dad works from the house and is always there when she arrives from school.

"Let's sit down in the living room and talk about your day."

*Oops, trouble. Dad usually doesn't ask me to sit with him to talk, especially in the living room. I hope he didn't discover the gummy bears. Make up a reason quick to—* "Hey, everything went okay. I've got a lot of homework."

"I just want to talk to you. Come on into the living room and sit beside me."

*Now I know I've got to tell him about the gummy bears. Am I going to tell the truth or not? I know it was wrong. Why did I take them in the first place? I shouldn't have. I'll just admit it. I know Dad will be disappointed, but he won't be mad* [the video clips are running at warp speed]. *He'll say something like,* "Why did you do it?" *or* "Can you promise not to do it next time?" *or something weird he's been saying since we've been to that dumb counselor:* "When you want to break the rules, just tell me before you want to break them." *I haven't done this yet; seems kinda crazy.*

Dad's right next to her now, gently touching her arm, directing her toward the living room. "This will just take a couple minutes."

Sitting on the couch now by Dad, Ava thinks, *It's going to pop....* "I know what this is about. I took two more gummy bears than I should have. I'll never do it again."

With a slight wrinkle in his forehead and just a little more volume, Dad says, "You did? I didn't even notice...."

*Oh no! Here I could have gotten away with it. Oh well, I feel better about it now.* "Are you sure you didn't know?" *I know Dad thinks it's cute when I give him my "daddy's little girl" eyes. Seems like he gets nicer when I—*

"Yeah, I've missed touching base with you. That's why I wanted just to talk a little bit. But I'm sure proud of you for telling me the truth." *Wrinkles gone, voice just right. Whew.* "Think you can try harder to tell me when you want to break the rules or sneak something next time? And remember, if you do something wrong, you can admit it to me, and there will be few or no consequences. When I was your age, I got into the habit of lying, and my dad made this kind of deal with me. You know how your grandpa was always using the stuff he did as a therapist with his clients on us kids. Sounded kind of weird, but it really worked. Few or no consequences made me less scared, and I started to tell the truth."

> Stay in the healthy frustration zone and you'll reap quite a harvest.

"Yeah, Dad. I'll try harder next time."

That's a demonstration of healthy guilt. Ava felt valued and maintained a feeling of "I'm good" as she was working on correcting unacceptable behavior. There are several important lessons in this example:

- Stay in the healthy frustration zone and you'll reap quite a harvest. Both Dad and Ava stayed below a level 5. Remember, in this zone there are no loud or mean words (maybe a few now and then but rapidly corrected), and facial expressions are not harsh—all essential behaviors for fostering healthy guilt. Another video clip was in Ava's video library with a very important underlying message: "I can admit my unacceptable behavior, change it, and still feel 'I'm good.'"

- Understanding and support work best. In her self-talk, you will notice Ava was supportive to herself as she worked through what she did wrong, and without harshness decided to admit her wrongdoing to Dad. This lack of harshness came from multiple video clips where Dad was not harsh to her when she was wrong. These video clips always ended with a neon sign that flashed "You will continue to feel 'I'm good' even when you've done something wrong and are working to improve it."

- Parents need to have the right mix of support and firmness. Dad showed his support by thanking her for telling the truth and firmly encouraging her to tell him the next time she was tempted to sneak something or lie. Just a brief point about this technique for owning up to a possible sneaky behavior before it happens: If your child is sneaky, stay in the healthy frustration zone with plenty of validation and sometimes give your child what she's thinking about sneaking—not always but maybe 5 percent of the time. Nothing like something good coming out of something bad. Eases the pain a little bit.

Now that we have a good feel for what healthy and shameful guilt look like, may I invite you into a brief classroom session?

## A Parent's Most Important and Difficult Task

If I had to pick the most difficult yet most important parental-love task, establishing healthy guilt would be at the top of the list. Why?

Healthy guilt = "I'm good"
Shameful guilt = "I'm bad"

It's so important because teaching healthy guilt to your child is the foundation of parental love (parental actions and words that consistently transfer the message—through devotion, tenderness, and affectionate attachment—that your child is lovable or good). It's so challenging because handling your child's being wrong, dealing with his misbehavior, and still maintaining "I'm good" within him can be as tricky as walking a tightrope across Niagara Falls.

Healthy guilt = "I'm good"

Shameful guilt = "I'm bad"

Ava's dad pulled this off when he said, "I'm sure proud of you that you told me the truth. Think you can try harder to tell me when you want to break the rules or sneak something next time?"

If Ava didn't improve, Dad would have to be firmer in the future while still getting the message across that he respected and valued Ava. Maybe a deprivation would be the next step: no TV for one night or requiring an extra chore to repay what she took. (We'll talk more about this later.)

Did Dad's response come naturally? You already know the answer. Shameful guilt is easy to express; healthy guilt is tough to communicate. The first week or so of the practicing period is always hard; that just comes with the "stages of change" territory. But after this initial learning and practice period, it gets easier and more rewarding. Better yet, the rewards are significant; you will not want to go back to your old ways. Let's pull our noses out of the textbook for a moment and see what this looks like in real life.

## Court Is Now in Session

Here's what happens within your child when shameful guilt occurs. In a child's mind there's no separation between the child and his or her behavior; the behavior and the child are the same. In your child's way of thinking, *If my behavior is bad, I'm bad.* That's what children regularly tell me: "Daddy yells all the time; I'm so bad." A parent's shameful guilt expressed in words and facial expression is experienced by the child as an attack, not only on the behavior but on the child. That's what we learned about unhealthy frustration, the energy source of shameful guilt: The attacks are painful and hurt a lot, as much as or more than physical injury. There's not one ounce of good in this type of guilt.

Guilt is the result of an internal human legal system—a system that identifies right and wrong and what happens when a person is wrong, a system learned primarily from parents. As I've said before, the easy part is learning what is right or wrong; the hard part is learning how to deal with being wrong and at the same time feel valued and respected.

Here are the nuts and bolts of the human legal system: We are all born with a vacant courtroom, with open positions for a judge, lawyer, and jury. The healthy guilt job descriptions for these positions are as follows:

> In your child's way of thinking,
>
> *If my behavior is bad, I'm bad.*

- Judge: determines right and wrong, determines consequences of wrong behaviors, and is the keeper of detailed rules on how to think and act in the best way possible.

- Lawyer (the best one possible): values and protects the basic worth of oneself when one may or may not have done something wrong.

- Jury (the best one possible): provides reasonable, fair, broad-based judgment about whether one is right or wrong.

The parent's tried-and-tested legal system serves as the child's legal system during the first year to year and a half. As you know by now, whatever you do and say eventually becomes the foundation for who your child is. Likewise, your legal system eventually becomes the basis for your child's legal system. During the first year to year and a half, there's not a lot for the parental judge to do.

By the time the child is two, the parental judge is working overtime with no extra pay. At this point your child is talking, walking, and commanding a lot of attention. Suddenly, you find yourself saying no many, many times each day. Your child seems to have developed a mind and will of his or her own almost overnight, and it's becoming more and more difficult to view your child as a precious little angel! There's a lot for the parental judge, and eventually the parental lawyer, to do.

By the end of the third year your child has filled the judge and lawyer positions; your child has internalized his or her own basic judge and lawyer from your legal system. Many cases have been tried in the child's internal courtroom. Multiple video clips have been taken; multiple consequences have occurred when the child has done something wrong. The foundation of your child's legal system has been established.

The jury part of your child's human legal system develops more toward the preadolescent years and is fully developed during the adolescent years. It's during this period that your child starts to consider seriously other people's judgments or points of view when determining what is right and wrong. That's the jury part of your child's human legal system. Our focus in this chapter will be on the younger years, when the judge and lawyer part of the human legal system become well established.

Through parental love a healthy guilt legal system is being established. The internal judge and lawyer consistently and accurately assess wrongdoing in a way that is supportive, appropriately firm, and reasonable. Your child has multiple experiences of several key healthy-guilt procedures: knowing what is right and wrong, being able to identify when right and wrong happen, and learning how to correct wrong behavior while maintaining self-respect and feelings of "I'm good." The child is learning that his or her behavior is caused by emotions, but at this age, the child doesn't quite have a grasp of who he or she is as a person.

Let's visit the courtroom trial of two-and-a-half-year-old Elise, who loves to climb on coffee tables. Let's see how the parent judge and lawyer handle the case.

Every time Elise crawls onto the table, the parental judge says, "Get down" in a kind voice. When this doesn't work, the judge orders the security guards to remove the child gently from the premises— no handcuffs, no yelling. So far so good.

That's when the lawyer part of the child's legal system kicks in. Elise's internal inexperienced lawyer defends her rights by kicking and screaming. Translating from kid behavior into lawyer lingo: "Your honor, my client is just curious. She's not really guilty of anything. Isn't it obvious she's just having fun and needs to explore? Please let her crawl onto the table as often as she wants to." The two-year-old lawyer's argument isn't strong enough, and the parent judge responds, "Overruled." (The lawyer needs to go to a few more workshops.)

Just a side note on helping your child develop the lawyer part: Be careful with your judge response to the screaming, kicking behavior. When possible, support the underlying reasons and feelings for the behavior: "I know it's really fun to climb. And that table is the perfect challenge. You need to get down because you could get hurt if you fall," and so forth. (Judges usually don't talk like this, but parental judges need to.) This ensures separating the behavior from the child: The behavior's unacceptable, not your child. After all, your child's lawyer needs as much support as possible in the first courtroom appearances. A harsh response ignores the very important (to your child) underlying reasons and feelings for crawling onto the coffee table. A harsh response inadvertently teaches shameful guilt. And remember, the video camera is always on.

The parental-love judge (you) focuses on emotions first, behavior second. Emotions come from the center of your child, the good part. The best type of guilt is grounded in feelings of "I'm good" not "I'm bad."

> Validating your child's feelings apart from behavior starts as soon as your child is born.

Validating your child's feelings apart from behavior starts as soon as your child is born. As your child continually takes in the

validation of feelings, the healthy guilt lawyer part will be fully developed by adulthood. The end result will be the ability to verbalize
feelings: "I was hurt when I heard you say those things about me,
but I shouldn't have said those negative things about you." That's the
healthy guilt way to understand unacceptable behavior. Shameful
guilt explains unacceptable behavior this way: "I had every right to
say those things about you; you deserve it."

When the parental-love judge starts this training from birth, it's
possible for your child to express feelings apart from behavior, as
demonstrated above, by at least six or seven years of age.

What's the take-home lesson regarding this lawyer? Teach your
child's lawyer not to defend behavior automatically but first express
accurately the feelings causing the behavior and admit easily when
the behavior is wrong. You do this, of course, by demonstration.
When you've modeled this behavior, eventually your child will be
able to accept a healthy judge's consequence for the wrongdoing
readily: "Yeah, Mom, I did pull my sister's hair. I was upset. I need to
say I'm sorry."

If the consequence is unfair, your child's
lawyer will be able to argue his or her case
in the healthiest way possible, readily admitting his or her part in the problem but
asking the parent or authority figure to pay
attention to what the other person did that
may have been unacceptable. "Yeah, Mom,

**It's never too late to start healthy guilt training.**

I did pull my sister's hair. What made me upset was her making fun
of my freckles. Can you stop her?" After some support and Mom
doing something about the problem, the freckle-faced boy said, "I'm
going to say I'm sorry." Sound impossible? When the parental-love
judge presides, I've witnessed this type of behavior multiple times
from children as young as six or seven.

Always remember to determine your expectations based on your
child's temperament. For the difficult child, seeing his or her part in
the problem will take a lot more time to achieve, but it can happen.

For example, only attempt this admitting part at a level 3 and below, never at a level 4 and above, and always in the least threatening situation possible.

Are you hearing an echo in the above take-home lesson from the last chapter on anger and fear? (Hint: monitor, regulator, separator.) A fully developed internal lawyer uses the regulator to separate feelings from thinking and behavior so we can think straight. With the regulator doing its job, the monitor can be turned on so we can first look at ourselves and accurately see what part we play in a problem before we look at the part the other person has played. Is this last skill ringing a bell? It's one of the four characteristics of self-confidence: accurately understanding oneself and others.

So, back to the courtroom. Elise has been found guilty as charged; she shouldn't be crawling on the coffee table. The parent judge must deliver a sentence, but will it be based on shameful guilt or healthy guilt? Will it be handed down in a loud voice, coming from a mean-looking parental judge who says, "You know you're not allowed up there…" or "How many times have I told you…" while the security guards drag the child kicking and screaming to her cell to calm down?

Or will the sentence come from a supportive, understanding parental judge who approaches the child with a calm voice, a kind look, and a favorite toy: "That's so much fun, isn't it? I know you really want to do this, but it's dangerous. Let's go play with your blocks instead." Lifting her screaming from the coffee table, Dad takes Elise to the play area, gets down on the floor, and starts building a tower for his daughter to send crashing down.

Just a word of encouragement before we continue with this tough subject. No parent demonstrates this healthy legal system perfectly all the time. At best we can aim for instilling healthy guilt most of the time. The center of your child is where good things happen. Your child thrives when you are there with him or her, particularly when conflict occurs. Once you get the hang of it, you'll feel very good about what you have accomplished with and for your child. The satisfaction is immense when you see the reflection of your validation in your child's face and behavior.

As I've mentioned before, the basics of a child's internal legal system are established between the ages of two and three. Some people refer to this age period as the "terrible" twos, but I like to think of them as the "terrific" twos. Sure, this time is full of challenges, but the challenges are about the rapid development of the child's personhood. Understanding what's going on developmentally and knowing how to handle the behavior in a healthy way can make this time terrific rather than terrible—most of the time.

If your child is way past this age and you feel you have communicated way too much shameful guilt, be kind and gentle to yourself. I've said it before, and I'll say it as many times as I need to: It's never too late to start healthy guilt training. Your child's underlying need to feel good never goes away—even throughout adulthood—and your child is always receptive to your validation of his or her goodness.

## In the Lab with Nathan

Just to get a better grip on this challenging healthy guilt task, let's take a little more in-depth look at how to teach healthy guilt to four-year-old Nathan. He has two noticeable temperament traits—activity level and intensity of reaction—that are both at a 4 on the 1–5 temperament trait scale. Sounds like a challenge, doesn't he? Well, fasten your seatbelt; I'm driving.

The biggest struggle for Nathan's parents is Nathan wanting to continue what he's doing when he needs to stop. That's true to some degree for all four-year-olds, but Nathan's particular temperament traits make the challenge even greater. Right now, playing in the sandbox is his favorite pastime, and he flies to a level 7 (FTS) in a millisecond when he's asked to come indoors.

Here's what happened in the most recent sandbox episode. Five minutes before Nathan needed to get ready for his half-day preschool, Mom prepared Nathan to leave the sandbox by playing with him and his brand-new dump truck and tractor. "Wow," she said, "that tractor sure has big tires."

"Yeah, Mom," Nathan replied, as he dumped a huge load of sand into the dump truck.

"I'm going to dump the truck. And then after another load, we need to get ready for school."

"No! No school!" (level 6.5 and climbing). Nathan dumped one more load of sand into the truck that was already full.

On her way to dump that load, Mom said, "We'll get an orange lollypop while you dress." (Mom has learned that a motivator is necessary in difficult situations like this one, and the lollypop makes Nathan feel good in a difficult, potentially "I'm bad" situation.)

"No" (level 5.5). Nathan pushed the tractor faster than ever for the biggest scoop of sand he could get to load onto Mom's truck.

The five minutes were up. Nathan had to stop his play and go into the house. "Mommy knows you want to play a little more." She validated, trying to help Nathan to feel a little bit of "I'm good." "I've got the lollypop in my pocket for you when you can come in by yourself. If you can't, I'll carry—"

"No!" (level 6.5 maybe 7).

Mom gently took his hand (Mom at level 4) and with the other hand held out the lollypop just beyond his reach (the carrot-on-the-stick approach). "Here's the lollypop when you can walk by yourself, and you can take the tractor [attempting to maintain 'I'm good' with a motivator; good idea] with you to school for show and tell. You really like that tractor, don't you?"

Nathan responded by kicking sand and yelling, "No! No school!"

Nathan threw the tractor down as hard as he could, spraying sand up in Mom's face. Mom's FTS level spiked to 6; she took a breath and brought it down to a 4.9. Mom quickly picked up the tractor without Nathan seeing her. (*Oh, if I only had four hands.*) She stepped out of the sandbox, pulling and lifting Nathan with her. Nathan tried to grab the lollypop. "Not until you can walk on your own" (a stretch but doable, maybe).

Nathan said more calmly, now walking by himself (level 5) and reaching, not grabbing, for the lollypop, "Give me lollypop."

He wasn't fighting nearly as much, so Mom handed the lollypop to Nathan, and with a gentle hand to his shoulder and trying to make eye contact said, "Thank you for handling your frustration by walking next to me and not yelling. Mommy loves you" (plenty of "I'm good" now).

Once in Nathan's room, Mom put the tractor on Nathan's bed and helped him change his clothes. "You can take the tractor in the car with you." (Keep the "I'm good" feelings coming.)

Nathan smiled (level 3). Mom thought, *Whew, another training session over. I could sure use a punching bag to release all the stuffed frustration. Will it ever get easier?*

### Setup for Success

I'm sure you've experienced this kind of situation if you have a child with Nathan's temperament traits. Don't be discouraged if you can't be this successful all the time. No one is. Remember, set up realistic expectations for yourself that will help you to be 98 percent successful. Mom was fairly new to the parental-love concepts. She'd only been working on them for a month or so, but she had prepared well. She was ready with a motivator, plenty of validation, the right mix of talking and firm limit-setting action (leading Nathan out of the sandbox), and being aware of and regulating her frustration level. Set your sights on noticeable improvement over time, and don't give up when some of your best-laid plans don't come together in the way you'd hoped they would. Every positive step, no matter how small, builds more "I'm good" feelings in your child.

Even though it wasn't obvious to Mom, Nathan was internalizing a valuable lesson

> Set your sights on noticeable improvement over time, and don't give up when some of your best-laid plans don't come together in the way you'd hoped they would.

through the sandbox encounter. He was learning his behavior was unacceptable, but he was acceptable—the essential lesson about unacceptable behavior and result of healthy guilt. His emotions were continually validated even in the toughest time when Mom was lifting him out of the sandbox and saying, "Here's the lollypop when you can walk by yourself, and you can take the tractor with you to school for show-and-tell."

Nathan also witnessed healthy guilt demonstrated by a parent. Mom showed Nathan that during a conflict a person can stay in the healthy frustration zone and be fair, kind, and respectful. A healthy-guilt judge was taking shape within Nathan.

> Imparting healthy guilt to your child = continual validation of feelings underneath the behavior + firm supportive limits to stop unacceptable behavior.

Mom did one other thing well; she used the stages of change information (chapter 6). She really played the motivator card to the max: a lollypop to get him out of the sandbox and a tractor to get him to forget the sandbox and think about preschool. It did take planning to make the change happen. Remember, a successful change plan requires maximum motivators and minimal barriers. She also minimized yakking and maximized acting.

### Setup for Failure

Let's briefly see how a shameful guilt system would look in Nathan's situation.

It was time for Nathan to stop playing in the sandbox and get ready for preschool. Mom stood at the door and called him. "Nathan, time to come in! It's almost time for school."

Nathan didn't even look up.

"Nathan! You get in here right now or we're going to be late!"

Nathan continued to fill his dump truck, still ignoring Mom.

Mom's frustration level escalated with every step she took toward the sandbox. By the time she reached her son, she was at level 6. She grabbed him by the arm and yanked him out. "I know you heard me, Nathan Scott Powers. Why don't you ever listen to me? Let's go."

Nathan screamed and squirmed, trying to break free of his mother's iron grip.

Dragging her son into the house, Mom said, "I was going to give you a lollypop, but you're being so naughty, you don't deserve it. I'm so sick of this!"

It looks so ugly on paper, doesn't it? But it's even worse in real life. And unfortunately, we've all lived through these types of scenarios. Of course, an occasional outburst like this isn't the end of the world. Problems arise, however, when most of the parent's corrections are done with shameful guilt. As you know by now, shameful guilt from the parent becomes shameful guilt for the child.

If Mom had responded to Nathan as in this second scenario most of the time, Nathan would automatically take this shameful approach into his legal system for future use when he thinks of doing or has done something unacceptable. When an unacceptable behavior would occur, Nathan's shameful guilt judge would make humiliating and embarrassing comments through his self-talk, at least in the 6.5-plus range: "How could you be so stupid?" And his lawyer would be practically useless, feebly explaining, "You are guilty as charged; you *are* really stupid." The internal judge would pass on a judgment something like, "I sentence you to a life of nobody caring for you and you not caring about yourself."

How do I know this? I hear it every day from kids five years old and up. You may say, "That's just because you're treating sick kids." Perhaps, but part of the reason these kids are suffering is because their parents have, inadvertently, fallen into the trap of parenting most of the time with shameful guilt, creating this type of internal legal system within their children. The heat and material of this weld is incredibly strong. Kids want to be valued, but when they are not, they become convinced (convicted) they are bad; the lawyer in them can't defend them against their own accusations.

# Two Essentials for Establishing Healthy Guilt

Before completing this chapter I'd like to share two important tips that make a big difference in terms of whether your child acquires healthy guilt.

1. Use the terms "unacceptable" or "acceptable" behavior in place of "wrong" or "right" when a mistake occurs.

2. Teach your child to own his or her part in a conflict before blaming the other person. Most of healthy guilt is dependent on this skill. This is the thinking skill of monitoring that we've talked about before. Remember, this skill is one of the four cornerstones of our self-confidence definition (accurately observing oneself and others).

## Why Wrong Is Wrong

Let's deal with the word *wrong* first. What's the big deal about using it? Parents often put it this way to me: "Wrong is wrong; our kids will face 'wrong' in real life; why not get them used to it now?" They're right. Children do need to get used to people using the word *wrong*, but not at two years of age; and you probably don't need to mention the word until your child is six or seven. Even then, use it sparingly throughout your child's teenage years. The only purpose for using it is to let your child know that's the word most adults use to describe unacceptable behavior.

Here's what's wrong, I mean unacceptable, about using "wrong" when your child is two. When the word *wrong* is used, it's usually said at an unhealthy frustration level—usually 5 and above—and is usually too much Tabasco for almost anyone, no matter what age. It burns with "I'm bad" far too often. When "wrong" is used, the judge imparting the verdict rarely validates the person, which puts us squarely in the area of shameful guilt. The internal lawyer either

> Use the terms "unacceptable" or "acceptable" behavior in place of "wrong" or "right" when a mistake occurs.

gives up ("Who cares?"), becomes self-destructive ("I always mess up"), or attacks others ("It's all your fault"). Why use a sledgehammer and railroad spike when the situation calls for a tack hammer and an eight-penny nail?

One side note: When I was involved in the leadership side of a business several years ago, my partner told me, "Never say 'You're wrong' to me or our coworkers. Hearing those words makes people immediately feel defensive. Telling someone he's wrong never gets him to change his viewpoint." My partner was right. People feel attacked, threatened, and bad when told they're wrong.

Notice how the word is used most of the time: "You're wrong." Rarely do we hear someone say, "Your behavior is wrong." There really is no good reason to make "wrong" our primary communication when a mistake is made, and there are many reasons for finding another way to help someone change his or her behavior.

"Unacceptable" and "acceptable" are two of the best nonjudgmental terms I've found when trying to change a child's behavior. Here's how it sounds when we validate feelings first and deal with behavior second: "I know you're really upset, and you should be. Dealing with your upset feeling by slamming a door is an unacceptable way to handle your anger. The acceptable way is to tell me how mad you are. If your upset is too strong, don't say anything, but go to another room and find something to distract you until you are less angry and can talk about it."

One last point about "wrong" as it relates to the parental judge who eventually becomes the child's judge. Make sure your parental judge is a supportive judge. Sounds weird, doesn't it? How can judging be supportive?

In real life when a judge takes the time to listen and understand both sides of the issue, all parties involved have a better experience.

In parental-love jargon, being a supportive judge means a parent teaches the child the difference between unacceptable and acceptable behavior in a firm, clear, limit-setting way while still being understanding and caring.

*Owning Your Part*

Now let's turn to the second tip that really makes a difference in your child's acquiring healthy guilt: training your child to own his or her part in a conflict first and then dealing with the other person's part. Let's see how this plays out with twelve-year-old (going on sixteen) Rachel, who has always been a more willful child and is now exerting her independence by arguing all the time and, worse yet, being rude to her mom.

Here's how Rachel is being trained to deal with her unacceptable behavior by owning her part in a conflict. The example that follows had been practiced with both Mom and Rachel in counseling and multiple times at home during a two-week period.

Mom asked Rachel to tell her friends to go home, and Rachel responded sharply in front of her friends: "We're not done playing, and they don't need to go home. Their parents aren't bossy like you are!" The friends froze, not quite sure how to respond.

Mom answered firmly (FTS level 4.9999). "That's unacceptable. Go to the family room and think this over, and we'll talk later. Girls, it's time to go home."

Rachel reluctantly went to the family room and turned on the TV while the girls quickly gathered their things and slipped out the front door without a peep. Mom waited ten minutes before approaching Rachel, then went into the family room, sat down next to her daughter, and opened the conversation.

"I know you get really frustrated when I ask you—"

"Mom, you're always—" (level 6 and climbing).

"Rachel, remember what we're working on: owning your part first and listening instead of talking."

Rachel put her head down, obviously trying to keep from talking.

As kindly and gently as she could, Mom continued. "Remember it's okay to tell me, 'Mom, that makes me frustrated.' You should be frustrated. I know you feel strongly about things, and it's hard to say it right…"

"Can I just finish this program? It's over in fifteen minutes" (level 5 and possibly lowering).

"Yes, you can. You know what I want to—"

"Mom, I know. You want me to own my part and make it up to you for what I did."

Mom nodded in agreement and stood up to leave. "Thank you for thinking this through." (Mom gave Rachel an opportunity to move to change stage 2, willing to think.)

Fifteen minutes later, Rachel approached Mom in the kitchen and said, "I'm sorry. I was rude to you. I shouldn't have said that in front of my friends."

"Thank you, Rachel. That really feels good. Let's talk about another way I can tell you what to do in front of your friends." They talked about alternatives, and Mom accepted one of Rachel's ideas and promised to use that approach the next time.

What you just read may be hard to believe, but I've seen it happen hundreds of times within several weeks of parents sticking with the procedures outlined in this book. Here's the progression for establishing "owning my part first in a conflict":

1. Validated emotions = I'm feeling respected and valued.

2. Feeling respected, valued = "I'm good" and the ability to think without defending.

3. Problem solving from "I'm good" = the best chance to own my part in a problem.

Remember: "Owning my part first" is a cornerstone characteristic of self-confidence. I often tell my clients that if people could acquire this one healthy guilt characteristic, therapists would not have jobs.

One side note on the story of Rachel and her mom. Are you thinking that Mom allowing Rachel to watch an additional fifteen minutes of TV is ridiculous? Sounds like it, but it fits with "I'm good." The purpose of Mom's leaving Rachel is not a "punishment," nor is it a way for Rachel to get the upper hand ("Mom's doing what *I* want now"). Rather, it provides Rachel with an opportunity to regulate her emotions, separate emotions from her thinking so she can think straight, and then accurately monitor what she did and then what Mom did.

"Owning my part first" is a cornerstone characteristic of self-confidence

The TV is a distraction, a great way to reduce unhealthy frustration to a healthy level. It's okay that Rachel knows Mom is being good to her by allowing her to watch TV; it makes her feel "I'm good." Thinking from the "I'm good" spot gives Rachel the best chance to know and own her part in the conflict. Even though Rachel is watching TV, she's thinking about her behavior and what to do about it.

That's it for the two healthy guilt tips: (1) use the word *unacceptable* in place of *wrong*, and (2) teach your child as soon as possible to first own his or her part in a conflict. It also really helps for you to own your part in a conflict with your child as much as you can. We all know the power of "walking the walk" rather than just "talking the talk."

## The Eternal Question

I'd like to end this chapter with an answer to the question I'm almost always asked when I present this material.

*I can see how this supportive-judge stuff helps a child to feel good when he or she is wrong or thinking about doing something wrong. I can see how that might help a child to be nicer to others when he or she needs to solve a problem with someone who has wronged him or her.*

*But here's where I differ big time. I think to teach kids to solve problems by being only nice to themselves and others is a disservice for two reasons.*

*First, I think kids often need and benefit from a rougher approach that focuses only on their behavior. I don't mean name-calling or belittling or spanking necessarily. More like when they lie, saying, "That's*

*wrong and disrespectful" and saying it at a level 6.5 on your Frustra-*
*tion Tolerance Scale.*

*Second, very seldom will my kids ever have this nice approach hap-*
*pen in the real world with friends and teachers. When they get the*
*shameful guilt approach, as you call it, they won't be prepared for the*
*real world. Wouldn't they then be devastated and really feel "I'm bad"?*
*I don't know; your approach just doesn't wash for me.*

Let's start by addressing the statement that a child with a supportive, understanding internal judge will not be prepared for the
real world. Actually, when your child is validated in the way we've
been talking about, he or she gets to know the core of his or her own
being really well and becomes very sure and comfortable, resulting
in self-confidence. Great self-confidence provides the best responses
to the real world. Let's review self-confidence characteristics:

- Comfortableness with knowing and expressing one's feelings and
  thoughts
- Minimal defensiveness
- Accurate understanding of oneself and others
- Assertiveness

This foundation of self-confidence makes the child tough and
able to sort out the meaning of an adult or other child being unfair
and mean to him or her. The child starts with how he or she feels,
knowing this is certainly "who I am." With "who I am" very clear, the
child then looks at and feels what's going on with the other person.
With this balanced understanding the child can assertively (without
being aggressive or attacking) engage in effective problem solving.

Without this self-confidence, your child will feel threatened
when a conflict occurs. Unhealthy frustration, with its attacking and
defending characteristics, will occur. Blaming the other person is
typical. There is no place for your child in this low self-confidence
position to own his or her part easily; it's too painful to admit "I'm
bad."

If a parent instills self-confidence and never exposes the child to the real world, the child would have a startled reaction at first. While you are providing the parental-love approach, expose your child to the negative side of problem solving. There are plenty of opportunities for this: newspaper articles, TV, and so forth. A self-confident child will not be devastated by someone dealing with conflict in an unhealthy way.

For example, a ten-year-old, Christopher, comes home from an afternoon at the swimming pool and says, "An adult chewed me out good for running when I was supposed to be walking. I know I did the wrong thing, but why did he get so mad and call me 'stupid' for running? You and Mom hardly ever get that mad at me. I even apologized like I'm supposed to, and the man just said, 'Well, don't do it again; it's irresponsible behavior,' and he just left in a huff."

Christopher's father says, "A lot of adults handle their anger by using a really angry voice and mean words. That will happen quite a bit in your life. Always know that mean words and voice are really that adult's problem, and just because someone growls at you doesn't mean you're a bad person—even though you may have made a mistake. Try to focus on whether your behavior was unacceptable and own up to it. It's really hard to do this, but with practice it gets easier. I'm glad you admitted you made a mistake."

Now, a point about firmness in response to the objection: "I think kids often need and benefit from a rougher approach that focuses only their behavior." The parental-love approach calls for the highest level of firmness possible when correcting unacceptable behavior. Firmness and limit setting are essential parts of parenting. Teaching the healthy-guilt system requires parents to be firm about expected behaviors while at the same time continually conveying respect by validating the child's emotions. Re-

> The parental-love approach calls for the highest level of firmness possible when correcting unacceptable behavior. Firmness and limit setting are essential parts of parenting.

spect comes first and then setting firm limits to correct unacceptable behavior. The parental-love approach instructs parents when too much firmness results in feelings of "I'm bad."

I've only met a handful of parents who have been able to practice a mostly healthy internal legal system. The internal guilt system changes dramatically with counseling. Some form of the unhealthy legal system is really the norm, and it's the automatic response when we are in the unhealthy frustration zone. Remember, we can all change to the healthy-guilt system no matter how old we are. It does, however, take awareness, disciplining ourselves to change, and then monitoring ourselves for achieving permanent change.

There's an important deceiving initial outcome related to the unhealthy legal system and unhealthy frustration. Initially, on the surface, it seems to work. Humiliation and shame, most of the time, for the moment stop unacceptable behavior. Unfortunately, the mid-term and long-term results are always stunted self-confidence—results you don't want.

Let's summarize: You want your child to learn how to distinguish between right and wrong, make the right choices, handle a conflict by owning his or her part first, and treat others in a responsible manner—in the best way possible and as soon as possible. Healthy guilt is the answer. Feeling "I'm good" is the best basis for these results.

Now you have your manual for helping your child learn healthy guilt and make healthy guilt the foundation of his or her being. Healthy guilt continually produces feelings of "I'm good," and "I'm good" always generates joy, the ultimate human experience.

The next chapter is all about "I'm good"—finding and helping your child establish his or her passion. We've been talking about some pretty heavy, troubling stuff. Not so with passion! Passion is as uplifting as the updrafts that support a soaring plane—only blue sky, bright light, and fluffy clouds. "I'm good" is the source of passion, where joy resides. Let's get some soaring experience while we explore how to find and establish your child's passion.

### CHAPTER 10

# Mine the "Extra" Good:
# Find the Passion

FOUR-YEAR-OLD KEVIN came running to his dad with his newest and "bestest" Lego creation ever, eyes wide, his smile making it almost impossible for him to form the words. "Daddy, look at the airplane I made."

Dad was putting the final touches on his presentation for the next day's business meeting. He stopped working, reached both hands out, a perfect landing field for the airplane; his smile reflected Kevin's; his eyes followed the backward loop, and the plane landed safely in his hands—barely. "Wow, that's cool. I really like the way you put the wheels toward the back of the plane. I've never seen that design before."

Kevin's eyes sparkled, and he and his plane sped around the room as he said, "Look at the three wings. They make the airplane fly real faster."

"It does go faster. You really have great ideas for planes. Show me more." As Dad's enthusiasm continued, Kevin flashed nonstop smiles. Joy lit up the room, like the Christmas tree in Rockefeller Center in New York City.

*Does it get any better than this? Kevin gets so excited when he builds these planes. I'm so glad we just bought him that 100-piece special airplane Lego kit. It was worth every penny. I'm glad, too, we cleared off the top of our china cabinet for him to put his newest cre-*

*ations on. Paying all this attention to his building sure has helped him feel better, especially since he's had to start those shots for his diabetes. So fun to see the smiles. And I feel so good inside. Sure beats the acid feeling when Kevin is sad.* (Yes, dads, you can feel deeply just like moms do. It's the gold, the good in you, and the extra good in Kevin all wrapped up in one awesome package. It's there. Let it out to your child.)

Now that's passion, with all the emotional and feeling frills—enthusiasm, excitement, and joy. And how about the key supporting cast, Dad. What a demonstration of how the parent-child relationship can result in "I'm good" glowing brightly.

Not too far away, just down the street in another home, ten-year-old Julianne has just put the final touches on her sunset drawing. She runs to the kitchen at warp speed, barely clearing the last corner, where Mom is struggling to get breakfast done before the school bus comes. Bouncing up and down, voice almost screeching, with that radiating smile showing all those pearlies, Julianne says, "Mom, Mom, look. Remember the sunset we saw out at the lake yesterday on our walk? This is it." She pushes her picture into Mom's face, barely missing the pan frying the eggs.

*There's no way I can look at the picture. There's no time...bus in ten.... How do I tell her...? No, no, Gary said mine the good, no matter what.*

Mom pulls Julianne and the picture away from the stove. She examines the picture closely and then locks eyes with her daughter. "How did you get the color below the sun to look so pink and purple? That's beautiful."

Julianne's face beams as brightly as the sun she's drawn.

Spending just a few seconds more in silence looking intently again at the drawing, Mom points to the orange autumn weeds and the two sailboats. "The color of the weeds is just the way I remember it, and those boats really stand out. How did you catch that one boat's name, *Windsteamer II*, written on the sail? Let's put this on the refrigerator—uh-oh, it's already full of pictures. Let's tape it to the edge of the counter." After the artwork has been strategically placed, they both stand back to admire it. Mom shakes her head in wonder and says, "Awesome."

The moment ends with a mutual hug. Julianne breaks free and says, "I know, I'll get dressed...." Her voice trails off as she runs back to her room, and Mom quickly gets back to the eggs, which are looking a bit well done by this time.

Warmth fills Mom's heart and radiates throughout the room—and not from the stove being left on. She glances at the picture once more as she transfers the eggs from pan to plate. Tears well up. *Wow, does she love to create. I'm so thankful she has this joy. That must be what Gary means when he says joy is the evidence of the good. I'm so glad she's got this joy to balance her sadness about not having any close friends at school. Oops! There's the toast.*

Are you soaring from the joy and enthusiasm expressed in the scenarios of Kevin and Julianne?

It's great to be talking about what's good about your child instead of what's wrong.

Joy is the emotion, the fuel, and the energy source of passion. Joy is the emotional expression and feeling of "I know I'm good"; it's the total experience of passion. And there's an extra bonus: Joy leaves little room for the other four core emotions that aren't any fun at all—anger, fear, disgust, and sadness.

> Joy is the emotion, the fuel, and the energy source of passion.

So how do you focus on, find, and establish the extra good in your child? In this chapter, rather than covering rough, mountainous terrain, we're simply going to glide through bright, sunny skies, experiencing together the joy of establishing and developing your child's extra good.

When I was a kid, I always liked it when the preacher told us ahead of time how many points he had in his sermon. As he covered each point, I knew I was getting closer to getting out of there. I just wish he would have said how many minutes each point would take.

So, for the rest of this chapter I'll be elaborating on three points. (How long each one takes depends on how fast you read!)

1. The critical importance of showing and encouraging excitement and enthusiasm

2. How to make sure you are at your child's center

3. What you need to look for and do to find and establish your child's passion

Let's start with excitement and enthusiasm.

## Being Your Child's Cheerleader

I've pointed out before that emotions and feelings are the driving force, the energy source, that plays the biggest role in determining your child's behavior and beliefs. Enthusiasm and excitement are the visible, emotional, and physical evidence of joy, the emotional energy source of passion. Your excitement and enthusiasm are two powerful transforming feelings that communicate directly to the center of your child, "You are good." Your child receives your excitement, and the transformation is instantaneous within your child to "I'm good."

This transformation is similar to what happens when a solar panel receives the sun's light and transforms this energy source into electricity to be used throughout the house. The powerful energy in the light of your enthusiasm and excitement is received at the center of your child and is transformed into "I'm good," the source of power for developing your child's self-confidence. Here's the extra-good news: When the transformation happens enough, your child's "I'm good" increasingly generates its own enthusiasm and excitement. Your child requires less and less outside

> Enthusiasm and excitement are the visible, emotional, and physical evidence of joy, the emotional energy source of passion.

enthusiasm and excitement to maintain feelings of "I'm good." Now, that's exciting!

Julianne's and Kevin's experiences radiated enthusiasm and excitement, and their parents reflected those emotions really well. This reflecting part by parents is essential because through it children learn what joy looks and feels like. When you reflect, here's what your child thinks and feels: *When I see and feel these feelings from you, I know "I'm good." It's totally clear you love my high voice, my waving arms; and I know the tingly, inside feelings are what come along with what I do that's really fun and makes you so happy. And I can't seem to stop those happy sounds that come out of me. You looking at other people, smiling and raising your voice when I do something fun, makes me feel those fun feelings even more, and I want to do what I'm having fun doing even more, and …*

> The powerful energy in the light of your enthusiasm and excitement is received at the center of your child and is transformed into "I'm good," the source of power for developing your child's self-confidence.

As you're well aware, enthusiasm and excitement are both a physical and emotional experience all at once. The emotional intensity manifests itself in a physical response. Dad reached out to receive Kevin's airplane; his smile reflected Kevin's; his eyes followed the movements of the plane and his son. Julianne bounced into the kitchen, showing all her "pearlies," and Mom took the time to examine the picture carefully.

I think we can safely conclude that passion's lifeblood is enthusiasm and excitement. The more you show these feelings through body language and comments, the more your child will do the same. All of these physical and emotional experiences add up to proof that you are together with your child at his or her center, where the extra good is found, experienced, reinforced, and eventually established.

And don't forget validation times three, the three "Vs." Did you notice how Kevin and Julianne's parents validated their children, commenting on the details of their creations? Dad said, "I really like the way you put the wheels toward the back of the plane." And Mom asked, "How did you get the color below the sun to look so pink and purple?" Validation punctuated with enthusiasm and excitement—you can't find a brighter light!

Just a side point. Try to make these two "E" words and the three "Vs" part of your daily responses to your child as you focus on the overall good in him or her. Shoot for at least 75 percent of your daily interactions to be validating and punctuated with the two "E" words, and not more than 25 percent dealing with what's negative. It's another 75/25 rule.

Now that we've covered enthusiasm and excitement, let's look at how to get to the center of your child.

## Living in the Center

You've read it a time or two (or three) already in this book, but I don't think I can stress it enough: Make sure you are at your child's center. You accomplish this by making sure the passion you are focusing on is your child's, not your own.

We talked about unconscious projection in chapter 3. Let's look at it more closely for a moment. You may be passionate about reading. Because of the joy, excitement, and enthusiasm you feel, it's only natural that you want your child to feel the same passion. That's why so many parents inadvertently (unconsciously) expect their children to develop passions similar to their own. If your passion ends up being your child's passion, great! If, however, your child's initial enthusiasm and excitement start to diminish after a month or so, you will know your passion is not your child's passion. Be aware of your unconscious projection. Even though it's normal, it can be one of the biggest barriers to finding your child's passion. (You may find it helpful to review chapter 3 for a refresher on unconscious projection.)

# Finding the Treasure at the Center

What do you need to look for and do when you are at the center of your child? You need to be aware of three critical parts found there: temperament traits, learning style, and the psychological developmental characteristics of your child's age. Joy is at its peak brilliance when your child's passion fits snuggly into these three parts.

Let's start with temperament traits, which you know a lot about already.

Fitting your child's potential passionate activity into his or her temperament traits is essential. Make sure you know and accept these traits. (You might want to do a quick review of the list found in chapter 4.) A child who is more shy (approach/withdrawal) may not do well in team sports but really well with individual sports such as golf or tennis. A more emotional/sensitive child (intensity of reaction) may be a good dancer but not have any interest in math club. Your distractible child may not have much interest in homework but significant interest in skateboarding. (Stimulating activities will significantly decrease distractibility.)

> Fitting your child's potential passionate activity into his or her temperament traits is essential.

Just like with temperament traits, your child's passion needs to be oriented to his or her particular learning style. There are three types of learning styles or combinations of learning styles: auditory, visual, and hands-on (tactile/experiential). A visual learner may have a great interest in making and editing movies but little interest in building things (hands-on). Your hands-on learner may spend hours creating Lego castles but have little interest in lecturing (auditory) or reading material (visual). Your auditory learner may quickly pick up foreign languages, public speaking, or music.

As you can imagine, not all children fit nicely into just one of these learning styles. Most children, however, do have one dominant learning style. As your child's passionate activity emerges, help your child shape the activity into his or her learning style. Let's say your twelve-year-old is interested in making home movies (a visual learner) and is distractible. Get the easiest editing program you can find to start out the editing experience. Something your child finds too boring or takes too long wouldn't work. Maybe your child is interested in golf and is a hands-on learner who favors visual learning more than auditory. Get a coach who uses videos rather than lectures.

This covers the classroom work. (And I promise you, my three points took much less time to cover than the preacher's did!) Let's summarize what you've learned so far:

1. Show your child plenty of enthusiasm and excitement as he or she explores possible passionate activities.

2. Do not unconsciously project your passion onto your child. Be aware of your child's response to your passionate activity. Drop it if that activity really is not your child's passion.

3. Fit your child's passionate activity into his or her temperament traits and learning style.

You've already noticed that we didn't cover the third aspect of what's at the center of your child: the psychological developmental characteristics of various ages and stages. We'll dig into that material in the next section.

## Going Underground

For this part of the chapter, we need to bring our glider in for a landing and head into the mine to uncover the extra good. Oh, you won't need a head lamp; your enthusiasm and excitement will provide plenty of light. Our mining activities include three stages: exploring possible interests, expanding the interest found, and encouraging the interest. That makes a total of five "E" words involved in our passion mining:

- Excitement
- Enthusiasm
- Exploring
- Expanding
- Encouraging

Exploring your child's interests before two years of age is of great importance, but the interests are more general and basic, oriented to engaging your child in all types of stimulating learning and physical activities—auditory, visual, and hands-on.

A wise miner always takes into consideration the kind of terrain he is digging in and uses the appropriate tools to get the best results. Our "terrain" is your child's psychological developmental characteristics. Since these characteristics are such a critical part of the terrain, I've provided quite a bit of detail on what your child is working to accomplish psychologically in the three age ranges: 2–5, 6–12, and 13–18.

We'll look at the two older age ranges, but our focus will be on two- to five-year-olds, and here's why. You can learn all of the mining activities while your child is quite young and gain a good idea of what your child's passionate activity is by age six. If your child doesn't seem to have settled on something by that age, however, you'll be able to use the same skills to continue your exploration of your child's passion throughout the next two age ranges.

What about the birth-to-two-year-old range? Exploring your child's interests before two years of age is of great importance, but the interests are more general and basic, oriented to engaging your child in all types of stimulating learning and physical activities—auditory, visual, and hands-on. Actual potential passionate activities typically start to show up around the age of two. That's why I'm starting with the two-year-old.

Many clients ask me when a child's passionate activity tends to become clear. From my own experience, well over half the children I know—both as clients and children outside my office—have not found a passionate activity by age thirteen. Some people do not find their passion until their late twenties, and some find it much later in life. We all know people who never find their passionate activity. Why? There are three main reasons: late bloomers, low self-confidence, and parents who have not adequately focused on developing their child's passionate activity. Be patient if your child is a late bloomer. Keep up your parental love. Your child's passion will emerge.

Please don't be discouraged if you have not focused on your child's passionate activity to the degree presented in this chapter. A parent's lack of focus on passion development typically has little to do with lack of love. There simply are no widely available guidelines that I am aware of for how to find and establish your child's passion.

> Be patient if your child is a late bloomer. Keep up your parental love. Your child's passion will emerge.

If your child has not yet developed fully his or her passion, don't despair. Here's what children consistently demonstrate in my practice—and your child is not an exception: No matter what, your child will always be extra-receptive to your validation, excitement, and enthusiasm about his or her extra good.

## 2–5-Year-Olds: "Me Do It"

Before we get into the mining activities with two- to five-year-olds, let's set the stage for what's happening developmentally with children this age. In this section you will notice that I will present a lot of information on developmental aspects. Why? Developmental aspects are a critical part of what's happening at the center of your child. Understanding these aspects and knowing how to develop them to the fullest is essential if you are to accomplish your parental-love goal: establishing "I'm good" within your child. It's within this terrain of "I'm good" that your child's passion will be found. That's why we must spend enough time to understand these developmental aspects.

The main psychological developmental aspects of the two- to five-year-old child are the establishment of trust, autonomy, and a guilt system developed through multiple self-initiation experiences. Doubt and shame can easily occur and need to be avoided.[1] For the first time, your child thinks (sort of), *I actually can try things on my own without Mom and Dad. But I want to know for sure that when I need them they will be there right away, especially when I'm scared. And when I do something they don't like, I don't want their faces and words to be too scary. I want to know they still think I'm good.*

> The main psychological developmental aspects of the two- to five-year-old child are the establishment of trust, autonomy, and a guilt system developed through multiple self-initiation experiences. Doubt and shame can easily occur and need to be avoided.

*When I do new things, everyone seems pretty impressed. But when I walk and run to places I've never been before and can't see Mom or Dad, I don't want to feel scared. It's so fun to run fast. Problem is, when those legs and feet don't work just right, boomie; falling hurts. I always want to know for sure Mom or Dad can take the hurt away.*

*Those hands of mine sure can grab stuff and make things with clay. And my arms? They're so strong I can throw stuff across the room—and break things. When I talk, people listen. I can get their attention, and they do what I want. I feel like that action figure Mom calls the Incredible Hulk. Looking in the mirror, I think I might be his brother.*

*All of these things I can do work with other kids, at least sometimes. It's fun to be with other kids, as long as I get to do what I want.*

Even though your child can't articulate his thoughts and actions quite that well, the above gives you a pretty good idea of what he or she is thinking at some vague level.

By four and five years of age, all these basic activities have become second nature—walking and running, talking and basic thinking, use of hands and arms, and relating to others—and the child begins to be able to handle more complex activities. *I can run or walk anytime I want, and I can run in sports like soccer. I can use a pencil or crayon to put things on paper that are in my head, and people really think it's great.*

*Don't tell Mom, but I can poke other kids. I can have a temper tantrum and get my way, sometimes. I can make people sad, happy, or angry, and sometimes things come out of my mouth that get me in trouble. I can hit my brother if he makes me mad. It gets me in trouble sometimes, but it sure feels good. Hey! He deserves to be hit if he's means to me.* (Honest, this is what extroverted, active kids tell me all the time.)

*What's really fun is being with other kids, playing together with them, and seeing how they talk and do things. Before, during, and after something happens I can figure out in my head (kind of—doesn't make too much sense) what's going on and decide what to do about it.*

Now that we know what is happening with your child during this age range, let's overlay that information on what's involved with the three mining activities: exploring, expanding, and encouraging.

## Exploring

Explore with your child a wide variety of activities as soon as possible. Exploring fits right in with two of the top developmental priorities of this age range: curiosity and mastery. Try involving your child with some activities throughout this age period from each of the following activity categories: athletic (kicking a ball, rolling a ball, and later maybe soccer), artistic (drama, music, art), intellectual (reading, discussing how things work), emotional (caring for people or animals, healthy problem solving—you never know, your child could become a therapist), social/family (play dates, establishing friends, and regular family events), physical (exercise).

> Watch carefully as your child explores each activity. When you see piqued interest in one activity, that's when you should begin expanding and encouraging.

Remember, no matter what age your child is, explore with him or her some activities from each of these categories, even if the interest is not particularly high.

Watch carefully as your child explores each activity. When you see piqued interest in one activity, that's when you should begin expanding and encouraging. I'm sure you have already done these things to some degree, maybe plenty.

## Expanding and Encouraging

Let's say Abigail starts choosing drawing more than other activities. Start expanding and encouraging. Go to a thrift store or garage sale and get a small table for drawing. Set up Abigail's drawing table in a fun place in the house, from now on known as "Abigail's Art Studio." Get a supply of paper and more variety of crayon colors, colored pencils, or markers. Make wall space available for pictures when there's no space left on the refrigerator door. Send grandparents pictures every other week. You get the idea: Put the mining activities of expanding and encouraging into your daily agenda. And don't forget the other two "E" words: Show plenty of enthusiasm and excitement along the way.

Before giving you a detailed example of how all this works in real life, let's pause for a quick summary of what we've learned:

- Get to and stay at the center of your child.
  - ✔ Be careful not to let your unconscious projection get in the way of seeing your child's passion.
  - ✔ At the center of your child, help your child fit the developing passion into his or her temperament traits and learning style.
  - ✔ Know your child's psychological developmental characteristics.
- Spend time with your child. Shine your excitement and enthusiasm on the good at the center of your child and enjoy the bright reflection of "I'm good" back to you. Joy will be abundant.

- Use the three mining activities to find and establish your child's passion: explore, expand, and encourage. Try to involve your child in some activities in each activity category: athletic, artistic, intellectual, emotional, social/family, and physical.

One more point: You can't control the exact outcome of your child's extra good or when it will emerge enough for you to notice it. It could be by six years of age; it could be at thirty. The extra good needs to be your child's. Remember, set aside your feelings and start where your child is. Explore for the vein of extra good, help your child expand the extra good, and encourage the extra good until it's at the highest level of purity.

> You can't control the exact outcome of your child's extra good or when it will emerge enough for you to notice it.

### Emma's Passion

I would like to introduce you to three-and-a-half-year-old Emma. Mom is an accountant, and Dad is a graphic artist. Mom's interests are reading and horseback riding. In high school Dad excelled in tennis and continues to play weekly. (Just a cautionary note about this example: You will notice that almost all of my examples are on the ideal side. I've mentioned this before, but the reason I do this is to show you the possibilities, not to hold these examples up as a standard.)

Here's what Mom and Dad had accomplished by the time Emma was three and a half. They made sure to show plenty of excitement with all the new walking, running, and communicating skills. They noticed the more enthusiastic they were with each new advancement, the more Emma smiled and wanted repeated praise. You've experienced this joy. You know how satisfied Emma's parents felt. Emma's joy is proof that her parents were at Emma's center.

They made sure to have many age-appropriate toys for mastering hand, arm, and leg movement and all the coordination aspects. They noticed Emma had a special interest in dancing whenever she heard music. Actually, she started moving her body to music at about eighteen months. It was so cute! Whenever she heard music—whether at a store, on the radio, or at home—she really could make the moves, right in sync with the music, too.

As Mom and Dad noticed this, they turned on the spotlights of enthusiasm and excitement. The reflection from Emma was dazzling—giggles, pirouettes, and even a few moves they hadn't seen before. By the time Emma was four, a lot of expanding and encouraging was going on. They had purchased some of her favorite music and had a dance "recital" after dinner every Friday night. She gave her first "public" recital to her grandparents on Christmas Eve just before her fifth birthday.

During this period Emma's parents were watching carefully for her learning style. By the time Emma was four, Mom and Dad noticed she learned better by actually doing the activity she was trying to learn, i.e., the hands-on orientation to learning. She had a hard time learning things when someone just showed her things to do (visual learner) or by someone telling her what to do (auditory learner). It didn't help that she had a little stubborn streak.

Emma's hands-on learning style was really noticeable when Mom tried to teach Emma about emotions while they played with homemade playdough one day. Emma was about three at the time. Mom showed Emma some pictures of people's faces with different emotions. At first Mom pointed to the sad-face picture (visual and auditory) and said, "Make this sad face on the playdough." Emma looked confused and couldn't do it; her interest was rapidly waning (why be curious when no mastery is possible?).

Since Mom was becoming more aware of learning styles, she tried the hands-on approach. She helped Emma trace the sad mouth on the picture and then make the same mark on the playdough. Mom had found the light switch of joy at the center of Emma. The switch was on, joy radiated; curiosity and mastery were working. Emma ended up doing two more playdough faces all on her own, first tracing the picture and then making a similar face on the playdough.

Emma's parents used the hands-on approach with other activities, as well. When they went over this incident with their doctor, she confirmed their thoughts: Emma was probably a hands-on learner, not an auditory or visual learner. Mom and Dad made sure to favor this learning style in all of Emma's experiences and at the same time encouraged Emma to improve her visual and auditory learning abilities.

You might be wondering, *What does this learning-style example have to do with finding a child's passionate activity, and why so much attention toward how to help Emma do things according to her learning style?* Keep in mind that mastery and curiosity are the top priorities of your child during this age period. You want to unleash curiosity and mastery to allow "I'm good" to flourish and for the extra good to be found and established. When exploring is done within your child's learning style, mastery and curiosity are enhanced. Your child's passion will be developed to the fullest.

How does knowing all about Emma's learning style apply to her dance passion? When her parents were looking into lessons after Emma's fifth birthday, they found a teacher whose teaching style relied primarily on physical demonstrations of dance, not on verbal instruction or visual aids such as video instruction. The dance lessons were a snug fit with Emma's learning style and resulted in continual excitement and joy.

Feelings of "I'm bad" can result if you are trying to help your child master an activity with a learning style that doesn't work. Let's look back at the example where Mom was trying to get Emma to put facial expressions of emotions on the playdough through verbal and pointing instruction only.

Let's say Mom got frustrated when Emma could not do it and said, "I give up. Let's do something else." (I know most parents would automatically do the hands-on, but I'm trying to make a point, so bear with me here.) Emma would see Mom's frustration and receive it as "I'm bad." Her curiosity to make a face on the playdough would have stopped, and mastery would have been dead in the water. A possible "I'm good" experience would have turned into an "I'm bad" experience. Some of this happens to all of us and is not a big deal; repeated instances, however, can reinforce "I'm bad"—a very big deal.

What about temperament traits and how they fit into finding Emma's passionate activity? By four years of age one temperament trait was obvious: emotional intensity (intensity of reaction)—great for her dancing but not so great when she didn't get her way. That's what brought them into counseling. After four sessions, the parents were able help Emma learn how to regulate her upset feelings adequately.

Feelings of "I'm bad" can result if you are trying to help your child master an activity with a learning style that doesn't work.

One time she brought her favorite CD and danced for us all. Her joy filled the room. It was so fun to see the enthusiastic body language from her parents during her two-minute performance and to see the joy on Emma's face in response to her parents' joy. Three smiling people in a therapist's office with that much joy was sure great for a change!

Two other strong temperament traits were apparent by age three: moderate adaptability and great concentration. Emma's parents could see that these two traits were a great match for her dance passion as they contemplated starting dance classes during her fifth year.

Part of the encouraging activity was involving extended family and friends so Emma could enjoy their excitement and enthusiasm. Emma's parents did this every time they could. The grandparents were so enthusiastic and excited after they experienced Emma's Christmas Eve recital that they offered to pay for a whole year of dance classes! They made the announcement the next day at the family Christmas dinner. Isn't it a joy when your parents enjoy your children! (None of the grandparents' other adult children were married yet, so there was no problem with jealousy from them.)

As I said before, Emma's parents picked a dance teacher who fit just right with Emma's temperament traits and learning style. By the time Emma was six, she was considered the best dancer in the dance studio. Mom and Dad did so many things to show their enthusiasm. Of course, neither one missed a recital. And every time a professional dance show came to town, all three of them attended.

Oh, by the way, Dad did explore tennis lessons when Emma was five and a half. At first Emma was really excited, but after two months of diminishing interest, Dad was clear; he would not have a tennis partner. He reluctantly remembered one of the mining requirements: When your child's interest diminishes, it means you've discovered "fool's gold." *Oh well, so much for that effort. But, after all, it's about Emma and not me. Kind of hard to remember sometimes.* And Mom didn't even try to interest Emma in horseback riding; Emma never showed any inclination, so Mom let it rest.

This concludes our discussion about finding the passionate activity for two- to five-year-olds. Now let's briefly see what it's like to explore a passionate activity for six- to twelve-year-olds and then conclude with thirteen- to eighteen-year-olds. Remember, your child's extra good will be found more easily and quickly when you understand the developmental terrain of each of these age ranges.

### 6–12-Year-Olds: "I Can Do It…or Can I?"

Six through twelve years of age is the time period when the little bird is pushed out of the nest; papa and mama bird are making sure the first experiences of flying are 98 percent successful. (Birds must know the 98 percent rule.) This is the age when independence gets its first test. (Adolescence is the final test; we'll go there next.) Here are the psychological developmental challenges facing your six- to twelve-year-old:

- Trying out behaviors Mom and Dad taught me on kids and teachers

- Practicing making choices in brand-new situations based on what I've learned about right and wrong and admitting when I'm wrong

- Expressing feelings in an acceptable way and practicing self-control

- Experimenting with how to make and keep friends (Friends are a lot more fun than my sister or Mom or Dad...well, most of the time.)

- When I try to learn at school, do I fail a lot and feel bad or am I successful a lot and feel good?

- Practice being sure of myself when I'm different than other adults and kids

Psychologist Erik Erikson summed up this age well by calling it a period of industry (competency) versus inferiority.[2] It's filled with so many opportunities to succeed and so many opportunities to fail. In parental-love language, this age provides so many opportunities for parents to reinforce their child's good and work through the inevitable "I'm bad" situations.

Uncertainty is very high: *Can I read this page? Why can't I write like my friend? It's so embarrassing when the teacher tells me in front of the whole world to stop talking.* Even more reason for finding the extra good. The extra good is the best anchor during the inevitable stormy times. If soccer is a developing passion, make this the anchor for your child. Does your child seem to enjoy reading? Expand the interest by going to a Saturday book club at the local library or find an exciting book series or every Tuesday night after dinner establish a time for your child to give a little talk on a new book he or she has read.

> The extra good is the best anchor during the inevitable stormy times.

If a passionate activity has not developed yet during this age range, turn up the light of your excitement and enthusiasm, take a closer look at an expanded activities category list, and explore some more. And this time look for any slight glimmers of passion. Maybe skateboarding is a possibility for your daughter, but you thought it was too boyish or too risky; get over it and find a way to make it happen. Maybe your son is interested in dance, but you thought it was too feminine. Reconsider. It's about him, not about you.

Your child's interest, no matter how vague it may initially appear, is the wick in his or her life candle that is waiting to be lit. Once that interest is ignited, your child will have a light source for his or her life that will never stop. Keep looking for passion's light flickering down deep in your child. Your child's passion will eventually shine for your child and for others to enjoy.

### 13–18-Year-Olds: "Who Am I?"

By adolescence, all the basics of independence are potentially in place. Your little fledgling is now a bird who can fly away from you for much longer periods of time and will wing to potentially dangerous places. If the tasks of the last age range are not quite complete, don't worry. Maturity levels vary. Just be patient. With your continued validation, your child will eventually mature with all the necessary skills to function in a healthy manner.

Adolescence is the final experimentation and application stage before a child permanently leaves the nest. "Who am I?" seems to be the constant question demonstrated though actions and words. Most often, the answer is: "I'm going to find out—apart from my parents." It's the time of test-driving everything: "I'm going to learn on my own now; I don't need you [Mom and Dad]—at least for now, but you'd better be there when I do need you." So goes the self-talk of the adolescent.

> By adolescence, all the basics of independence are potentially in place.

Challenging? Yes! But stimulating and rewarding—most of the time—for all involved when parents focus on the good, especially the extra good. The anchor of a passionate activity is even more important now. Staying at the center of your adolescent is tricky, and you can expect in this soaring adolescent flight some pretty steep dives that come close to the ground, as well as some exhilarating updrafts that take you and your child to unbelievable heights! Understanding the following developmental aspects will prepare you for most of the ups and downs.

## Rebellion

*I need to know who I am, and the only way I'm going to do it is to be apart from my parents. To be or not to be?* (That's not what Shakespeare had in mind). *Do I need to be opposite of my parents or the same as them? I'll choose opposite; the other way is boring for sure.* This is the rebellion part of adolescence. Expect it. Focus on and support the need to be different as good (not the behavior necessarily). You know, emotions first, behavior second. At this point, your child is thinking, *Being who I am apart from Mom and Dad is essential to find the real good inside me.* And their thinking is right on!

## Self-Centeredness

*A lot of the time I'll not care about anyone else and only think about myself and do just what I want to, even if it bothers someone else. I guess I need to do this sometimes to get to know myself. I don't understand why everyone calls me selfish or wrong when I'm doing what I want. Feels good to me. Isn't that what that counselor is saying all the time?* Well, not quite, but it's the adolescent interpretation, taking what's said and making it fit into the self-centered adolescent way of thinking.

This kind of thinking and the resulting behavior is called "selfish," "bad," or "wrong" by most adults. The fundamental aspects of this thinking really are *not* bad or wrong. The expression of this thinking is trying and tricky for parents to handle. But being centered within yourself is a necessary phase the adolescent needs to go through to find the good. That's why I label this behavior as self-centered. (It tastes a little better that way, a little bit like the Tabasco˚ sauce in the anger chapter.) Some people never get over this phase. Not a good thing. When there's too much "selfishness" for too long a period, self-centeredness becomes too spicy for everyone involved, no matter how normal self-centeredness is supposed to be. When this happens too much, get the stop sign out and say firmly, "That's enough."

> When there's too much "selfishness" for too long a period, self-centeredness becomes too spicy for everyone involved, no matter how normal self-centeredness is supposed to be.

*Ambivalence*

As I'm having fun knowing who I am, I seem to think a certain way for a while, and then the next day I might think a completely different way. How weird is that? Oh well, I'm still an adolescent. One thing that happens a lot is that one day I'll think I don't need my mom and dad at all and I'm almost mean to them; then the next day, seems like I want to be with them a lot.

*Kind of Confusing*

That's ambivalence—feeling two opposite ways at the same time. It's part of finding out "who I am," the adolescent goal. One thing to remember about ambivalence in your adolescent: You see and hear only one side of the ambivalence. The other side is there, but hidden in the unconscious. (See figure 10.1.) Your daughter may say with the boldest attitude, "I'm thinking about starting to use marijuana."

## Adolescent Ambivalence

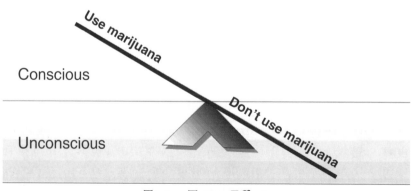

**Teeter-Totter Effect**    FIGURE 10.1

You are stunned! Your daughter is not that type of person. Count on your daughter feeling the opposite thought (hidden in the unconscious): *Marijuana is not a good choice.*

What should your response be, knowing your daughter has these two opposite feelings? "Sounds like you're really grappling with an important decision. Tell me more." (As a parent of an adolescent, always dress with a loose-fitting blouse or shirt so your child can't see your racing heartbeat, and don't forget deep diaphragm breathing.)

That covers the three critical aspects of adolescence: rebellion, self-centeredness, and ambivalence. Let's see how these developmental aspects affect your adolescent's passionate activity. Our example is Jacob, a fifteen-year-old budding artist. He's won numerous awards and loves drawing—at least everyone thought so....

"I really thought I liked drawing, but I'm thinking of giving it up. It's not fun anymore."

*What! After all those lessons! Don't look stunned. Is this ambivalence? Are there now mixed feelings about what looked like a passion? Oh yeah...ask a feeling question; gives me time to look normal.* "Tell me more about what you're feeling." *Wow, I'm pretty good at this now, and I kept it at a level—*

"I just don't like the teacher I have at the fine arts center anymore. I'd just like to quit."

*I've spent over a thousand dollars in the last two years on this passion* (level 7 but still inside). *He'd better.... No, no focus on the feelings. Get back to the change stuff. What's the step? Oh yeah. Thinking. I'm too upset. I need some time to think. Don't force the action stage:* "You have to do this or else." *Abort mission.... Plant a seed.* "Let's talk some more about it later. Tomorrow we can talk about all the possible options, like quitting [*I can't believe I said that. Should I retrieve it? No, keep going.*], maybe taking a break for a few months...."

You get the picture. Hard to face, but easier when you know what's going on in an adolescent's head. If your adolescent hasn't found a passion, keep doing the exploring, expanding, and encouraging. Just because your child is an adolescent doesn't mean he or she doesn't thrive on mastery and curiosity. Guide your adolescent to opportunities that stimulate curiosity and result in mastery. And don't get discouraged. Your job is to encourage, not control. Be patient; the extra-good candlewick is there; it's just not ready to be fully lit—yet. And the light of your excitement and enthusiasm will eventually light up your adolescent child's passionate activity.

That's it for this chapter. We've landed—and safely at that. Whew, quite a trip, this passion business! Let's do a quick review:

Now you know about the energy sources of passion: joy, enthusiasm, and excitement. You've also learned about passion-mining activities: exploring, expanding, and encouraging. To make sure you find and mine the richest vein of good, your child's passion needs to fit into his or her temperament traits and learning style. Knowing what your child's psychological developmental tasks are in each age range is essential. When all of these passion puzzle pieces are put together, you and your child will find a passion. Count on it being a vibrant, bright picture of the extra good in your child—passion that has the potential to be experienced for a lifetime, an everlasting source of joy.

> If your adolescent hasn't found a passion, keep doing the exploring, expanding, and encouraging. Just because your child is an adolescent doesn't mean he or she doesn't thrive on mastery and curiosity. Your job is to encourage, not control.

CHAPTER 11

# Discipline
# from the Good

THE BEST PROBLEM SOLVING occurs when parents establish guidelines about why the new behavior is better and how to change the behavior—keeping "I'm good" at the center of it all. Although this may seem like an insurmountable task, there are procedures available for *ensuring* that each person feels respected and valued during a discussion about differences. I know, "ensuring" is a strong word. But it's true. Using these procedures always results in mutual respect and feeling valued.

Two of the best procedures come from Imago therapy and Ross W. Greene's Collaborative Problem Solving Method. I've blended these two procedures into one, which I call the discussion procedure.

There are three huge benefits to this procedure: (1) problems get solved with mutual satisfaction, (2) bonding is strengthened, and (3) feelings of "I'm good" get reinforced one more time. The overall result? Self-confidence is increased.

The discussion procedure is based on the idea that problem solving has two stages: the concerns stage and the solution stage. Usually, problem solving with children is done by only one person, the parent demanding a solution. Not so with the discussion procedure.

The procedure guides each person in the conflict to verbalize and listen to the other's concerns first (concerns stage) and then find a mutually satisfying solution (solution stage). The procedure focuses on each person feeling heard and understood, valued and respected. Mission impossible? No, not if you follow the procedure.

Here's the concerns stage in a nutshell (these steps are for the parent, the receiver):

- Step 1: Listen.
- Step 2: Repeat.
- Step 3: Agree.
- Step 4: Validate.

> The discussion procedure is based on the idea that problem solving has two stages: the concerns stage and the solution stage.

Remember Sophia from chapter 8? She and her dad were having a disagreement, to put it mildly, regarding Sophia's curfew. Let's see how Sophia and her parents learned and implemented the discussion procedure. Later we'll cover the solution stage, but you'll see that most of the work for problem solving is done during the concerns stage.

As with any situation, remember to apply parental-love dialogue requirements while you're solving a problem together. Let's quickly review them before we get to Sophia's situation:

- Avoid judging. Focus on what's right and not what's wrong.
- Avoid negative comments.
- Be calm. Stay within the healthy frustration range. Being calm teaches your child how to use the regulator thinking tool. Then the separator and monitor can work.
- Talk no more than 25 percent of the time (75/25 rule).
- Make only one or two points at a time.
- Keep the transaction brief. Try to put your comments in question form to keep you in the 75/25 range.
- Acknowledge your mistakes and what you will change.

If this procedure sounds clumsy and awkward to you, you are not alone. In my whole career I've never had a parent who had heard of or used this procedure unless he or she had already been in therapy and used it. (Often marital therapy uses approaches similar to the discussion procedure.) When parents understand the procedure and see the results, they are always pleased. Like I've said before, you will need to stick with it for at least three weeks to learn it well.

## Preparing the Family

Here's how Sophia's parents described the problem in the first session:

Dad began the story. "Sophia has been driving for about four months. She regularly misses her Friday and Saturday eleven o'clock curfew. I've tried lecturing, grounding (two weeks at a time), taking things away (cell phone, computer social networking, car privileges, nothing left), and rewards. Nothing's worked. The straw that broke the camel's back—and almost my back for that matter—was when Sophia started climbing out her window at night to go to her friend's house. That's when we called you."

> When parents understand the procedure and see the results, they are always pleased.

In the second session we worked on the parental-love approach and the discussion procedure.

The discussion procedure gets a big boost when the parents can feel and see the benefit of using it in their own relationship. Mom had a problem when Dad always blew his top (level 7) about Sophia coming home past curfew. Naturally, Mom pointed this out.

I asked Dad, "What would it be like if your wife would first agree with you in some way and validate your emotions with something like 'I agree that Sophia's situation is so frustrating that it's next to impossible for you not to swear, for now. What can I do to help with your frustration instead of criticizing you?'"

Tears welled up in Dad's eyes. "Yeah, that would be nice." Mom reached over to squeeze Dad's hand, and their eyes met. "Until now I really did not get it. I promise to try to be more supportive," she said. A priceless moment! Validation of Dad's feelings and understanding, and *bam!* In a millisecond she went from the behavior to the center of Dad's heart. It's so much easier and more productive to solve problems from a position of empathy.

I spent the third session with Sophia, listening to her side of the situation and briefing her on the discussion procedure. Her response to this approach of mutual listening and understanding was "Are you kidding me? That will never happen." By the time these sessions were completed, Mom and Dad were ready to invite Sophia into the next session. They had worked hard in between sessions with parental-love assignments.

Just before we asked Sophia to join us in my office, I asked Mom and Dad to review out loud their notes from their previous sessions. Here's what they reported:

- Steps 1 and 2: Listen and repeat. No "buts" or defending. Throw all our defensive points out the window, for now.
- Step 3: Agree with something.
- Step 4: Validate with as much positive emotion as possible.
- Remember all parental-love points.
- Change stages: Try to get her to stage 2, thinking; keep comments in the healthy frustration range; make comments fit within her highly emotional temperament trait (intensity of reaction); follow all the dialogue requirements, especially minimal talking and avoid "I'm right; you're wrong."
- Expect all the adolescent stuff: rebellion, self-centeredness, and ambivalence.

Bottom line: All of these procedures focus at the center of Sophia, where the good is found, not on her behavior. Validate and respect, validate and respect.

Warm-up's done. Dad looked at Mom while he reached out to hold her hand, and almost in unison they both took a deep breath. Dad looked at me and said, "National anthem's done; let's play ball."

## Sophia's Session with Her Parents

Each parent-child interaction has multiple differences, and the outcome doesn't usually come as fast as you see in my examples. Expect gradual success rather than immediate perfection.

As everyone settled in their chairs, I said, "Just a couple of points before we get started. If at any time you think I don't understand your point, please correct me right away—especially you, Sophia. Your feelings and thoughts are especially important in here." She gave me the "what planet are you from" look and cracked her gum extra loud. "As each person gives a point, I will completely believe you until there is evidence that I should not believe you—even if the other person's point is opposite of yours. Nobody's allowed to interrupt. And one other thing, Sophia: Anything you say in here cannot be held against you outside this office."

Sophia rolled her eyes and said, "Oh yeah, fat chance of that happening."

"Is keeping everything in here acceptable to you, Mom and Dad?"

Both parents agreed.

I continued. "Sophia, tell your parents why you want a different curfew time than eleven o'clock. Remember, only a couple of points at a time."

"You guys just don't get it. All my friends stay out until one or two o'clock. I should at least get to stay out until one."

Dad looked at Mom, his face contorted as if he had a severe stomach pain, and whispered, "What?"

Sophia saw her dad's expression and then said to me, "It's true! *Nobody* has an eleven-o'clock curfew."

Dad looked at me, then at her, and raised both hands in surrender. "Okay, Okay, I blew it, I just...."

I could see where Sophia got her emotional temperament trait.

I gently supported Dad. "Dad, you get to give your point in just a little bit. This is really hard to do, but it's important that we hear Sophia out completely."

Dad exhaled loudly and sat back, barely below level 6.

"Continue, Sophia. You're doing exactly what you're supposed to do. It's hard for Mom and Dad to hear this, but they need to listen." (I tried to sneak a fast glance to see whether the g-force of those comments was too much. Nope. Everybody was still conscious.)

"Yeah, Dad, you never listen to me." Tears welled up in Sophia's eyes, which meant she was starting to feel valued. "Finally someone's hearing me," she said as she darted a glance from her dad to me. Dad's jaw tightened as he struggled to remain quiet and not react to his daughter's lie.

Looking and acting more powerful, Sophia went on. "As I was about to say, only losers have to come home at eleven. Do you know how embarrassing it is to say in the middle of a movie, 'Sorry, guys, I need to go home'? Everyone looks at me like I'm some freak. I did that once. I'm not doing it again—evvver."

I raised my hand. "Sophia, let's stop for a minute. You've said a lot of important things. Are you interested in seeing if Mom and Dad heard you?"

"Yeah, maybe they will hear me—for once."

Sophia was becoming more and more disrespectful, but I wanted to stay at her center. "Sounds like you're really mad and really feel completely misunderstood." I was working hard to remain in the eye of the storm, demonstrating to the parents where they needed to be instead of where they were—as far inside the hurricane protection center as possible.

Mom and Dad looked like two tasered zombies. They were trying so hard to keep quiet and not show their emotions, even though they knew Sophia was *dead wrong about everything*. Looking at them, I said in the most supportive tone and words I could muster, "I know how hard it is to hear stuff like this when you have really important points to make. You're doing it just right. You're listening and taking in Sophia's words. Now, Mom, I want you to repeat what Sophia said—just her words, not your point; your turn is coming later." Dad looked away, trying to find his regulator and doing a good job as he studied the beach calendar hanging on the wall to his right. *I wish I could be on that beach....*

Mom took a deep breath, moved her eyes from me to Sophia, who looked like an angry judge, arms crossed, ready to pronounce "guilty" before Mom even opened her mouth.

"Here's what I heard you say: None of your friends have to go home at eleven, and you want your curfew to be one o'clock. I know that already. You—"

"Mom, just keep with what Sophia said—no commentary."

Mom fidgeted a bit, trying to find a more secure spot on the couch. "Okay, I get it, I slipped. Whew, is this hard." She looked at me, a little perturbed, then put on a smile and faced her daughter. "Okay, did I hear you right?"

"Yeah, Mom, you heard most of it, but you didn't get the embarrassing part. You'd never know how embarrassing it is. You—"

Again I gently stopped Sophia, starting to train her to use her regulator. "Sophia, let's give Mom a chance to repeat that part. It's really hard not to keep trying to convince your mom of your point—"

"For sure," she said as she looked back at her mom with that extra-full-of-myself glare.

Mom continued. "So, you're really embarrassed when you have to leave something like a movie and the rest of the kids stay. I guess now that I think about it, that would be embarrassing, but—"

I carefully stopped Mom, helping her to maintain her accomplishment of sticking with the step-2 "repeating only" requirement.

"Mom, you did that really well. Now, ask her if you heard all of it."

I glanced at Dad. He looked a lot more comfortable; Mom was on the hot seat instead of him.

Mom went on. "Did I get it all this time?"

"Yeah, finally, but I know your just hearing it won't change anything. You and Dad are really old-fashioned; I know you'll never budge on this. Grrr."

Mom replied, "I know you're sure this is hopeless, but we're try-ing something different here, so let's keep going."

Turning to Mom, I asked her to move to step 3. "Can you agree with at least one thing Sophia said?"

"Yeah, matter of fact, I can," Mom said with a surprising degree of calm. "That embarrassing part. I can remember that happening to me when I was about your age." Mom was validating emotions, and I was happy to see it—as long as it didn't go on too long.

I glanced at Sophia. It was working. She was nodding and whis-pering, "About time."

"Great job, Mom. You're keeping your comments all about So-phia. So, what do you agree with, in just one or two sentences?" (The clearer the agreement, the more strongly Sophia will feel "I'm good.")

"I agree that being asked to leave your friends in the middle of a movie is really embarrassing."

"Great job again. Now for step 4, validating Sophia's emotion. You've already done some of it, and look at Sophia. Do you think what you said has already affected her?"

Mother and daughter exchanged brief smiles, and Mom replied, "Yeah, you should have been embarrassed. I know I was when it hap-pened to me as a teenager. I don't know how we're going to go about fixing it, but I don't want you to feel embarrassed."

"It's easy, Mom. All you—"

"Sophia, hold on. The fixing comes after they give their points to you."

"Okay, I guess I can wait."

I glanced at Dad. He seemed ready for a gentle question. "Dad, what do you think?"

"It's really hard. I want to say so many things. But I know ev-erything I want to say is wrong for what you're trying to teach us. Anyway, I just want to listen. I'm getting how it works. I just can't see how we'll get to a solution. But keep going."

"It does seem impossible, doesn't it?" Sophia frowned at my comment. "Sophia, stick with this. I'll help all of you, including Dad, to find a solution."

That's a typical first attempt at the discussion procedure by the parents. With refereeing, there's always noticeable success for both parents and children. I'm always excited about the outcome, no matter how many times I facilitate these conversations. It's feeling and seeing parents and a child communicate at the child's good center that does it every time.

Now for a summary of Sophia's listening to her parents' concerns. When children and adolescents are receiving their parents' comments in the concerns stage, ignore steps 3 and 4. Here's why: Listening and repeating is an adequate basis for the concerns stage and a huge step forward. Developmentally, your kids will have a tough time with the agreeing and validation steps (3 and 4). Feel free to experiment with these stages, but I find that requiring the agreeing and validation steps complicates the problem solving unnecessarily. The self-centered part of an adolescent can make these steps really hard.

One last point: You can attempt to replace step 3, agreeing, with understanding, but try it only when your child's emotions are at a level 4 or below. Make an attempt to see whether your child understands your point: "Can you see why I get frustrated when you don't do your chores like you promised?" Your fourteen-year-old may respond with "Yeah, that would make me mad." If he does, you've witnessed a huge accomplishment.

Now, on to the session in which Sophia was required to listen to her parents. I had the parents start by repeating what Sophia had said, what they agreed with, and what they validated in the previous session. Nothing like starting at Sophia's center. And the parents did a great job giving just a few validating comments!

As you can imagine, Sophia had a hard time listening and repeating. And the parents needed help with limiting the number of points and keeping them brief. When they made their points, the parents mixed in validating comments to Sophia about how difficult it was for her to stick with the curfew. Make sure to validate when you make your points. It will help your child's regulator and separator by getting emotions to a lower level so their thinking can kick in. At the end of the discussion, the parents' concerns boiled down to these four:

1. We need to be able to count on you coming home when you promised.

2. We need to know where you are.

3. We need to be comfortable with the friends you are with.

4. If you are at someone's house, we need to be comfortable with the parents.

At first, Sophia did a lot of interrupting, but with two or three reminders she did well. At the end she even agreed with her parents about needing to count on her being home when she promised: "I guess I would be scared too if I was a parent, but—" I interrupted her so she could experience agreement without her "but" comments. Her agreement with her parents' point was huge.

This family even started the solution phase during the same session: "If you can follow the existing rules we just expressed for two weeks, we will move your curfew to midnight for one weekend night." A suggested possible solution like this is a good idea to add at the end of the concerns stage—that is, if everyone is at a level 4 or lower. Don't even think about it if the FTS level is higher. In this case floating the idea helped Sophia start thinking (change stage 2) in preparation for the solution stage. At home, it's a good idea to do the solution stage at another time, especially if the frustration level is hovering around 4.5 to 5.

Here's the short form of this concerns stage before we go to the solution stage:

What you do (your child sending concerns and you receiving):

- Step 1: Listen to your child without interrupting.
- Step 2: Repeat what your child says and identify feelings.
- Step 3: Agree with something your child says.
- Step 4: Validate your child's feelings.

What your child does (you sending concerns and your child receiving):

- Step 1: Your child listens to you.
- Step 2: Your child repeats what you said.
- Step 3: Your child understands your point. Gradually start implementing this step from about age six and up.

## Solutions for Sophia

Now we are ready for the solution stage. There are two overall requirements:

- The parents clarify they have the final say in determining the solution, but most of the solutions will involve the child's ideas. Shoot for this happening at least 80 percent of the time.
- The suggested solution must include the concerns presented by each person during the concerns discussion. It can be initiated by parent or child.

Here's the main point: Your child needs to feel validated and respected throughout the procedure, and the solution needs to reflect his or her points as much as possible.

> The suggested solution must include the concerns presented by each person during the concerns discussion.

The steps for the solution phase are as follows:

Step 1: The parent sets a high-level requirement for the solution before suggestions are given. This requirement needs to leave open the opportunity for your child to make choices. (Choices reinforce feelings of "I'm good.") For example, your five-year-old loves to play with her horse collection just before bedtime. It's always a fight, however, to get her to put the horses away and get ready for bed. You tell her she can still play with the horses, but only right before or after dinner. Her choice. Or you have a ten-year-old who wants his friends to come over every day after school. The current rule is no friends in the house on school days. New requirement: Your son can pick two days out of the week for after-school play times after his chores are done. His choice.

Step 2: Parent and child suggest a solution. The solution must represent both the child's and the parent's concern. If not, another solution must be presented.

Step 3: Parent and child discuss solutions, focusing on the same steps as in the concerns stage: 1, 2, and modified 4. Brief validating is enough since this is the solving stage. Too much validation can get you sidetracked. Decision making is the focus. Step 3, agreement, is left for the final decision, when the agreement about the solution occurs.

Step 4: Decide on a solution. As you listen to solutions, either pick the solution your child gives or create a solution that includes enough of your child's ideas so the child feels ownership in the final solution.

What happens if a mutual solution cannot be reached? Parents make the decision, pointing out that the choices are still available, as well as other choices the child may think of later. All choices must fit within your high-level requirement. But maybe your requirement is too rigid. If so, modify your requirement to get participation from your child. Maybe video games can be played for one hour on one night during the school week instead of not at all. Maybe two sleepovers a month would be acceptable instead of one.

Now that you know the solution steps, let's look back in on Sophia and her parents to see what they decided.

Sophia immediately took her parents up on their offer of extending her curfew by an hour. But after she thought about it for a moment, she presented a counteroffer: "I want a two-hour curfew extension for one night instead of the one hour."

The parents agreed, with the following qualification: "Let's take it in steps. Keep to the rules the first two weeks and you can then stay out until midnight on one weekend night. If you can stick to this rule for another two weeks, you can earn the right to stay out until one on one weekend night. But the one o'clock curfew has to be for a special reason like prom or a rare late movie."

Sophia agreed.

This family used the discussion procedure regularly from that time on with great results. Even better, they found that after using the procedure for a week or so, they only needed it for big disagreements. But whenever they worked through their differences, they made sure to remember the ultimate purpose of the discussion procedure: to hear, understand, and validate Sophia.

On the flip side, they made sure Sophia heard them and often asked her to repeat what they said. They worked hard to keep their points brief in order to increase the possibility of Sophia understanding. They knew better than to expect Sophia to understand and acknowledge their points frequently, but they appreciated every small victory.

Here's the short form for this solution stage:

*Step 1*: Parent sets high-level requirement.

*Step 2*: Parent and child give suggestions for a solution.

*Step 3*: Parent and child listen, repeat, and validate to discuss possible solutions.

*Step 4*: Both parties agree on a solution that reflects everyone's concerns whenever possible.

Parents often ask me whether the discussion procedure can be used with younger children. Absolutely. And do you always need to follow each step perfectly? No. You use the underlying concept of the discussion procedure: Both participants feel their thoughts and feelings are respected and valued. Apply discussion-procedure steps according to your child's age level and according to the severity of the prob-lem. A less severe problem does not require each step be used to the tee. Here are some examples:

> Apply discussion-procedure steps according to your child's age level and according to the severity of the problem.

Your two-and-a-half-year-old keeps throwing food off his high chair. Well, you don't need to listen in this situation, there's nothing to repeat, and you combine the concern stage with the solution stage in one fell swoop. You just need to talk while you act, doing step 3 and 4 in one or two sentences with an ade-quately stern look: "You like to throw things [validation]. It's fun." You're agreeing even as you reach out and keep him from throwing more. See? You're already at the solution stage. "We don't throw food on the floor," you say as you shake your head, and your child gets it. He's listening and understanding—steps 1 and 3 at the same time. Understanding? Well, maybe not right away, but with repeated "no"s from you—if you stay in the level 3 range—your child's behavior will show you he understands and that a solution is in place.

In the above exchange your son felt his thoughts and feelings were respected and valued. The steps were there but modified for a two-and-a-half-year-old.

How about a less severe problem. Eight-year-old Adeline repeat-edly fails to feed her dog before school. Here's what Mom's response was before learning how to use the discussion procedure: "You kids don't take any responsibility around the house. Do you know what I do for you guys?" (level 6).

Adeline interrupts defiantly: "It doesn't matter if I feed her before or after school."

Neither Mom nor Adeline felt their thoughts and feelings were respected.

After learning how to use the discussion procedure, Mom modifies the procedure: "Muffy will get hungry during the day if you forget. Is that fair for Muffy?" Mom only gives her concern and focuses on Adeline understanding her.

"Yeah, Mom, I guess you're right. She'd get pretty hungry." Now Mom moves to the solution stage, sets a requirement, and gives a choice: "Feed her before breakfast or just after you leave the breakfast table. Your choice." Result: Both Mom and Adeline feel respected. I know this situation could get complicated really fast. If it does, go to the full-fledged discussion procedure. But as you know, this modified approach often will work, especially if the discussion procedure has been used in its entirety with more difficult problems.

That's it for the discussion procedure. It's the fundamental parental-love tool for working through differences and maintaining "I'm good."

Before we conclude our journey together, let's look at how you can effectively take the parental-love principles beyond the four walls of your home—to school and to Grandma's house. Chapter 12 will help you learn to advocate for your child with those who are unfamiliar with the parental-love approach.

### CHAPTER 12

# Advocate for the Good: Teachers and Family

MOM HANDED ME THE email as she and Dad started their fourth session of counseling. "We're really making improvement at home, but school is getting worse for Lily. As you can see from the message from her teacher, Lily's still being disrespectful, not completing her homework, and on it goes. We have to go to yet another meeting to hear about how awful our daughter is. With all those teachers and staff people there, it feels like we're on trial. We never know what to tell them, and nothing ever improves. What can we do?"

"Sounds like you're feeling pretty discouraged. I've worked with many parents who've faced similar challenges, and I have a tool I think will help you. I call it the 'GEP Advocacy Steps.' 'G' stands for 'gap assessment'; 'E' is for 'educate'; and 'P' stands for 'plan.'" I handed them a copy of the steps, and we discussed them in detail.

## Advocating at School

The GEP advocacy steps work extremely well in an educational setting.

### Step 1: Gap Assessment

This one seems almost too obvious, but you'll bring a great deal of clarity to the situation if you begin by determining the gap between teacher and child. Do this by (1) listing behaviors expected by the teacher, (2) listing the behaviors of your child, and (3) identifying mutually agreed-upon outcomes.

Dad spoke up first. "Without knowing it, we've already done the first step. The teacher's newest email actually answers the first two points of the gap assessment."

Here's what she wrote:

> Math is really the main problem. When we do class work, Lily doesn't do the work. She often will start doodling, which is not allowed. When I ask her to do the work, she crosses her arms, looks the other way, and sort of growls at me. The more I remind her, the more she refuses to do anything. At times she'll talk back, saying something like "Who cares." Respect for authority is one of our core values at school. Disrespect will not be tolerated.
>
> I expect her to look me in the eye when I give her instruction and to accomplish at least some work. Please help! I'm out of ideas!!!!

Dad continued. "And for the last point—agreed-upon end behavior—I think we can both agree that we want Lily to eventually do her work. Does it sound like we're starting right?"

"That does cover the first step," I said. "Whew! The teacher's FTS level must be pretty high with four exclamation marks. Now let's look at step 2 and see if we can't align behavior and expectations and make everybody's lives a little easier."

### Step 2: Educate

Step 2 involves four main tasks:

1. Ask for the teacher's observation about the child's behavior and cause.

2. Acknowledge that teacher, parents, and child are responsible for specific behaviors. The teacher will need to take the lead in changing his or her approach to ensure 98 percent success from the child.

3. Identify your child's temperament traits and learning style.

4. Communicate to the teacher what works at home (starting where the child is, dealing with emotions first, etc.).

Mom spoke up. "It looks like the first point of this step is really about starting where the teacher is, right?"

"You've got it. For step 4 you will need to fit what you do at home into where the teacher is; find a way to agree with and validate the teacher—the discussion procedure ideas. For example, you could say, 'We find this stubbornness really annoying, too, but we've found a way to deal with it.'

"Tell the teacher what worked best was for you, the parents, to make the changes first and then focus on what Lily's changes needed to be—with the clear implication that teacher changes need to be made first. Be prepared for the teacher to want Lily to make most of the changes first. Won't work. Then you can present the temperament trait and learning-style information and then what works at home.

> Acknowledge that teacher, parents, and child are responsible for specific behaviors. The teacher will need to take the lead in changing his or her approach to ensure 98 percent success from the child.

"Here's the most important point for successful advocacy. Show the teacher what works at home by example; don't tell or lecture. Make sure you prepare a point or so that speaks directly to what the teacher says is a problem."

"We've done the temperament scale assessment and can take that with us," Dad said. "She's at a 4 on adaptability and intensity of reaction, and her learning style is visual, really poor on the auditory. So that takes care of that point.

"Let's see.... What example can I give that fits what the teacher is facing? What we've learned in counseling is that you can't just say something directly to Lily when she's at an FTS level of 5 or above because of her adaptability and intensity of reaction issues. We can tell the teacher that when Lily is too upset, reasoning doesn't work; that way too much talking and confrontation ends in failure for everyone. I notice the teacher is too direct. You've got to say things indirectly to Lily. When we need to leave the house in ten minutes and we know she won't be ready, we set a timer, tell her when we're leaving in the shortest, most neutral way possible—no judgments or lecture, calm voices and kind facial expressions—and then go away for a couple minutes. Would that be the way to demo the parental-love approach to the teacher?"

"Perfect! Here's something to watch out for: Don't mention the consequences. Most adults rely on consequences as the only answer for change. Address the consequences in step 3, the plan."

### Step 3: Plan

Implement step 3 by changing only one or two targeted behaviors at a time.

1. Agree on the end result.

2. Identify teacher behaviors for desired outcome in measurable behavior terms: stretch but doable outcome; modify until 98 percent successful.

3. Identify parent and child behaviors.

4. Establish accountability system to monitor progress.

"Okay, here's how I'd work out step 3," Mom said. "Of course we need to be prepared for suggestions from the teacher, but if possible we need to give our suggestions first. That gives the teacher a chance to see how we would suggest applying what we do at home to the school situation. First, I'd say that we have the same outcome in mind as the teacher, that Lily eventually does class work like the rest of the kids and that we want to make Lily as responsible as possible, given her starting point.

"Then I'll suggest something like this. In a calm way maybe Lily could be told something along this line: 'Class work is important to do.' I'd let the teacher know how this indirect approach works much better with Lily, and when Lily is at a level 6, direct comments will make her clam up.

"Then I'd suggest the teacher say something like 'I'll come back in a couple of minutes to see how you're doing. I'd like for you to get this much done in the next ten minutes—maybe half of the work for today.' I'd also suggest to the teacher that she may need to do more visual explaining to deal with Lily's visual learning style.

"What do you think about that? I'm stumped on what consequence to suggest to the teacher if Lily doesn't start."

"You're right on track. Here's where you introduce the consequence part. If Lily hasn't started after a couple of minutes, the teacher can say quietly, 'If the work I asked you to do doesn't get done, I'll email your parents, and this will be addressed at home.'

"If Lily doesn't do any work and starts doodling, the teacher says nothing and emails you guys. Ask the teacher to try this for a week, with daily feedback to you. That takes care of the last point, the accountability plan. What do you think?"

Both parents nodded, and Mom replied, "I think we're good to go as long as we can give you a brief SOS call for last-minute strategies." They left the office, appearing confident in their ability to advocate for Lily.

I got a call from them a week later, just after their meeting. "The teacher accepted the plan," Dad said, "and best of all, the psychologist really gave us a lot of support. She acted like she knew a lot about what we were trying to do. Thank you so much! See you next week."

That's it for the GEP advocacy program. What about advocating the parental-love approach with family members, both immediate and extended?

# Advocating at "Home"

Moms whose husbands refuse to buy into the need for counseling or changing their parenting style often want to know how best to approach their spouses. I've heard many variations on the following:

*Brian refuses to come to therapy. He thinks the ADHD diagnosis is bogus and that Austin never doing chores right and always doing his projects at the last minute is because Austin is lazy and irresponsible. By the way, I think he's ADHD and is having a hard time admitting it. What should I do?*

Here are a few tips for influencing men (or women, for that matter) such as Brian:

First, find some common ground. Usually you can agree on the overall behavioral outcome: finishing chores well and in a timely manner and schoolwork being done on time.

Next, apply parental-love techniques to Brian's case: Start where Brian is. Using the stages of change information, try to get Brian to start thinking about the causes of the problem (stage 2). Maybe give him information on why ADHD kids act the way they do and how to parent kids like Austin.

Lastly, *you* move ahead with appropriate parenting even if Brian refuses. Tell him you're going to try the ideas and ask if he will at least watch how the techniques work and not interfere. This is the "show, don't tell" rule. Most dads hate to be told what to do because they consider themselves to be the fixers.

If the most discouraging ending happens—Brian refuses to change—keep showing and showing some more. Children thrive on healthy parenting, and they can grow a lot even if both parents are not on board. Of course, if Brian's resistance is long-term or his behavior is continually destructive, you need to insist that he attend at least one counseling session—if not with Austin's therapist, then with a therapist of his choice. You must be involved. But try the previous ideas first. Most of the time a spouse will come around.

Parents aren't the only ones who refuse to follow the parental-love approach. Sometimes grandparents or other extended family members purposefully or inadvertently impose their parenting methods on the younger generation. Here's an example:

*My mom is a terrific grandma to our twelve-year-old, Kayla, but my problem is there's too much love. I know that sounds crazy, but here's what I mean. First of all, Mom has such a great relationship with Kayla I don't want to ruin a good thing. But my mom caves in on almost anything Kayla wants. Kayla's just a little overweight, and Mom lets her eat junk food whenever she wants to. Mom also lets Kayla use her cell phone to text message—sometimes for several hours at a time—and that's not allowed in our home. The other day Mom allowed her to set up a MySpace account, which we had made clear to Kayla that she could not do. Even though Mom was aware of our rules, I haven't really said much to her until this MySpace deal. On that one I got too mad and hurt my mom's feelings. How do I approach her in a way that keeps her love going?*

> Children thrive on healthy parenting, and they can grow a lot even if both parents are not on board.

Thank goodness for loving grandparents. Establishing "I'm good" gets a huge turboboost from loving extended family members. There's a special place in all of our hearts for a loving grandma and grandpa. A lot of time and undivided attention are just a couple of the gifts a child receives from extended family. You don't need to spend too much time with a child, however, before that child begins to test the limits. That's where clear, regular communication about problems needs to be the rule.

This dilemma is a common one—how to keep the love flowing and at the same time maintain your family values and guidelines. Here are four critical guidelines to help you navigate this relational tightrope:

1. Give extended family written, regularly updated guidelines regarding safety (bicycle use, seatbelts, etc.), nutrition (types of food, snack times, etc.), discipline, and parental-love guidelines.

2. Don't micromanage in your guidelines or your feedback to extended family. Allow flexibility for grandparents to implement your guidelines.

3. Start where grandparents are. First identify all the positive behaviors and how you cherish their love for your children. Then discuss your concerns—no judgmental labels, just behavior—and arrive at a mutually satisfying solution.

4. Monitor agreed-upon solutions and celebrate successes. If you're concerned about a particular situation, don't assume it will correct itself. Meet face to face and communicate.

> Start where grandparents are. First identify all the positive behaviors and how you cherish their love for your children. Then discuss your concerns.

These advocacy guidelines for teachers and family members have proved helpful for many families. Be clear and concise about how you want others to treat your child. I'd advise writing down these expectations. Then commit to insisting, diligently and graciously, that your expectations be met in all settings. When your child sees you as an advocate, he or she will feel respected and valued. "I'm good" will be even more deeply ingrained.

We're almost done with our journey together. Before you close the book, I'd like to share with you stories of four adults who experienced the power of unleashed love.

# Thanks for Loving Me

AH, THAT OCEAN AIR...*sun just ready to set.... Where's my camera? Lucky nobody's found this great spot.... Shade's just right.... Just like the times Mom, Dad, my brother, and I would watch the sunset over a lake after we'd been sailing. I can hear Captain Dad yell, "Let 'er loose" when we were going really fast. Sure miss 'em all. This is amazing...like the ocean never ends. Wow! That breaker must have been ten feet high.*

*Didn't think college could be so exciting. It's been scary at times too. Got to have a plan for handling my suite mate before I walk back. He leaves the lights on all hours of the night.*

*Can't believe what it's like to do whatever I want, especially when I turned in a paper I got done at the last minute, and I did it handwritten, when it was supposed to be typed. I could just see my mom trying to hide a frown. First one-legged A I've ever got. The prof got a little carried away, covering half the cover page with that ugly, big, fat red letter. His note was kinda funny: "Did you leave your Mac at home?"*

*I was surprised when I told my new friend Mike about what I did. He looked really uptight and said, "I'll bet your folks would be really ticked. Course, who'd be dumb enough to tell a parent?"*

*I didn't say anything, but I imagined what they would say. Something like "Independence is quite a teacher, isn't it?" Come to think of it, they never made a mountain out of a molehill. Dad would say ever*

233

*since I can remember, "Watch for the molehills. Keep 'em small, and don't let 'em become mountains."*

*Yep, I'll use my Mac from now on.... Best part of the sunset, half the sun left, spilling rainbow colors all over the place. Dad and Mom never micromanaged, but Mom let me know what the end result would be, like for college: "You pay for the next semester if you end up with anything below a C average." That's pretty cool how they let me figure things out myself.... Wow, that freighter is huge. I wonder what country it's from.*

*Have to get Mom and Dad to sit with me in this great spot when they come next week. Better start back to the dorm. Let's see.... What should I say to my roommate? "Is there a time that would work for you to have our lights out?" Yeah, that'll do it. He'll get mad and probably find something wrong with me. I saw that when one of the other suite mates confronted him.*

*Oh, well. That's his stuff. I'll hear him out and own my part if I need to—another Mom-and-Dad deal. I can just hear Dad: "Own your part first, then worry about the other person." I hated it at first, but it really does work. Most of the problem goes away. It takes the wind out of the sail, as my mom used to tell us.*

*All these thoughts about Mom and Dad kinda choke me up. They really did know how to love. I think I'll email them tonight and tell them thanks.*

IN A SMALL MOUNTAIN community near Durango, Colorado, twenty-eight-year-old Nicole had just tucked her five-year-old son into bed. *I'll turn on the outdoor lights to watch for a minute. Look at all those snowflakes. Wow! Quarter size...falling like fancy cotton balls. And those huge pine trees look like white arrows piercing the dark sky.*

*Today sure was full of challenges. Jack hit someone today—second time this week. It's getting worse. He gets so frustrated, and I know just how he feels.*

*That's me in kindergarten, not hitting but yelling. Everyone got so mad at me…except Mom. She got pictures of all kinds of "feelings" faces, and she would stop me when I started to yell. She'd say, "You must be really upset, and you're handling your feelings by yelling."*

*What a wonder. So many snowflakes, every one separate, like they know their place, and landing so gently. Feelings words at first made me yell more, but eventually I actually started naming the feelings out loud. I didn't yell that much by the last part of first grade.*

*Teasing really got bad by Christmas break of first grade. After Christmas break, that's when Mom and Dad told the teacher the same thing they had told me a lot: "Nicki feels things a lot and lets out her emotions easily." Now I know Mom and Dad found a way for me to feel good even though my behavior wasn't working. Amazing how that worked. I got to be in the meeting. I remember the teacher looked really kind and said to me, "We'll take care of that, sweetie."*

*Next day the teacher asked the kids to be kinder to me. She said, "Sometimes kids' emotions are strong. We can all help Nicole, and teasing is not going to happen anymore." Kinda scary the way she said it. Everybody knew she meant business.*

*From then on, the teasing gradually stopped. Up to then I can remember I really felt something was wrong with me. I felt bad all the time except at home. I hated everything about school and tried to stay home as often as I could. I'd tell Mom about it at bedtime, and she would always listen as she rubbed my back and say stuff like "You're really sad. I'm sad too. I love you." Mom sure had calm ways of bringing my emotions down slowly until they were okay. Kinda like the snowflakes. I'll just watch some more and remember. She's amazing.*

*She'd say, "We'll keep talking with the teacher and keep helping you to say the feelings instead of yelling." Then by the end of first grade I started wanting to go to school, my grades got better, and I made a good friend I still have. I was happy most of the time. And the last day of school I got the "most improved student" award. I've still got that certificate.*

*Here come the "love tears." That's what Mom called them. "Let 'em flow," she'd say. "They're coming from the heart." I'll love Jack like my mom loved me. It's been fun to reflect with Mom on those days. I'm calling her right now to tell her thanks again for loving me.*

AT FIVE THE NEXT morning, another story was unfolding. The lights were already burning in a small manufacturing plant in Topeka, Kansas.

*I think I've figured out how to tell the guys about the downsizing I have to do—the 15 percent reduction in pay and letting Gordon go. Jeremy and Dan will take it in stride. Allen will get really quiet. He tends to complain about his hurt and anger about my decisions with the other guys and not to me directly. That's just him, but I know it helps to support his anger ahead of time and let him know I expect it. Anyone would feel it.... Jim'll be here any minute.*

Frank leaned back, took a deep breath, and reflected for a few moments. *Boy, last night I was all over the place. The old feelings of "I'm bad," it's all my fault, if I'd been a better...blah, blah, blah. What happened in all those therapy sessions with Adam is what I can always depend on. Together we found what was me—and it wasn't a shameful idiot.*

*Pictures and feelings from counseling sure are brighter than the old junk. My not doing well in school wasn't because I was stupid. My drug abuse wasn't because I was bad. It started after my mom died when I was halfway through high school. My dad got so distant.... But Adam valued and respected what was deep inside me. I actually felt unconditionally loved for the first time.*

Frank was pulled from his reverie as the door banged open.

"Hey, Frank, whatcha thinking about? That Porsche you're going to buy when this business turns around next year?" *That's Jim. Sure glad I found him to be my manager of the shop. He always puts a light spin on things.*

"Yeah, right. Maybe one of those plastic model Porsches. Hey, man, we've only got about twenty minutes until the meeting. Let's huddle so I can get your feedback about what I've decided to tell our employees."

After reviewing the cuts in pay with Jim, Frank concluded. "I want to tell you I'm sad that we're in this situation, and I have a certain amount of fear about whether we're going to pull through. But with these reductions I've told you about, we can definitely keep going for another quarter. I feel confident about the next three months at least. And I think going from five eight-hour days to four nine-hour days will lessen the sting of the pay reductions on the guys. How are you feeling about your salary reduction?"

"Hey, I saw it coming. I've got a few more notches in my belt to tighten. I'm not sure you should let them know you've got some fear about the future, though. That might spook 'em. And I don't know why, but saying stuff like you're sad…well, I don't know. But I like the confidence in your voice about the next quarter. That'll go a long way with them. I know it makes me feel a little more secure."

"I hear what you're saying about mentioning fear, but I know we're all feeling scared, and I know for sure all of us are feeling sad, and for that matter several of the guys will be angry, and they should be. I really do need to mention the feelings stuff. You make a good point; it's delicate to bring up. I'll make sure to temper it, though. And I'll let them know that whenever anything starts to get worse or better, we'll meet and discuss it openly."

Jim breathed in, nose in the air. "Smells like cinnamon rolls."

"Yeah, picked 'em up just half an hour ago." They divided one and chatted a minute before the team came in for the meeting.

Afterward Frank reflected, *Whew, went as well as could be expected. Feel good about the meeting. I'm so thankful for the experience I had in therapy. Kinda weird, but without me experiencing in therapy that I'm good and not sewage, as Adam often pointed out, that meeting wouldn't have happened.*

The phone rang, and Frank turned his focus to the business of the day.

LATER THAT DAY IN a town just outside Boston just before sunset, Johanna was taking a walk. *Colors dance off of those leaves, so vibrant and full of life. That's how I felt after discussing with Connor how I want another baby. I knew he felt differently, and I was feeling scared, that he'd put me down. That's all I knew as a kid, and it still always happens with my mom.*

*Fact is, he never puts me down. Okay, maybe a couple times in the last five years, but nothing we couldn't work out together. Feeling wrong pops up still when I have a different opinion than Connor does.... Look at those two deer, silhouetted by the sun.*

*I'm still amazed how the technique he learned as a kid in some family counseling works. Like today, he didn't interrupt once—and I talked awhile. He agreed with a lot of what I said, and I really felt he understood why I wanted a baby, even though he's not totally in favor of it.*

*Wish my folks would have treated me this way. It's taken years for me to feel that what I've got to say is worth something. Didn't start until I married Connor, and now I'm really feeling good more and more about who I am. It's excitement I never really felt as a kid. I don't say it much, but I'm going back right now to thank Connor for loving me so much.*

Love's unleashed power always generates joy in abundance.

# Parental-Love Monitoring Forms

USE THIS FORM EACH week for three weeks to evaluate and monitor your progress. There are two sections: situation description and parental-love requirements evaluation. (Only one week will be presented in this sample.)

## Situation Description

Prepare five brief reports each week: (1) what happened; (2) what I said; (3) what went well; (4) what improvements are needed; and (5) here's the way I want to say it.

### WEEK 1

*What happened*: Tommy handles his anger by hitting his sister. The prearranged consequence was grounding Tommy from friends if he hit his sister. One hour after I told him about the consequences, he hit his sister. According to our prearranged agreement, the consequence was imposed the next day right after school when Tommy asked to play with a friend.

*What I said (no need here to write down what Tommy said)*: I started with a calm voice: "You hit your sister. You were told you would be grounded." When Tommy talked, I stuck with my point and gave him a lecture about how hitting will not be allowed in our house. I talked for at least three minutes straight. He kept interrupting, and I kept arguing. Once I made at least four points without stopping. It ended with me yelling.

*What went well*: I had a prearranged consequence and discussed it with Tommy. I'm evaluating myself to see how I can improve. Even though it seems almost impossible to change my old way of doing things, I can see how the requirements will really help Tommy and me. I'm trying to meet the last dialogue requirement: acknowledge my mistakes and offer to change.

*What needs improvement (Pick one or two improvements for now. The most common problem is picking too many improvements and becoming discouraged.)*: I have so many things to improve, but I'll start at the beginning. I need to feel, acknowledge, and validate Tommy's feelings. Also, I'll try to talk only 25 percent of the time. The next time Tommy hits his sister, I will work extra hard to focus on Tommy's feelings, stay calm, and stick to my guns with the consequence. I'm going to practice what I want to say with my husband at least several times.

*Here's the way I want to say it*: "Something must have happened that made you very upset. What happened?" After Tommy responds, I will say, "I can see how that would be upsetting. I would be upset too. Most kids would feel like hitting someone. What's another way to handle being upset?" If there's no response, I'll say, "How about handling your upset by saying, 'I'm frustrated,' and then leave? You can tell me what happened, and I'll handle your sister." I will encourage Tommy to say as much as possible, so he feels validated.

# Parental-Love Requirements Evaluation

## WEEK 1

*Did I start where my child was?* Remember: Emotions first, behavior second.

- Feel, acknowledge, and validate emotions.  <u>No</u>  Partly  Yes
- Choose a 98 percent successful modified behavior.  <u>No</u>  Partly  Yes

*Comment*: I didn't realize how much I talked and argued. I didn't acknowledge his feelings once. I've got a long way to go. I'll impose the consequence tomorrow and see whether it's 98 percent successful.

*Did I follow the dialogue requirements?*

- Avoid judging (describing behavior, not labeling).  <u>No</u>  Partly  Yes
- Avoid negative comments.  <u>No</u>  Partly  Yes
- Be calm.  No  <u>Partly</u>  Yes
- Talk no more than 25 percent of the time (75/25 rule).  <u>No</u>  Partly  Yes
- Make only one or two points at a time.  <u>No</u>  Partly  Yes
- Keep the transaction brief.  <u>No</u>  Partly  Yes
- Acknowledge your mistakes.  <u>No</u>  Partly  Yes

*Comments*: I did start out calm but couldn't keep it up. Now I see why most of my problems with Tommy occur. I really hardly ever do any of these dialogue procedures. Right now it seems like a big hill to climb, but I can see now doing these things will really help.

# Parental-Love
# Monitoring Forms
## (BLANK)

Use this form each week for three weeks to evaluate and monitor your progress.* There are two sections: situation description and parental-love requirements evaluation.

## Situation Description

Fill in the four parts of the situation description each week: (1) what happened; (2) what I said; (3) what went well; (4) what needs improvement; and (5) here's the way I want to say it.

# Situation Description

## WEEK 1

*What happened:*

*What I said:*

*What went well:*

*What needs improvement:*

*Here's the way I want to say it:*

# Situation Description

## WEEK 2

*What happened:*

*What I said:*

*What went well:*

*What needs improvement:*

*Here's the way I want to say it:*

# Situation Description

## WEEK 3

*What happened:*

*What I said:*

*What went well:*

*What needs improvement:*

*Here's the way I want to say it:*

# Parental-Love Requirements Evaluation

## WEEK 1

*Did I start where my child was—emotions first, behavior second?*

- Feel, acknowledge, and validate emotions.            No   Partly   Yes
- Choose a 98 percent successful modified
  behavior.                                            No   Partly   Yes

*Comments:*

*Did I follow the dialogue requirements?*

- Avoid judging (describing behavior, not labeling).   No   Partly   Yes
- Avoid negative comments.                             No   Partly   Yes
- Be calm.                                             No   Partly   Yes
- Talk no more than 25 percent of the time
  (75/25 rule).                                        No   Partly   Yes
- Make only one or two points at a time.               No   Partly   Yes
- Keep the transaction brief.                          No   Partly   Yes
- Acknowledge your mistakes.                           No   Partly   Yes

*Comments:*

# Parental-Love Requirements Evaluation

## WEEK 2

*Did I start where my child was—emotions first, behavior second?*

- Feel, acknowledge, and validate emotions.      No   Partly   Yes
- Choose a 98 percent successful modified
  behavior.                                       No   Partly   Yes

*Comments:*

*Did I follow the dialogue requirements?*

- Avoid judging (describing behavior, not labeling).   No   Partly   Yes
- Avoid negative comments.                        No   Partly   Yes
- Be calm.                                        No   Partly   Yes
- Talk no more than 25 percent of the time
  (75/25 rule).                                   No   Partly   Yes
- Make only one or two points at a time.          No   Partly   Yes
- Keep the transaction brief.                     No   Partly   Yes
- Acknowledge your mistakes.                      No   Partly   Yes

*Comments:*

# Parental-Love Requirements Evaluation

## WEEK 3

*Did I start where my child was—emotions first, behavior second?*

- Feel, acknowledge, and validate emotions.        No   Partly   Yes
- Choose a 98 percent successful modified
  behavior.        No   Partly   Yes

*Comments*:

*Did I follow the dialogue requirements?*

- Avoid judging (describing behavior, not labeling).  No   Partly   Yes
- Avoid negative comments.        No   Partly   Yes
- Be calm.        No   Partly   Yes
- Talk no more than 25 percent of the time
  (75/25 rule).        No   Partly   Yes
- Make only one or two points at a time.        No   Partly   Yes
- Keep the transaction brief.        No   Partly   Yes
- Acknowledge your mistakes.        No   Partly   Yes

*Comments*:

# Temperament Trait Characteristics: Comparison and Goodness of Fit Plan

THE GOAL OF THIS worksheet is to help you to establish a better fit between your temperament traits and those of your child. *

*Instructions*

1. Circle the numbers on the scale that best describe the traits of both you and your child.

2. Comment on whether you are unconsciously projecting your trait onto your child.

3. State your feelings and thoughts about the result of each scale.

4. Refer to the example below for further help.

*Example*:

**Activity Level:** Your child is either more active or more quiet.

|  | Quiet |  |  |  | Active |
|---|---|---|---|---|---|
| Parent | 1 | 2 | 3 | 4 | ⑤ |
| Child | ① | 2 | 3 | 4 | 5 |

*Comments*: I really didn't realize we were this much different. I'm always thinking or saying, "She needs to be more active in getting things done. She's so poky." After uncovering my unconscious pro-

*Permission is granted to photocopy forms in appendixes A and B for personal use only.

jection of "being active is the way people are, so what's wrong with her?" I can see I've been projecting who I am onto her and expecting her to be just like me. Wow, what a mistake!

1. **Activity Level:** Your child is either more active or more quiet.

| | Quiet | | | | Active |
|---|---|---|---|---|---|
| Parent | 1 | 2 | 3 | 4 | 5 |
| Child | 1 | 2 | 3 | 4 | 5 |

*Comments:*

2. **Regularity:** Your child's behavior is regular (predictable) or irregular (unpredictable) related to physical functions: eating, sleeping, etc.

| | Regular | | | | Irregular |
|---|---|---|---|---|---|
| Parent | 1 | 2 | 3 | 4 | 5 |
| Child | 1 | 2 | 3 | 4 | 5 |

*Comments:*

3. **Adaptability:** Your child shifts from one thing to another easily or with great difficulty.

| | Quick to adapt | | | | Slow to adapt |
|---|---|---|---|---|---|
| Parent | 1 | 2 | 3 | 4 | 5 |
| Child | 1 | 2 | 3 | 4 | 5 |

*Comments:*

4. **Approach/Withdrawal:** Your child approaches new situations easily with confidence or is more uncertain and withdrawn.

| | Initial approach | | | | Initial withdrawal |
|---|---|---|---|---|---|
| Parent | 1 | 2 | 3 | 4 | 5 |
| Child | 1 | 2 | 3 | 4 | 5 |

*Comments*:

5. **Physical Sensitivity:** Your child tolerates physical sensations well or is highly sensitive regarding taste, sight, hearing, smell, touch.

| | Low sensitivity | | | | High sensitivity |
|---|---|---|---|---|---|
| Parent | 1 | 2 | 3 | 4 | 5 |
| Child | 1 | 2 | 3 | 4 | 5 |

*Comments*:

6. **Intensity of Reaction:** Your child's emotional reactions to events, either internal or external, are experienced somewhere on a continuum from mild reactions to high intensity.

| | Mild reaction | | | | Intense reaction |
|---|---|---|---|---|---|
| Parent | 1 | 2 | 3 | 4 | 5 |
| Child | 1 | 2 | 3 | 4 | 5 |

*Comments*:

**7. Distractibility:** Your child experiences distractibility somewhere on a continuum from very distractible to not distractible.

| | Not distractible | | | | Very distractible |
|---|---|---|---|---|---|
| Parent | 1 | 2 | 3 | 4 | 5 |
| Child | 1 | 2 | 3 | 4 | 5 |

*Comments:*

**8. Positive or Negative Mood:** Your child's mood is experienced on a continuum from positive to negative.

| | Positive mood | | | | Negative mood |
|---|---|---|---|---|---|
| Parent | 1 | 2 | 3 | 4 | 5 |
| Child | 1 | 2 | 3 | 4 | 5 |

*Comments:*

**9. Persistence:** Your child can sustain his or her attention, effort, and energy for long periods or falls somewhere along a continuum toward weak persistence.

| | Strong persistence | | | | Weak persistence |
|---|---|---|---|---|---|
| Parent | 1 | 2 | 3 | 4 | 5 |
| Child | 1 | 2 | 3 | 4 | 5 |

*Comments:*

*Which of your child's traits are most difficult?*
(Your child's most difficult temperament traits are those with the highest numbers on the scale or those that show the greatest numerical contrast with yours.)

1.

2.

3.

*Which of your traits have you been unconsciously projecting onto your child?*

1.

2.

3.

# Follow-Through Steps

*Step 1: Display the Temperament Traits Worksheet you've just completed.*

Make several copies of the filled-out Temperament Traits Worksheet to place in various locations in your home for first-thing-in-the-morning and last-thing-at-night review.

*Step 2: Pick one temperament trait to focus on.*

Use the Monitoring Sheet to work though the problem (appendix A). Place a checkmark in the box beside the trait you will focus on in the next several weeks:

❏ Activity Level        ❏ Intensity of Reaction
❏ Regularity            ❏ Distractibility
❏ Adaptability          ❏ Positive or Negative Mood
❏ Approach/Withdrawal   ❏ Persistence
❏ Physical Sensitivity

*Step 3: Periodically review the other temperament traits that are a problem.*

Awareness will help a lot. If the problems persist, use the Monitoring Sheet to solve the situation.

*Step 4: Review the Temperament Traits Worksheet with your child without the comment section.*

Tell your child that you are going to work on significantly reducing your frustration with him or her. Do not expect agreement from your child about the scores. Usually your child will respond negatively to the negative scores because your child will feel bad about the score. If you get this response, don't be discouraged. The sole purpose of this step is to let your child know you are doing something positive about your frustration—not to get your child's blessing and approval that you are doing the right thing. Tell your child something like the following:

> As you know, I've been frustrated a lot of times with you. Now I know why. It's because we have some differences in the way we do things. These differences have ended up making you feel bad and making me not like part of you. I'm really sorry about how I've been acting. I've found a way to deal with these differences in a positive way. I'd like to share with you a sheet that shows how we're similar and how we're different. By knowing about these differences, I will be less frustrated and get along with you a lot better.

# Parental-Love Requirements

1. Set your thoughts and feelings aside temporarily, at the beginning of a problem-solving situation.

2. Start with your child's feelings first and then address behavior second. Be at the center of your child, where thoughts and feelings reside. Start where your child is, not where you are.

3. Establish behavioral expectations that will enable your child to be successful 98 percent of the time. (Forget about your behavior requirements for success.)

4. Dialogue effectively:
   - Avoid judging.
   - Avoid negative comments.
   - Be calm.
   - Talk no more than 25 percent of the time; allow your child to talk 75 percent of the time (the 75/25 rule).
   - Make only one or two points at a time.
   - Keep the transaction brief.
   - Acknowledge your mistakes.

# NOTES

## Chapter 1: Love Works

1. Daniel Goleman, *Emotional Intelligence* (New York: Bantam Books, 1995).

2. Paul Ekman and Wallace V. Friesen, *Unmasking the Face* (Major Books, 2003).

3. Haim G. Ginott, *Between Parent and Child* (New York: Three Rivers Press, 2003).

## Chapter 3: When Good Beliefs Go Bad

1. Judith S. Beck, *Cognitive Therapy: Basics and Beyond* (New York: Guilford Press, 1995).

2. Bruce H. Lipton, "The Intelligence of Your Cells," *Peak Vitality: Raising the Threshold of Abundance in Our Material, Spiritual, and Emotional Lives*, J. M. House, ed. (Santa Rosa, California: House Elite Books, 2008).

3. Anna Freud, *Ego and the Mechanisms of Defense* (New York: International Universities Press, 1971).

## Chapter 4: Temperament Traits, Part 1: Understanding Goodness of Fit

1. A. Thomas and S. Chess, *Temperament and Development* (New York: Brunner-Mazel, 1977).

2. Ibid.

3. Ibid.

## Chapter 6: Go for the Gold: Invest in Change

1. Maxwell Maltz, *Psycho-Cybernetics: A New Way to Get more Living Out of Life* (New York: Pocket Books, 1989).

## Chapter 7: Change from the Inside Out

1. B. F. Skinner, *About Behaviorism* (New York: Knopf, 1974).

## Chapter 8: Good Anger? Good Fear? Good Grief!

1. Peg Dawson and Richard Guare, *Executive Skills in Children and Adolescents: A Practical Guide to Assessment and Intervention* (New York: The Guilford Press, 2003).

## Chapter 10: Mine the "Extra" Good: Find the Passion

1. E. H. Erikson, *Childhood and Society* (New York: Norton, 1993).

2. Ibid.

# INDEX

# ABOUT THE AUTHOR

GARY M. UNRUH, MSW LCSW has been a clinical practitioner, providing counseling and mental health services to children, adolescents, and families, for nearly forty years. He also consults with clients' teachers and administers training for programs related to ADHD, bipolar disorder, and behavior management. He lives in Colorado Springs with his wife, Betty; they have four grown children. In his spare time, Gary enjoys sailing and gardening.

Give the Gift of

# Unleashing the Power of Parental Love

*4 Steps to Raising Joyful
and Self-Confident Kids*

**to Your Friends and Family**


CHECK YOUR

LEADING BOOKSTORE

OR ORDER ONLINE AT

www.unleashingparentallove.com